CHILDMINDING

A Guide to Good Practice

Christine Hobart and Jill Frankel

T

First published in 1999 by:
Stanley Thornes (Publishers) Ltd

Reprinted in 2001 by:
Nelson Thornes Ltd
Delta Place
27 Bath Road
CHELTENHAM
GL53 7TH
United Kingdom

01 02 03 04 05 / 10 9 8 7 6 5 4

A catalogue record for this book is available from the British Library

ISBN 0 7487 4023 6

Illustrations by Jane Bottomley
Page make-up by Columns Design Ltd

Printed and bound in Great Britain by T. J. International

CONTENTS

About the authors iv

Acknowledgements v

Introduction vi

Chapter 1 Childminding as a career 1

Chapter 2 Relationships with parents 14

Chapter 3 The needs of children 26

Chapter 4 Children's development and learning 40

Chapter 5 Understanding children's behaviour 60

Chapter 6 Caring for babies and toddlers 73

Chapter 7 Caring for the school-age child 87

Chapter 8 The safe environment 95

Chapter 9 Children with disabilities 111

Chapter 10 The sick child 119

Chapter 11 Child protection 136

Chapter 12 The professional approach 156

Chapter 13 Communication skills 168

Chapter 14 Observing and assessing children 180

Chapter 15 The business side of childminding 195

Chapter 16 A return to learning 203

Appendix A Developmental norms 214

Appendix B Sequence of language development 220

Appendix C NCMA principles of excellence in childminding practice 224

Glossary of terms 228

Further reading 231

Addresses and helplines 233

Index 236

ABOUT THE AUTHORS

The authors come from a background of nursery teaching and health visiting, and have worked together for many years training students to work with young children. They have written eight books encompassing most areas of the childcare curriculum.

ACKNOWLEDGEMENTS

The authors and publishers are grateful to the National Childminding Association (NCMA) for their help and co-operation in producing this book, and acknowledge NCMA as the source and inspiration of parts of the text.

The authors are grateful to NCMA staff for their valuable help and advice, and to Angela Dare for reading the manuscript and making useful comments.

The authors would like to express their appreciation of Neal Marriott, their editor, for his support and encouragement, and his willingness to listen to new proposals, and to his PA, Jane Beane, for her efficiency and friendliness.

NCMA guidelines' definition of a 'fit' person on page 4; the 'Conditions of the childminding service offered' questionnaire on page 11; the 'Children's development and learning' table on page 59; the 'Child record' form on page 103; the 'Permission to administer medicine/treatment' form on page 108; the 'Accident record' sheet on page 109; and the 'Existing injuries' sheet on page 144 are reproduced by kind permission of NCMA.

The extract from *All About Me* on page 193 is reproduced by kind permission of Sheila Wolfendale, the author, and NES Arnold, the publishers.

The 'Principles of excellence in childminding practice' (Appendix C) are reproduced by kind permission of NCMA and CACHE.

The statement of children's emotional needs on page 28 and the general guidelines for toilet training on page 33 from Beaver M. et al., *Babies and Young Children, Book 2* (2nd edition), 1999 and the table 'Sequence of Language Development' (Appendix B) on page 220 from Beaver, M. et al., *Babies and Young Children, Book 1* (2nd edition), 1999 are reproduced by kind permission of Stanley Thornes (Publishers) Ltd.

'The extent of violence involving children' on page 139, from 'Children and Violence: the Report of the Commission on Children and Violence' convened by the Gulbenkian Foundation, is reproduced by kind permission of the Calouste Gulbenkian Foundation.

The procedure for investigating a case of possible child abuse on page 148 is adapted from *Child Protection: A Guide for Midwives* by Jenny Fraser, published by Books for Midwives, 174a Ashley Road, Hale, Cheshire WA15 9SF.

The table 'What places children at risk of child abuse?' on page 150 is reproduced from *Child Abuse and Neglect: an introduction, Workbook one, making sense of child abuse* by kind permission of the Open University.

The extract from *Playladders* on pages 190–191 is reproduced by kind permission of Hannah Mortimer, Educational Psychologist, North Yorkshire LEA.

The 'Checklist to assess children's social development' on page 192 is reproduced by kind permission of D.E. McClellan and L.G. Katz.

The authors and publishers have made every effort to trace the owners of copyright material. Should copyright have been unwittingly infringed in this book, the owners should contact the publishers who will make corrections at reprint.

INTRODUCTION

This book is written for people who are thinking of entering the childminding profession, and for experienced childminders who are updating their skills. These individuals may wish to commit themselves to training courses such as the three units of the CACHE Certificate in Childminding Practice or to gaining a level 3 National Vocational Qualification in Early Years Care and Education. The activities introduced throughout the book could be used by individuals, members of child-minding groups or study groups. They could also contribute to written evidence for a National Vocational Qualification (NVQ) portfolio, allowing an assessor to evaluate understanding and knowledge.

The National Childminding Association (NCMA), which was established in 1977, has approximately 45,000 members. The Association promotes good child-care practice and offers information and support to childminders and parents. NCMA has a strong commitment to training and the need to take a professional approach to childcare.

The government has made a commitment to increasing provision in childcare and education. Family daycare – registered childminding – is one of the favoured options. From September 2001 the Office for Standards in Education (Ofsted) will take over responsibility from local authorities for the registration and annual inspection of childminders in England. Many of the staff currently working for local authorities' registration and inspection sections will transfer to Ofsted's Early Years Directorate.

At present, the government is consulting on proposed new standards for the regulation of childminding. The final standards will be published in the spring of 2001. Ofsted will register and inspect childminders on the basis of these new standards.

Since the vast majority of childminders are female, we have referred to the childminder as 'she' throughout the book. We have referred to the child as 'he' in odd-numbered chapters and 'she' in the even-numbered ones.

1 CHILDMINDING AS A CAREER

This chapter includes:
- Advantages and disadvantages of childminding
- What makes a skilled childminder?
- Registration
- Preparing yourself and your family for childminding
- Support systems
- Training

There are several reasons why you might choose to become a childminder. You might have given up a career while you stay at home to look after your own young children, and need to earn some money. You might have a childcare and education qualification that you wish to use at home. You might 'like children', and miss the constant company of your own children now they have started school. You might be looking after your grandchild with great enjoyment, and feel that a companion for him would be a good idea. You might prefer working in your own home and being self-employed. For whatever reason, you have decided to make childminding your career.

Childminding is the largest form of daycare provision outside the home for under-fives. There are approximately 100,000 registered childminders in the UK. They provide the equivalent of more than 200,000 full-time places for under-fives, although the actual number of children cared for is higher, as many attend on a part-time basis. Childminders also provide care for a substantial number of school-age children outside school hours and during school holidays.

Advantages and disadvantages of childminding

The advantages are:
- it is a useful way of earning money while remaining at home and of gaining experience with children of various needs and ages
- it is a satisfying career, providing personal fulfilment
- it is a flexible job, where you can set your own hours and organise your own work. It gives you independence
- it provides companionship for your own children, and satisfies your wish to play a role in children's development
- it offers possible access to some training programmes and can lead to training for a professional qualification
- through the National Childminding Association (NCMA), it provides help and support through local groups.

The disadvantages are:
- possible poor pay and long hours
- interference with your family's social life
- wear and tear on your home and furniture
- some families find it difficult or are unwilling to pay, and it can be embarrassing to chase defaulters
- a possible sense of isolation and a lack of adult company
- needing to buy a number of expensive safety items of equipment
- possibly having to deal with difficult parents without immediate support.

Activity
What would you consider would be the greatest advantage and disadvantage for you, in becoming a childminder?

Parents who work often choose childminders to care for their children because, apart from the flexibility of the hours, they prefer their children to:
- be in a domestic setting
- be cared for by one carer consistently
- have the opportunity to play with a small group of children.

What makes a skilled childminder?

Before starting the process of registration and training, you should consider the nature of the job. Childminding involves:

- working in partnership with parents, recognising that they have the main role in their children's upbringing
- being prepared to understand and accommodate various child-rearing practices, always putting the welfare of the child first
- educating children, supporting and stimulating their learning and development by offering a wide range of activities and play opportunities
- ensuring equality of opportunity, recognising each child as an individual, giving them opportunities to develop their full potential
- commitment to children and their families, preparing to offer stability over a period of time
- anti-discriminatory practice, presenting a positive role model and helping children to develop positive attitudes towards others from a variety of cultures, backgrounds and religions, and towards those with disabilities
- adopting safe and hygienic practices
- playing a part in protecting children from abuse and neglect
- developing a professional approach, and the ability to work in partnership with other professional workers
- being open to scrutiny, personally and in your home

You need to ask yourself whether you have the qualities required for a caring and demanding profession. While it is not totally necessary to have previous experience of working with children, it is sensible to have some knowledge of different age groups and some experience of how children behave in groups of two or three. You will need to be able to tolerate a high level of noise, enjoy messy activities, be patient, firm and consistent. You should be open-minded and responsive to other child-rearing practices.

You need to be in good physical and mental health. Looking after children is a strenuous physical job as well as an intellectually stimulating one. Young children are prone to many minor illnesses and you will need to build up resistance to coughs and colds very quickly. Recurrent back problems or eczema are examples of chronic medical conditions for which you may wish to seek medical advice before pursuing a career in childminding. A neurotic or depressed personality will not be able to offer a happy, stable environment to the children.

Men and women who represent the ethnic groups within the local community have much to offer as childminders. Men are generally under-represented in early years work.

If you have outside interests and hobbies, such as a love of music, enjoyment of reading, skill at various crafts, an understanding of art, or an interest in nature and animals, you will be able to share these experiences with the children. This will widen their horizons and aid their learning and development.

As well as caring for the children, you will find yourself working closely with the parents, social services staff and perhaps other professional people. Confidence in yourself is the key, whether you have a quiet, calm manner or a lively, impetuous nature. A sense of humour is especially important when working with children and with other people.

Activity
Draw up a profile of yourself using the table on page 5.

Registration

It is illegal to care for other people's children under the age of eight in your own home for two or more hours per day for reward, unless you are a close relative, or unless you are registered as a childminder. The Children Act 1989 requires local authorities to be satisfied that a person proposing to look after children under eight is 'fit', or in other words, suitable to do so. The purpose of the registration process is:
■ to protect children
■ to give reassurance to parents
■ to ensure quality
■ to provide a framework that parents understand.
NCMA guidelines' definition of a 'fit' person is someone who:
■ 'enjoys being with young children and has experience of dealing with them
■ is aware of the possible long-term commitment required in caring for other people's children and is prepared to make such a commitment
■ has a practical understanding of the social, physical, intellectual, communication and emotional development of young children
■ can create a warm, caring, relaxed atmosphere and has the ability to provide a stimulating environment which fosters children's development at each stage
■ is prepared to care for children in harmony with parents' practices and values, respecting the special relationship between children and their parents, and to share information with parents on a regular, planned basis while keeping confidences about information concerning families
■ has a commitment to and understanding of equality of opportunity and will value and respect each child as an individual
■ will not discriminate against children and their families on any grounds such as racial/ethnic origin, cultural/religious background, gender, disability, marital status or sexuality
■ will encourage children to question stereotyped views and to reject prejudice against other people
■ can provide a healthy and safe environment and a nutritious diet as agreed with parents
■ is physically and emotionally able to cope with the demands of caring for young children
■ is able to keep appropriate records
■ does not have a past history or a relevant criminal record, which could indicate that s/he was or is unfit to care for young children'.

(Reproduced by kind permission of NCMA)

SELF APPRAISAL

	Strengths	Weaknesses
Health record		
Interests/hobbies		
Personality		

Communication skills:
    written
 	
    oral		

Reliability		
Knowledge of various cultures		
Experience of working with children		
Ability to organise own work		

This page may be photocopied. © Stanley Thornes (Publishers) Ltd

The registration will also assess the suitability of the domestic premises, inside and outside. A registration officer will assess:

- access to outside play space and safety factors
- safety with regard to electric fires, sockets, gas fires, open fires and radiators
- safety with regard to windows
- safety with regard to floor coverings
- safety with regard to glass
- safety in the kitchen and stairways
- the use of safety equipment, such as stair gates and cooker guards
- cooking facilities
- arrangements for the care and control of pets
- the cleanliness of the premises.

STAFF/CHILD RATIO

One childminder can care for:
- up to three children under five years of age. (NCMA recommend that only one of these children should be under the age of one year, except in the case of multiple births)
- up to six children between the ages of five and seven
- up to three children under five and three children between five and seven.

These figures include the childminder's own children.

The size and suitability of the premises will also be a factor in determining the number of children allowed. Two or more childminders may be jointly registered and work together in the same premises if the premises are suitable. Planning approval for change of use of premises may be needed for larger groups of children.

A childminder may work with an assistant. The assistant must be registered as such by the local authority. Working with an assistant does not increase the number of children minded. The assistant must not be in sole charge of a child except in an emergency.

In some families the partner of the prospective childminder may also apply for registration. This will provide emergency cover only (unless the partner is a registered childminder in their own right), and some additional assistance, but will not affect the number of children minded. All adults living in your home over the age of sixteen will be included in the process of checks carried out by the social services registration officer.

MAKING AN APPLICATION

Local authorities may vary in their procedure for registration; some for example may request attendance at a briefing meeting prior to application, while others start with the submission of the application form, together with a non-returnable fee. The application will be processed by a registration officer, who will arrange a schedule of visits to discuss the suitability of the applicant and of the home environment.

The local authority will carry out certain checks before registering you, which will include:

■   a police check on you and everyone over sixteen years who lives at your address
■   a medical check
■   a social services check
■   a dog check, making sure you have no dangerous dogs. Other dogs may have to be checked by a vet
■   at least two personal references being sought
■   several home visits being made to discuss numbers of children, to assess safety and hygiene in the home, and to ensure you can provide warmth and stimulation.

There may be visits from the fire prevention officer and the environmental health officer. Many local authorities will require applicants to complete a training course prior to registration.

The process of registration can be quite lengthy, particularly if alterations to the premises have to be carried out. You will be reminded that until you are registered you are not able to care for children legally.

REQUIREMENTS OF REGISTRATION

At the conclusion of the registration process you should be clear about:
- the number and ages of the children you are registered for
- what records concerning the children and the families you are required to keep
- safety procedures
- holding public liability insurance (available from NCMA)
- your requirement to attend training sessions
- your commitment to equal opportunities
- the time when you will be required to renew your registration during an annual inspection.

NCMA recommend that a home visit should be made within three months of registration, to observe the minder with the children. They also recommend that all visits should be carried out by the same person, and that childminders should be visited four times a year, and some of these visits should be carried out without notifying the childminder in advance, unlike the annual inspection, for which notice must be given.

Preparing yourself and your family for childminding

It is often difficult to combine a balance between employment and the needs of oneself and of the family. With childminding, this is even more difficult, as you will have a sense of obligation to the children and their families which might, on occasion, mean that you put the needs of your own family second.

POSSIBLE EFFECTS ON YOU

You will be:
- working very hard
- working longer hours
- taking on a professional role
- making relationships with people outside the family
- changing your routines
- finding it difficult to make time for yourself, such as having your hair cut, going to the dentist or meeting friends, and having less time for recreational activities and hobbies
- feeling stress from time to time
- managing a business
- having to assimilate new knowledge and understanding of children's needs and development
- feeling anxious about keeping another person's child safe
- having to balance the needs of your family with the needs of the children you mind.

POSSIBLE EFFECTS ON YOUR PARTNER

He may be:
- aware of other children in the house
- putting up with changes in the family routine
- involved with making the home environment safe
- expected to play a part in meeting the needs of children
- expected by you to register to provide you with emergency cover
- expected to do more chores around the house
- expected to submit to the registration checks
- expected to interact socially with the parents of the minded children
- expected to give up smoking in the house, or in front of the children
- expected to be up and dressed before the children arrive
- disturbed when trying to sleep, if he works shifts.

POSSIBLE EFFECTS ON THE CHILDREN

They may:
- have to share you with other children

- have to share their home and possibly their toys
- find it is more difficult for you to attend school events
- have to be tidier and keep their own treasured possessions stored away
- be expected to do some of the household chores
- have the opportunity to make lasting friendships
- have the opportunity to be caring towards younger children
- have the opportunity to enjoy the company of older children
- have the opportunity of learning about other cultures
- have more play equipment
- be restricted as to choice of pet.

POSSIBLE EFFECTS ON THE HOME

There may be:
- more wear and tear on the furniture and equipment
- extra space taken up by safety and play equipment and for storing nappies
- extra storage needed for catering for larger numbers
- additional cleaning
- a large investment in safety, which might include new safety glass in doors, bars or locks on windows, locks on some doors and cupboards, and fitting safety gates
- a need to make the garden safe and secure.

When considering becoming a childminder, you have to talk it through with your partner, your older children and other members of the extended family who may be in frequent contact with you. Childminding will make many changes in the life of everyone in your family, and it would be very difficult to carry out this demanding career successfully without the support and encouragement of everyone concerned.

> **Activity**
> Identify any particular difficulties you or anyone in your family will encounter, as a result of you becoming a childminder.

Completing the 'Questionnaire for a new childminder' on page 11, designed by NCMA, will help you to focus on what provision you are prepared to offer and you will find it useful in explaining your service to the parents.

Support systems

We all need support and advice, particularly when we start a new job. Many minders decide to choose childminding because they have had their own children looked after in family daycare. Many of these relationships turn into friendships, and most experienced childminders would be pleased to support new people in the field.

Conditions of the childminding service offered

A questionnaire for a new childminder

Complete this, filling in the conditions you are willing to offer as part of your childminding service. To help you decide, discuss the conditions with other childminders or your under-eights adviser. Think about your reasons for setting each condition. Use it to explain to parents the service you feel you can offer.

I can offer full-time care   Yes   No

I can offer part-time care   Yes   No

The earliest I am willing to start in the morning is ....

The latest I am willing to finish in the evening is ....

I am willing to work a maximum of .... hours in a day

I cannot offer a service on .... days

The meals I am prepared to offer are ....

I am willing to work in school holidays   Yes   No

I am willing to work at weekends   Sometimes   Never

I am willing to have children overnight   Sometimes   Never

The youngest child I am willing to care for is ....

The oldest child I am willing to care for is ....

I am willing to take children to
    and from playgroup/pre-school   Yes   No

The playgroups/pre-schools I am willing to go to are

    ....

I am willing to collect children from school   Yes   No

The schools I am willing to go to are ....

Reproduced by kind permission of the National Childminding Association

This sample form is for illustrative purposes only. Copies of the form can be obtained from NCMA.

Questionnaire for a new childminder

Seeking help and advice is not a sign of weakness, but shows maturity and an awareness of the difficulties of the job. Many minders will be able to call on family and friends to sustain and encourage them and they will be a source of strength in times of uncertainty. All discussions and conversations must observe the rules of confidentiality.

PROFESSIONAL SUPPORT

The National Childminding Association

NCMA acts as a support network to promote quality and to improve the status and conditions for childminders, the children and their parents. It is a public voice for childminding, lobbies political parties and uses the media to promote childminding. It also liaises with various government departments. It produces information for members, provides free legal advice, offers training, insurance and publications and business materials to help childminders run their businesses effectively. It is currently involved in setting up childminding networks that can make a major contribution to Early Years Development and Childcare Partnerships.

NCMA realise that childminding can be a lonely job, and encourages childminders to set up their own groups which offer childminders the opportunity to:

- meet other childminders with similar experiences
- discuss problems, issues and concerns
- borrow equipment and use the toy library
- participate in vacancy co-ordination schemes
- provide emergency back-up
- attend drop-in sessions or more formal meetings with speakers
- attend outings and social occasions
- participate in in-service training

Most childminding groups are affiliated to NCMA and are able to take advantage of the benefits this brings to their members.

Other professionals

Other people who support childminders are:

- social services under-eights advisers, who may be registration officers or development workers
- NCMA officers or co-ordinators
- NCMA county/borough committees
- health visitors (either your own, or those of the families you mind)
- infant and primary school teachers.

If you are discussing a child with other professional people, it is important not to pass on confidential information without gaining the permission of the parents first. By contributing support and help to other people, you are more likely to receive support yourself.

Training

'I hear: I forget. I see: I remember. I do: I understand'

(Chinese saying)

Many local authorities are now requiring childminders to attend preparation training courses as a pre-requisite to registration. Childminders can now prepare for a nationally recognised qualification by taking NCMA's 'Developing Childminding Practice' (DCP) Stages 1 and 2 which will give the childminder knowledge of child development and behaviour, child protection, making good relationships, equal opportunities, safety, record keeping and business needs. Childminders may then choose to do a National Vocational Qualification (NVQ) in Early Years Care and Education following the DCP. Some minders who are very experienced may choose to prepare for the NVQ without previously attending a training course.

Childminders will benefit from training by:
- valuing the skills of family daycare
- developing knowledge, skills and professional attitudes
- developing good childminding practice
- gaining greater self-esteem and self-confidence
- learning by participating in discussion and from the experience of others
- reflecting on their practice
- learning through observation how to assess children's needs in an objective fashion
- being able to offer support to other childminders
- gaining a qualification.

Discussion about training needs should be part of the annual inspection process. Training for one profession may lead to an interest in another. Gaining knowledge can become addictive, leading to a thirst for learning in other areas.

2 RELATIONSHIPS WITH PARENTS

This chapter includes:
- The parent as the child's primary carer and educator
- The first meeting
- Why women work
- The Children Act 1989
- Understanding various cultures and child-rearing practices
- Families under stress

As you have decided to embark on a career as a childminder, offering quality childcare and education, you will have realised how important it is to build good relationships with the parents of the children in your care. The words 'parent' or 'parent/carer' are used to describe all primary carers, whether they are the child's biological parents, foster parents, adoptive parents, grandparents or other relatives having responsibility for the child.

The parent as the child's primary carer and educator

From as long ago as the 1950s it has been acknowledged that the support and aspirations of the parents play a vital part in the educational attainment of the children. All the research shows the importance of parental interests and involvement and therefore parents need to be kept well-informed about their child's development and behaviour and understand your approach to their child's learning. The child will benefit most when the triangle of parent, child and childminder are all working together in harmony.

Parents spend time with their children and will know their strengths and weaknesses, anticipate their needs and will have made many decisions about their child prior to placing the child with you. Therefore it is sensible to work with the parents in all aspects of care and education for the benefit of the child. It will add to the security of the child to see parents and childminder working together and in regular communication.

The first meeting

With any professional relationship, there will be a certain amount of tension and anxiety felt by both yourself and the parent/s at the first meeting. The parents' range of emotions may include:

- guilt at leaving their child with a stranger
- anxiety about the safety of the child
- feeling that not knowing enough about childcare and education may prevent them from assessing the suitability of the minder
- doubts about the decision to return to work
- being unhappy at the thought of parting from the child
- being upset at possibly missing out on certain milestones, such as finding the first tooth, seeing the first steps or hearing the first words
- anxiety that the childminder will replace them in the child's affections
- anxiety about being able to cope with the logistics of running a home, doing a job, and developing a relationship with the childminder
- worrying how they will manage if the arrangement breaks down

The childminder's range of emotions may include:

- anxiety at a stranger's reaction to her home
- images of the parents as professional working people, and insecurity about her own status
- fear that she will not be able to form a satisfactory relationship with the parents
- fear that she may not like the child
- worries about cultural clashes
- worries balancing the needs of her family with those of the child she is about to mind

■ worries whether her knowledge and skills are sufficient to equip her to do the job satisfactorily.
■ anxiety about discussing business matters.

Realising that the first meeting can be an emotional one for both parties, try to arrange it at a time when you are not overwhelmed with other responsibilities, and you can sit together discussing all the issues in a relaxed, calm atmosphere. Making the parents feel welcome, by offering a cup of tea and some biscuits, and getting them to relax by engaging in some small talk, will help to build a positive relationship. If you manage the meeting successfully, the parent will be impressed by your professional approach.

The parents may come with a lot of questions and information for you, but, equally, you may find that they are new, inexperienced parents, who are not sure what to ask. NCMA has produced these checklists so as to help elicit information.

What the childminder needs to know about includes:
■ other members of the child's family, including pets
■ pet words and names and other vocabulary specific to the child
■ any special object or toy the child uses as a comfort object
■ what the child does and does not like to eat; what parents want and do not want the child to eat
■ anything the child finds alarming or unsettling, e.g. dogs, people in spectacles, beards

- the family's cultural, religious or traditional background, and the implications it has for caring for their child
- the parents' attitude to the activities you plan for the children, and how they feel about you taking them out (to shops, park, drop-in centre etc.)
- whether the child can use a cup; what eating implements she uses
- information about nappies and toilet training
- whether the child still has a nap; whether there are any routines which help the child to sleep
- the hours parents work and will need your services
- the address and telephone number where parents can be contacted in an emergency
- who will be collecting the child, and whether there is anyone who is not permitted contact with the child
- details of the family doctor and health visitor, the child's immunisation status and any allergies or health problems
- any new factors or special problems in the child's life.

See page 18 for a table in which to record information on the child's individual preferences.

What the parent needs to know about includes:

- where the children will spend their day. Show them the rooms (and any garden) to be used
- what the children will do during the day – play activities, meals, going out, television, stories, nap
- what sort of play equipment and materials you provide
- what sort of food you provide, and your attitude towards sweets and snacks
- something about your attitude to bringing up children, e.g. setting limits to behaviour, equal opportunities for all children
- what experience and training you have in looking after other people's children
- what safety equipment you use (including, if the children are to be taken in a car, the restraints used)
- what your plans are in the event of an emergency
- when your childminding services are available, and how much you charge
- details of your registration and insurance
- that you expect to use a written contract, signed by both parties
- your expectations about providing nappies, food, change of clothes, playgroup fees, etc.
- that you will not pass on confidential information about the family
- how many other children are being minded, and their ages
- your availability for taking children to and from playgroup, pre-school and school
- your policy if children are unwell
- that you will need their written permission to administer any form of medication, and for taking a child on an outing
- members of your family
- what sort of pets you keep and the children's access to them
- smoking in your home.

Child's individual needs

Child's name _____ D.O.B _____

Pre-school/Playgroup _____

School _____

	NOTES
Food Does the child have any allergies? Is the child given food choices? Is the child expected to finish the meal? What happens if the child refuses food?	
Dressing Can the child dress self? Does the child like privacy? Can the child tie own shoe laces?	
Toileting How often is the nappy changed? What is used to clean the baby? *During toilet training* How does the child indicate the need to use the lavatory? Will the child say s/he needs to use the potty? Are there special words or signals I should know? Is a nappy used when sleeping?	
Separation How does the child handle separation from parent? How is the child distracted? How does the child like to be comforted when distressed?	

Rituals
Is there a special way of doing things:
    at rest time
    at mealtime
    at other times?	

Preferences
What preferences does your child have for:
    food
    drink
    toys
    books
    persons
    stories
    games
    activities
    songs?	

For older/school-age children
Who are the child's best friends?
Is the child expected to do any chores?
What arrangements are there for:
    homework
    watching TV
    music practice
    outside activities?	

Medical concerns What past illnesses has the child had? Does the child have any allergies? Is there other information?	

As you develop your practice and become more experienced, you might like to build a portfolio, held in a ring-binder, showing your registration and inspection documents, insurance certificates, training certificates, any parents' testimonials, and a timetable of a typical day. This may be of interest to new parents, and make them feel more secure in their choice.

During this first meeting, you might take the opportunity to introduce the new family to your own family. If at all possible, time should be spent in exploring the suitability of the partnership before a final decision is made. Then the contract should be produced, as outlined in Chapter 15, and should be completed before the arrangement begins.

Once the decision has been made and the child is coming to you, you will need to discuss with the parents how you are going to help the child settle. Ideally, if the parents are not going straight back to work, you might suggest that they bring the child for short periods of time, staying with the child, helping her to become familiar with your home environment, your family and the other children you mind. The child can be left with you for gradually longer periods.

Remind the parents to bring the comfort object or a favourite toy in case she becomes momentarily distressed. Use this opportunity to communicate fully with the parents, to find out all you can about the family, and the way they like things done. Good communication will prevent problems arising and any that do arise can be easily dealt with at an early stage.

Case study

Pauline is in her late twenties and is a first-time mother. She has to return to work for financial reasons, and has settled her baby son of six months with Sarah, an experienced childminder. He is well and happy and thriving, but every morning Sarah observes Pauline crying as she walks down the road to the bus stop.

1 How can Sarah help Pauline?
2 Are there any outside organisations or professional workers that might be able to offer Pauline advice?

Why women work

Many of you will have made the decision to stay at home with your children, and not return to outside employment until all your children are much older. It is important that you respect the decision of others to return to work, even if their children are very young. If you express disapproval, it is likely to damage the relationship you hope to achieve with the parents. If you have your own children, remember that you are a working mother too!

There are many reasons why mothers work outside the home. Some women are leaving it later to start a family, and are usually quite well established in their careers. They are able to afford to pay for help with the children. Other women may have to work in lower paid employment so as to meet the family's basic needs. For some it may be temporary whilst their partner seeks employment. For some lone parents, a job may provide an antidote to isolation and depression.

From 1998, the Government is implementing a National Childcare Strategy to be put into place over the next five years, part of which will be a working families tax credit. To achieve success, and feel that the children are well cared for and secure, a good childminder who provides long-term care for the children and is happy with the family, is a major factor.

Increasing numbers of women are returning to work following childbirth. Research shows that two-thirds of mothers resume their careers within eleven months of having a baby and that they are returning to work sooner after giving birth. Eighty-one per cent go back within 28 weeks, and of these 20,000 women a year in the UK return to work after less than 14 weeks maternity leave. For many it is a financial necessity to maintain their standard of living, while for others it is important not to interrupt their careers for too long a period. Some employers operate schemes to help women employees to balance work and family commitments by providing opportunities for flexible working hours, job shares, dependency leave and workplace nurseries. These are in the minority, and most

mothers will retu   of their new
responsibilities or

The Childr

The Children Act 1989 has had a g   g to children,
affecting all children and their families.

Much of the old law was abolished and the emphasis of the new law was that
parents should have responsibilities for their children, rather than rights over
them. Parental responsibility is defined as the rights, duties, powers, responsibilities and authority that, by law, a parent of a child has in relation to the child, and
to his or her property.

The Children Act 1989 acknowledged the importance of the wishes of the
child. Parental rights diminish as the child matures. Parental responsibility is a
concept that is important when deciding who is in a position to make decisions
about the child and who should be contacted in any legal proceedings.

Those who can hold parental responsibility are:

- the mother, who always has parental responsibility, whether married or not.
  She can only lose it when an adoption or freeing order is made
- the natural father, who has parental responsibility jointly with the natural
  mother, if they are married to each other at the time of the child's birth or sub-
  sequently marry. He too can only lose it if an adoption or freeing order is made
- the unmarried father may acquire parental responsibility by agreement with
  the mother or by court order
- the step-parent can acquire parental responsibility by obtaining a residence
  order and will lose it if that order ends
- the local authority acquires parental responsibility when obtaining a care
  order or emergency protection order, and loses it when that order ends
- others, such as grandparents, may acquire parental responsibility by court
  order, and will lose it when the order ends.

Parental responsibility may not be surrendered or transferred. It can be shared
with a number of persons, and/or the local authority. Each individual having
parental responsibility may act alone in exercising it, but not in a way that is
incompatible with any court order made under the 1989 Act.

Local authorities have a responsibility to ensure minimum standards of childminding and day care for children under eight, by means of registration and
inspection of the care provided. Inspection must be carried out at least once a
year. The Department of Health and the Department for Education and
Employment have agreed principles of good practice for all children with childminders or in day care:

- the child's welfare and development is of paramount importance
- the child should be respected as an individual and treated in such a way as to
  meet her particular needs
- the parents' primary responsibility for their child should be recognised and
  respected

- va ⬛ ⬛ ⬛ ious and linguistic backgrounds should be ⬛ ⬛ ⬛ ⬛ ⬛ ⬛ ⬛
- childminders should work in ways which reflect the fact that parents are the first caregivers and educators of their child
- parents should have access to information about available services and be able to make informed choices.

Understanding various cultures and child-rearing practices

FAMILY TYPE

Children are brought up in many different types of families. These include:
- the nuclear family: a small family unit of parents and children, with no other family members living with them
- the extended family: this includes parents, children, and other family members who may live with the family or close by, and who are in frequent contact with each other
- the lone-parent family, sometimes known as the single- or one-parent family: the mother or father plus children. Roughly ninety per cent of these households are headed by the mother and ten per cent by the father. Of the women, about seventy per cent are divorced or separated, twenty-three per cent are single and seven per cent are widowed.
- the reconstituted family, sometimes known as 'blended': parents have divorced or separated and re-married or are living with new partners and perhaps their children
- homosexual family: two men or two women living together with the children of a previous heterosexual partnership, or in some gay relationships, their own children. The children may be adopted. All the research carried out since the sixties shows no differences in the social and emotional development of children living in these households, or to their gender orientation.

Other family types include communes, where many groups of people live together and support each other, and travellers, such as 'New Agers' and Romanies, but they are unlikely to use the services of childminders.

VARIOUS CULTURES

NCMA have stated that 'parents are central to children's lives and, in the interests of children's welfare, childminders should provide care which is consistent with that of home'.

Children's needs and parents' wishes may derive from a cultural or religious source or from medical reasons, or quite simply, that is what the parents want for their child. Parents' wishes and child-rearing practices must be respected and every effort made to comply with them.

Childminders and parents should discuss and come to agreements about matters relating to:

- food, its preparation and eating, for example whether it is to be meat-free or certain meats are to be excluded
- personal hygiene, for example using the lavatory and hand-washing
- skin- and hair-care, for example which creams and combs are suitable for some African-Caribbean children
- the question of clothing during play, for example maintaining modesty in physical play, covering very curly or braided hair for sand play, or protecting skin against strong sunlight
- periods of rest and sleep, for example what routines, comfort objects or activities such as massage are expected
- any other expectations
- managing unwanted behaviour.

Do not assume that because a family is part of a particular cultural group, they follow all the practices of that culture. It is essential to discuss all aspects of the child's care with the parents and find out what they want.

Activity

You are approached by a Muslim family who wish you to care for their three-year-old daughter and eighteen-month-old son.
1 What will you need to ask the parents?
2 How will you demonstrate to the parents that you can provide the care they wish for their children?

When parents explain what they want for their child, it may be necessary to discuss any compromises which have to be made in order to care for children from several different family backgrounds, and reach some compromise arrangements. Once agreement has been reached, respect parents' wishes and stick to the practices agreed. Not to do this would represent a betrayal of parents' trust and demonstrate a lack of respect for their views and child-rearing practices.

Families under stress

The families of the children you mind might be feeling stress for many reasons. This might occur once the children have started with you, or be long-standing. The parents may become:

- difficult to communicate with
- reluctant to fulfil the terms of their contract, such as being slow to pay you or unreliable about the time they should collect and deliver the child
- reluctant to discuss the needs of the child
- uninterested in the child's achievements
- depressed and unresponsive to offers of help
- angry and aggressive towards you.

The child might:

- be difficult to manage
- be clinging and fretful
- show anxiety at separation from the parents
- display mood swings, ranging from being withdrawn to being aggressive
- show an increase in comfort behaviour
- be reluctant to go home at the end of the day
- regress in development.

A situation in the family where the child you are minding is obviously unhappy cannot be left to resolve itself. This is also true if the parents are taking advantage of your good nature and not contributing to a positive working relationship. If you find yourself in this position you will attempt to:

- acknowledge your feelings
- seek opportunities to communicate with the parents in a non-threatening, non-judgemental manner
- be open and assertive. State your needs to the parents
- keep calm if you have to deal with an angry parent. Listen to what is being said and do not respond in an aggressive way
- keep meticulous records of the child's behaviour and incidents involving the parents
- employ stress management techniques and persuade the parents to do the same
- advise the parents about sources of help and support in the community.

If you are unable to alter the situation and the parents continue to be stressed, making the child unhappy, you have no alternative but to contact your daycare adviser or NCMA, making them conversant with the situation and asking for advice and support.

CASE STUDY

Sally is a busy, experienced minder who has been caring for Rosie, aged two, for the last three months. She has established a good working relationship with Rosie's mother. For the last month, Rosie's aunt has been collecting Rosie on a Wednesday. On the last two occasions, she has been very late and smelling of alcohol. Sally knows that Rosie's mother, who is a lone parent has to work late on a Wednesday.

1 How do you think Sally should handle this situation?
2 Describe any situations where a childminder might refuse to allow someone to collect a child.
3 How can Sally support and advise Rosie's mother?

GOOD PRACTICE IN WORKING WITH PARENTS

1 Respect all parents as individuals, and learn from them different ways of child-rearing. Their practice may be different from yours, but is no less valid. Be open to a variety of opinions.
2 Respect parents' values, practices and preferences.
3 Provide a welcoming and relaxed atmosphere in your home, encouraging

parents to settle their children in and to spend time whenever they wish.

4 Avoid patronising parents. Remember they are the experts on their own individual children.

5 Try to communicate, at the end of the day, the important aspects of the child's day, sharing negative and positive situations alike.

6 Be professional at all times. Never gossip about parents to other parents. Refuse to listen to other people's unsubstantiated hearsay.

7 Offer reassurance and encouragement to parents, always emphasising the central role they play in their children's lives.

8 Be clear about the service you are offering. The more time you spend in discussion with the parents prior to accepting the child, the less likely it is that there will be problems.

Activities

1 Describe how you make a good relationship with parents who have a different first language from you.

2 How do you work with parents to promote the child's confidence and self-esteem?

3 THE NEEDS OF CHILDREN

This chapter includes:
- **Developing relationships with children**
- **Routines**
- **Physical care routines**
- **Nutrition**

When working with children, it is important to understand that there is a variety of needs that have to be met before children are able to grow and develop satisfactorily and achieve their full potential. It is necessary to maintain a balance and adopt a holistic approach in caring for children. This means taking into account all aspects of development, care and education and the interaction of one upon the other. Children belong to many diverse groups, with various values, religions, and approaches to child-rearing. All children need love and security, stimulation and education, routine physical care and the right to protection. You need to be aware of children's needs, so that together with your knowledge of child development, you will be fully equipped to nurture the children's maximum growth and development.

Communicating regularly with the children's parents, building a relationship of trust and exchanging information, will keep you up to date with the changing needs of each child. Establishing routines throughout the day and bearing in mind each child's particular needs, will help to give the child confidence and security.

Developing relationships with children

You would not have become a childminder if you did not very much enjoy the company of children. Building trusting relationships does not happen overnight. You will have to work at it with every new child you take on.

A great deal will depend on your relationship with the child's parents. You will have spent some time getting to know them, reassuring them that you are a skilled professional worker, and that their child will be safe and well-nurtured in your care. You will have gathered all the essential information that you need to know, and answered all their questions about your practice. First impressions are important, and you will do your best to make sure that the parents and the child feel welcome in your home.

Settling in a new child needs a great deal of thought. Ideally, one or other of the parents will be able to stay for a while during the first week, and this will help the child to feel secure. The youngest babies will probably settle quite easily, but once the baby is eight months old or so he may feel a great deal of anxiety and distress. The longer the parent can stay and share the care with the childminder, the sooner the baby will feel secure and allow the parent to leave without fuss.

Older children vary a great deal in their response to a new environment. This is partly because of previous experiences and partly due to the personality of the child. A child who is finding it difficult to settle with you will be helped by the parent staying as long and as often as possible. It is sometimes helpful if you visit the child in his home, where he might see you as a family friend. Once the parent has to go, he or she should do so quickly, as the longer the goodbyes are drawn out, the more distressing it can be for the child. On the other hand, the parent must not sneak out, without the child seeing her, as this can lead to distrust and insecurity on the part of the child.

Once the parent has finally left, try to give the child as much of your attention as you can. Provide activities that are familiar to the child and that do not require too much concentration and effort. In the first few days, perhaps he could bring one or two treasured toys from home. Check that he has his comfort object with him and that it is available to him whenever he needs it. He may demand cuddles and hugs, and you will need to respond to this. Remember that some children do not like close physical contact with anyone except their mother, and this should be respected.

After a little while, the new child will have fitted well into your home, and this is the time to develop a loving, caring relationship. Children have many emotional needs and you will play an important part in helping them to develop emotional strengths, and enabling them to reach adulthood, confident in themselves and valuing their achievements.

From the moment of birth, the baby begins the process of attachment, bonding with the mother in the same way as the mother bonds with the baby. This love and mutual trust is the basis of emotional development, allowing the child to continue to make loving and trusting relationships with other members of the family, with you and later with the outside world.

Settling a child successfully into a new situation often needs careful handling. The birth of a new baby may lead to feelings of jealousy and rejection. Problems within the child's family, such as divorce, unemployment, death or addiction may distress the child and halt their emotional development, causing the child to regress and become emotionally less mature. Understanding the stages of emotional development is a critical factor in ensuring good practice.

The following is a statement of children's emotional needs (Beaver M. et al., *Babies and Young Children, Book 2*: *Work and Care*, 1999). 'Children have many emotional needs:

- affection: the feeling of being loved by parents, carers, family, friends and the wider social community
- belonging: the feeling of being wanted by a group
- consistency: the feeling that things are predictable
- independence: the feeling of managing and directing your own life
- achievement: the feeling of satisfaction gained from success
- social approval: the feeling that others approve of your conduct and efforts
- self-esteem: the feeling of being worthwhile.

The absence of any of the above can lead to unacceptable behaviour as children struggle to get what they need.'

You probably feel that you know what children need, perhaps having had your own, but looking after other people's children requires a more professional approach, and as you are in touch with more children you will gain a wider knowledge and understanding of the wide range of needs exhibited by children.

Routines

Routines refer to regular events, organised and planned within the day, such as hygiene practices, mealtimes, nap times, exercise and play. It is impossible to generalise and describe a childminder's day, as each one will be unique. Much depends on the ages and the number of the children, your established family routines, and personal preferences. Obviously, if you are caring for a school-age child, one of your routines will be taking and collecting him from school.

In your home, television programmes may be part of your routine. When used wisely, television is a useful educational tool, which also allows you to have a short time to relax. Be very selective in the programmes you allow the children to watch. It is a good idea to tape some programmes, such as *Sesame Street* or *Blue Peter*, and have them available to show the children at a time that suits you. The children will gain more from watching if you are with them to answer questions and to help them participate.

Undoubtedly, you will have to fit in some domestic routines in your busy day.

Encourage the children to help you, as this will lead to independence and teach them how to clear up after themselves. Many routine tasks can contribute to children's development and learning. For example, walking to school presents an opportunity for exercise and conversation and may expand the child's knowledge of the outside world.

Ideally, routines should take place at the same time each day, so that the young child feels secure by knowing what to expect. A childminder who is constantly changing her daily routines, and allowing herself to be overwhelmed by events, will find the children she is minding becoming fractious or even distressed. For this reason, you will need to arrange your routines carefully, allowing enough time for each one. Although not so tightly scheduled, you will also need to reflect on weekly routines, such as on what day Johnny has a music lesson, on monthly routines, which might include a major shopping trip, or getting your children's hair cut, and yearly routines, such as preparing for inspection or managing summer holidays, when everyone's holidays would have to be worked out. Time management is an issue for all childminders. A childminder's day can be very busy and complex, and there needs to be time built in for unforeseen events and for giving 'quality time' to individual children. This must be remembered when you are considering taking on additional children.

Physical care routines

Some routines require physical care. These include skin- and hair-care, sleep and rest, exercise, mealtimes, care of the teeth, and hygiene practices, such as hand-washing and toileting. Most children need adult help and supervision in their personal care requirements. Good standards of care are important to prevent ill-health, to increase self-esteem and gain acceptance by other children. The eventual goal is for the children to become independent and care for all their physical needs themselves.

SKIN- AND HAIR-CARE

The skin has many significant functions, including:
■ preventing injury to the internal organs
■ preventing infection entering the body
■ tactile awareness of hot and cold, and hard and soft
■ the secretion of sebum to lubricate the hair, and keep the skin soft and flexible
■ regulation of body temperature
■ disposal of waste products from the body in sweat
■ a role in producing vitamin D through exposure to sunlight, which is important for healthy bone growth.
Too much cleaning of the skin, particularly by scrubbing, removes the sebum and may make the skin dry and cracked.

Childminders should:
■ ensure that the children wash their hands and faces before and after handling and eating food
■ wash their hands after using the lavatory and after messy play
■ observe the skin for any rashes or sores
■ play a part in moisturising the skin of black children, taking advice from parents
■ protect the skin from excessive exposure to the sun, using hats, sun block or high factor sun-cream
■ play a part in treating skin problems, such as eczema and sweat rash, following discussion with the parents.
Hair will vary in colour, texture and style. There can be strong religious and cultural practices associated with care of the hair. Rastafarians, for example, will have long strands of braided hair, tied together. The girls will cover the hair with a scarf and the boys with a hat.

You are unlikely to have to wash children's hair unless it becomes very dirty following messy play. If you do, use a non-stinging gentle shampoo, rinse the hair well, and avoid using the hair-dryer. Prevention is better than cure, so have at hand some shower caps for the children when playing with sand, or with any other very messy material.

SLEEP AND REST

Sleep allows the body to rest and recover from its exertions, so it is important that children are encouraged to rest after vigorous physical exercise. Sleep consists of deep relaxing sleep and rapid eye movement (REM) sleep, when we dream. It is thought that children use REM sleep to make sense of their day, and if they are woken at this time they may become drowsy and disorientated.

Like adults, children appear to need differing amounts of sleep. You will need to discuss the sleep routines of babies and children with their parents and, where it is compatible with your other commitments you should attempt to follow this routine. You must remember that as the child is having a different and possibly busier day, he might require a nap even if this is against the wishes of the parents, and you will need to discuss his sleep needs with them.

Some children need to unwind and relax before they are able to sleep, and may need a comfort object to take with them for their rest. Even if children do not sleep during the day, there should still be a quiet period when they can look at books or just have a cuddle.

EXERCISE AND FRESH AIR

All children need exposure to fresh air and the opportunity to exercise during the day. This will:

- increase their oxygen intake
- reduce their exposure to the risk of infection
- increase their exposure to sunlight – needed for the production of vitamin D
- develop physical skills and co-ordination
- improve muscle tone and strengthen muscles
- burn up body fat
- enable them to sleep better
- improve their digestive and respiratory systems.

Allowing children to exercise every day will help them to establish this as a habit for life and may prevent future heart disease and obesity. Access to a garden is

obviously a great help in promoting fresh air and exercise, but even without one, it is possible to take the children to a park or playground regularly.

CARE OF THE TEETH

Childminders in consultation with parents play a part in encouraging good dental hygiene. They will:
- encourage children to brush their teeth after meals, using their own brush and a fluoride toothpaste
- provide a healthy diet, low in sugar, high in vitamins and calcium
- avoid giving sweet drinks, especially in a bottle or on a dummy
- restrict giving sweets to children
- not give sweet snacks between meals
- provide food, such as apples, carrots and brown bread, that has to be chewed.

One of the children may have a dentist's appointment in the near future. In partnership with the parents, prepare him carefully, discussing what is likely to happen, perhaps finding a book at the library about visiting the dentist. If you are nervous at the dentist, be careful not to pass any of your fears and anxieties on to the child.

TOILET TRAINING

There are many different theories and methods of toilet training, and you will need to discuss this fully with the parents before you take on the child. Toilet training can be a cause of friction between you and the parents who often do not realise that a consistent approach is vital for success.

You might find the following general guidelines (Beaver M. et al., *Babies and Young Children, Book 2: Work and Care*, 1999) useful. Beaver states that:

- 'the child must be aware of the need to use the toilet or potty. The central nervous system (CNS) must be sufficiently developed for the message that the bowel or the bladder is full to be understood by the brain. Babies of 12 to 18 months may know when they are soiled or wet, but are not yet able to anticipate it
- they must have sufficient language to tell their carer, verbally or with actions, that they need to go to the lavatory
- too much pressure at an early age can put the child off the idea completely and create a "battleground"
- there is a need to wait until the child is ready
- training should be fun! Carers should be relaxed and not show displeasure or disapproval about accidents which will certainly happen. The child may be more upset than the adult and deserves understanding
- seeing other children or adults use the lavatory will help the child to understand the process
- in theory, bowel control comes first: the child may recognise the sensation of a full bowel before that of a full bladder. However, most carers report that children are dry earlier than they are clean. This may be because children urinate more often than they have their bowels open, so have more practice
- you should have a potty lying around for a long time before it is used, and then it will become familiar. You should also watch for signs of a bowel movement and offer the potty, but not force it. If it is successful then congratulate the child and show them how pleased you are
- training is easier in warm weather when children can run around without nappies or pants. They can become aware of what is happening when they urinate or have their bowels open.'

Once a child is trained, he may still need reminding to use the lavatory, particularly before going to sleep or going out. Accidents can still happen, and you should just ignore them, keeping some spare pants available.

GOOD PRACTICE IN ENCOURAGING PERSONAL HYGIENE IN CHILDREN

1 Childminders should be a positive role model.
2 Establish routines that promote hygiene.
3 Make hygiene fun, by putting toys in the bath, having 'fun' toothbrushes and flavoured toothpaste.
4 Give each child their own flannel, toothbrush, towel and comb. Colour coding these is a good idea, to make sure they are kept separate.
5 Provide a foot-stool, so that the younger children can reach the basin comfortably and sit on the lavatory without fear of falling through the hole.
6 Teach them to care for themselves, and encourage independence in routines.

MEALTIMES

It is important for you to have a good understanding of nutrition and how to provide a well-balanced diet for the children in your care. A healthy nutritious diet plays a large part in promoting health, and in ensuring healthy development. The way you cook and eat, and the food you provide, will help the children to develop sensible eating patterns and will encourage children to try various types of food.

During your initial meeting with the parents, they will have told you of any special dietary requirements. You will need to have a good knowledge of special diets and understand why these are necessary, and this is covered in Chapter 10.

Eating is a basic human need and an activity that most people enjoy. It serves more than the need to survive and is tied into feelings of well-being. Eating at the table is a social activity, a time when relaxed conversations can take place, and news of the day shared.

Children's eating behaviour
Children's eating patterns develop from infancy and are shaped by their experiences. The attitude to food of the parents and carers is most influential. Adults might show concern and anxiety if a child refuses food, because they worry that the child might not thrive without what they feel is sufficient food. They might feel rejected that the meal they have prepared with such loving care has been refused. The child may come to the conclusion that whether they eat or not is of very great importance and therefore have a way of manipulating adults.

Provide a range of utensils for all the children, and they should then become skilled at using chopsticks and knives and forks. 'Table manners' are more important in some families than in others. It is up to you what behaviour you tolerate at the table. Remember that some cultures do not have the words in their language for 'please' and 'thank you'.

Appetites differ in children and are unpredictable. Children know their own hunger signs and it is more sensible to offer smaller portions, and provide more if the child requests it. If children say they are hungry in the middle of the morning, it is wiser to offer them a snack of fruit or raw vegetables, as filling up on milk, bread or biscuits will reduce the appetite for the midday meal.

Children have a shorter attention span than adults. Some find it very hard to sit at the table, and it might be a good idea to allow them to leave the table when they have finished, providing a quiet activity for them so as not to disturb the children who are slower. Allow children to eat at their own pace within limits.

Some children cause anxiety because they may:
- refuse to eat many foods
- linger for a long time over food
- refuse to swallow food
- display other poor eating behaviours.

If a child is causing anxiety, make a record of what food is being refused, how he behaves at the table, such as crying, complaining or throwing food, and what food he enjoys. Evaluate this information. You may see a pattern, such as too many snacks prior to the meal, and be able to resolve the problem. If the behaviour persists after you feel the child has settled with you, and there is no obvious reason, you will need to involve the parents and discuss how he eats at home.

CASE STUDY

Marion has recently registered as a childminder, and has her own child of nine months. She has started to care for Ben, aged two and a half years. She worked very hard at making a relationship with Ben's mother, and the settling-in period has gone well. There appears to be one concern: Ben sits at the table for long periods of time, chewing the same mouthful of food over and over again. He leaves the table with most of the food still on the plate, and the rest still in his mouth, which is later found in various places around the house.

1 Explain why this is a worrying situation.
2 Should Marion inform the parents?
3 Why do you think Ben treats food in this way?
4 How can Marion help Ben to enjoy his food more?

There is a fashion today for some parents to allow their children to 'graze'. This means eating continually, on demand, and usually walking around with the food. As a childminder, it is unlikely that you will be able to tolerate this, and you need to make this clear to the parents. Children are adaptable, and will probably accept your rules about eating food in your home.

Activity

How do you involve children in the preparation and clearing away of food? Why is this important?

GOOD PRACTICE IN ENCOURAGING HEALTHY EATING HABITS

1 Let children help themselves to food at mealtimes.
2 Allow children to help prepare food on occasion.
3 Encourage children to set the table and clear it.
4 Talk to children during the meal about the foods.
5 Encourage children to help mop up any spills.
6 Present food in an interesting way, mixing colours, flavours and textures.
7 Make your table look attractive, with a clean cloth and perhaps a small jug of flowers.
8 Encourage children to try new foods, presenting one new food at a time, when they are not tired or ill.
9 Set a good example by sitting at the table with the children, and showing your enjoyment of the food.
10 Never force children to eat new foods.
11 Never make children finish what is on their plates, or insist they sit at the table until they do so.

12 Make nutritious puddings as part of the meal and never use them as a reward or punishment.
13 Let children eat at their own pace.
14 Ignore fussy behaviour and praise hearty appetites.

Nutrition

When planning the meals you will offer the children, you must discuss them with the parents, as there are cultural, religious and medical concerns about certain foods that may not be acceptable to the family. You should respect any requests made by the parents, showing them the weekly menus, and abiding by their wishes. Do not assume because a child comes from a certain culture or religion, that the family will necessarily pursue the prescribed food regime. If you find it difficult to provide the diet requested by the family, ask them to bring in the food for the child. Never agree a certain diet, and then ignore it. See page 37 for information on dietary customs.

Prepare a variety of foods daily in adequate amounts, from the following food groups:
■ bread, cereal, rice and pasta
■ vegetables
■ fruits
■ milk, yoghurt and cheese
■ meat, poultry, fish, eggs, beans and pulses. Nuts provide protein but can be a hazard for young children. Before offering peanut butter, you must check with the parents that the child does not have an allergy.

Activity
How do you make sure that you offer children in your care a balanced, nutritious diet?

No single food can supply all the nutrients required by a child. Milk is an important food for children as it is rich in calcium, but it has little iron. Drinking too much milk may reduce the appetite for other important foods. Children over the age of two years, who eat well, may be offered semi-skimmed milk, rather than full cream. For children to have a nutritious diet, you must offer a variety of foods.

Water is an important nutrient and should be offered several times a day, instead of sugared drinks. Fibre or roughage is necessary in preventing constipation. It is found in brown rice, wholemeal bread or pasta, baked beans, pulses, potato skins, fruit and vegetables. Small children find it difficult to digest a great deal of fibre, but it can be offered in small amounts as a snack.

Fruits and vegetables are good sources of vitamins, especially when eaten raw. A variety is necessary, as they all contain different vitamins. Breads and cereals, especially whole grain products, are an important source of vitamin B and iron, and supply some protein.

DIETARY CUSTOMS

Food	Jewish	Sikh	Muslim	Hindu	Buddhist	7th Day Adventist	Rastafarian	Roman Catholic	Mormon
Eggs	No blood spots	✓	✓	Some	Some	Most	✓	✓	✓
Milk/Yoghurt	Not with meat	✓	Not with rennet	Not with rennet	✓	Most	✓	✓	✓
Cheese	Not with meat	Some	Some	Some	✓	Most	✓	✓	✓
Chicken	Kosher	Some	Halal	Some	✗	Some	Some	Some still prefer not to eat meat on Fridays particularly during Lent	✓
Mutton/lamb	Kosher	✓	Halal	Some	✗	Some	Some		✓
Beef	Kosher	✗	Halal	✗	✗	Some	Some		✓
Pork	✗	Rarely	✗	Rarely	✗	✗	✗		✓
Fish	With scales, fins and back-bone	Some	Halal	With fins and scales	Some	Some	✓	✓	✓
Shellfish	✗	Some	Halal	Some	✗	✗	✗	✓	✓
Animal fats	Kosher	Some	Some halal	Some	✗	✗	Some	✓	✓
Alcohol	✓	✓	✗	✗	✗	✗	✗	✓	✗
Cocoa/tea/coffee	✓	✓	✓	✓	✓ No milk	✗	✓	✓	✗
Nuts	✓	✓	✓	✓	✓	✓	✓	✓	✓
Pulses	✓	✓	✓	✓	✓	✓	✓	✓	✓
Fruit	✓	✓	✓	✓	✓	✓	✓	✓	✓
Vegetables	✓	✓	✓	✓	✓	✓	✓	✓	✓
Fasting (where not specified, fasting is a matter of individual choice)	Yom Kippur		Ramadan						24 hours once monthly

✓ Accepted   ✗ Forbidden

Adapted from *Nutritional Guidelines*, ILEA, 1985

Protein, found in meat, fish, poultry, beans and pulses, cheese and eggs, is important for growth and repair of body cells. This group also is a source of iron and other minerals. There is concern these days about the safety of meat, particularly if it is bought ready minced or on the bone. You will have your own view, but you should also discuss this issue with parents and respect their views.

To allow for their healthy growth and development, children have different nutritional requirements from adults. Children need a certain amount of fat in their diet. It is as well to offer less fat from animal sources, and more vegetable fat, such as frying food with oil instead of butter. Too much animal fat in the diet may lead to heart problems in later life.

There is controversy about the use of food additives. It is thought that some additives contribute to hyperactivity and allergies. Parents should advise you if they wish you to exclude certain foods from their child's diet. Many processed foods and drinks contain a great amount of additives, including salt and sugar. Looking at the labels will inform you of the amount of additives used in the product.

There is a view that some children, particularly the younger ones, or children who are unwell, benefit if they eat little and often. Snacks should certainly be offered if children are hungry, but try to discourage children from snacking less than two hours before a meal. Some examples of nutritious and enjoyable snacks are:

- fruit and fruit juices
- vegetable sticks, such as carrots, celery and cucumber
- yoghurt
- crackers
- oatmeal biscuits
- rice cakes.

Use sugar in moderation. If you are cooking with the children, try to cook something other than cakes and biscuits. Salt should be used sparingly in cooking, and should not be put on the table for children to help themselves.

It is quite common these days for families to be vegetarian and exclude meat from the diet. There are various types of vegetarians:

- lacto-ovo-vegetarians eat plant foods, dairy products and eggs
- lacto vegetarians eat plant foods and dairy products
- vegans eat no animal product of any kind
- fruitarians eat only fruit, including nuts and seeds
- the Zen macro-biotic diet is based on wholegrain cereals.

Problems rarely arise with the first two. A vegan diet is adequate with a supplement of vitamin B12. The latter two diets are not adequate for babies and children.

Activity

Write a menu for three children, aged between three and five years, for five days. One of the children is vegetarian. Roughly calculate the cost of the food.

All the children in your care, whatever their age, need your affection, consistency of care, understanding and an opportunity to play and learn. Respecting children's individual needs will increase the bond between you and their family.

4 CHILDREN'S DEVELOPMENT AND LEARNING

> **This chapter includes:**
> - **Developmental stages**
> - **Play**
> - **Activities with children**
> - **The early years curriculum**

Research has shown that close partnership between parent and carer encourages children's learning and development and extends their concentration and attention span. The amount of time the child spends in your care makes your role critical. A willingness to share information and discuss issues with the parents can help to identify possible concerns. Sharing your pleasure when milestones are achieved is good for the child's self-esteem, and helps to strengthen the partnership with the family.

Developmental stages

Children develop at different rates, and you may find that one of the children you mind might be advanced physically, being well co-ordinated and able to hop and jump at an early age, whereas others might be making more progress in language development than you would expect. Children vary in the age they attain a skill, but all development proceeds in stages. For example, a child learning to walk always goes through the following stages (see page 41):
- acquiring head control
- sitting with support
- sitting without support
- pulling to stand
- walking with support
- acquiring balance and walking.

Some children walk at ten months or even earlier, others may be delayed until eighteen months or later, whilst the majority walk between twelve and fifteen months. This is all within a normal range.

Development has been categorised under five areas: social, physical, intellectual, communication, and emotional (SPICE). See Appendix A.

SOCIAL DEVELOPMENT

A human being is born without any social skills and becoming a social being is learnt initially in the family, and then in the wider environment. Feral children

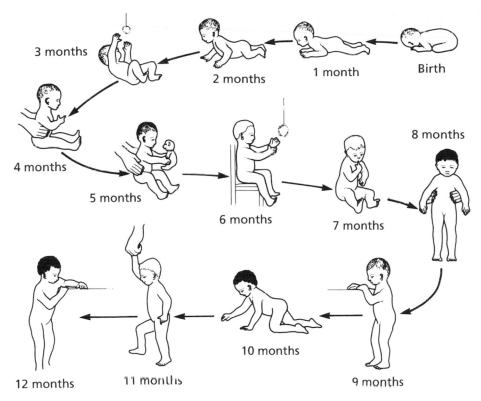

3 months

2 months

1 month

Birth

4 months

5 months

6 months

7 months

8 months

12 months

11 months

10 months

9 months

The development of locomotion

who are brought up by animals in the wild, or those children locked away with no human contact, not only do not develop socially but do not develop physical skills, such as walking and do not have any recognisable language. The existence of these children indicates clearly that all children need human contact to develop normally so that they can take their place in society.

Social development takes place alongside emotional development, and the importance of the environment cannot be over-emphasised. You will need to have a clear understanding of the stages and sequences of the child's developing relationships within society, the process of socialisation both within and outside the family, and the development of the child's social skills.

In our multi-cultural society, there is a variety of cultures with varying beliefs and values. Knowledge of these cultures will help you to appreciate the richness of the society and the difficulties sometimes encountered by children who are coping with more than one value system and many customs at a very young age.

Activity

Find out if any of the families you work with will be celebrating any major religious festivals during the next year. What might you do to help them celebrate?

PHYSICAL DEVELOPMENT

Physical development describes the acquisition of skills, such as the gross motor skills of running, sitting and throwing, all of which are to do with movement, and fine motor skills, such as feeding, threading and picking up objects, which are dependent on manipulation and hand–eye co-ordination.

Gaining physical skills is dependent on the opportunity for practise and the encouragement of the carer. The development of gross motor skills starts with head control, and works down the body, the child learning to sit, perhaps crawl, pull up and walk. She learns to balance and then to hop and skip. Fine motor skills are linked with vision and hand–eye co-ordination. These skills begin in the centre of the body, working outwards to the fingers, which increasingly take on more complex tasks.

Activity
Describe two activities that you provide for children to promote their fine motor development.

Physical development is often linked with growth, which is measurable; and relates to an increase in weight, height and head circumference. Potential growth is mainly genetically determined, although the environment will play its part. Better diet has resulted in taller and heavier people in most parts of the developed world. Babies are measured at birth, and this is used as a baseline for subsequent monitoring.

INTELLECTUAL (COGNITIVE) DEVELOPMENT

Intellectual development, sometimes called cognitive development describes the way in which we learn to think. It encompasses the ability to concentrate, memorise and understand information gained through the senses. As children develop intellectually, they are able to think logically and creatively and to relate past learning to solving present problems. There are many theories that show how this takes place, but most would agree that learning happens in stages and in a particular sequence, so it is important to recognise these stages and to encourage development in areas where learning is delayed.

Some theorists believe that most cognitive ability is inherited, whereas others think that the influence of the environment is more important. Piaget, the most influential of the theorists, argues that it is both.

Activities
1 Reflecting on some of the children you have minded, and perhaps your own children, do you think that intelligence is most influenced by inheritance or by the encouragement and stimulation of the parents and others who cared for and educated the children?
2 Describe two activities that you provide for children to help extend their concentration span.

Learning is aided by the child having opportunities to observe other adults and children and to observe and explore their world, by extending their language and by using their senses to the full. You will need to provide activities appropriate to the age of each child, so as to promote, encourage and extend children's learning and imagination. You will need to be conversant with the development of language and how this links with intellectual development.

COMMUNICATION (SOMETIMES CALLED LANGUAGE DEVELOPMENT)

Human beings are the only organisms that can converse fluently with each other and can read and write. The ability to communicate well is a key factor in happiness and achievement. The discovery of feral children has shown us that practising and exposure to language is essential from birth, and that without language it is not possible to grow and develop satisfactorily. Communication includes eye-gazing in babies, facial expressions, gestures, body language, reading and writing, understanding spoken language and speech.

In all countries and cultures language development follows the same sequence (see Appendix B). A good knowledge of language development will help you to detect a child whose language is immature or delayed, and you will know how to help a child yourself and when to suggest the parents seek help.

Children whose home language is not English have the enormous advantage of growing up speaking two languages fluently. When they first come to you they may need some support and additional help. Be careful not to assume that delay in acquiring English indicates that there is a delay in other areas of development. Access to books in their home language allows you and the parents to read with the children. Fluency in the home language will enable them to become fluent in English later on.

EMOTIONAL DEVELOPMENT

During your career as a childminder, you will realise how important it is to build relationships with children, helping them to develop emotional strengths, and enabling them to reach adulthood, confident in themselves and valuing their achievements. Your commitment to them will aid their emotional stability.

From the moment of birth, the baby begins the process of attachment, bonding with the mother in the same way as the mother bonds with the baby. This love and mutual trust is the basis of emotional development, allowing the child to continue to make loving and trusting relationships with other members of the family and later with the outside world. Childminders often have a part to play in giving young parents reassurance and helping them to bond with their baby. The relationship of the childminder and her charges never threatens the paramount relationships of parents and child.

There will be times in the lives of the children in your care when you will need to be particularly sensitive. Settling a child successfully into a new situation often needs careful handling. The birth of a new baby may lead to feelings of

jealousy and rejection in the older sibling. Problems within the child's family, such as divorce, unemployment, death or addiction may distress the child and halt their emotional development, causing her to regress. Your love and care will help build her self-esteem and give her a positive self-image, thus building confidence and leading to independence. Understanding the stages of emotional development is a critical factor in ensuring good practice.

SENSORY DEVELOPMENT

Initially, babies learn through their senses: vision, hearing, taste, smell and touch. As children grow older, the senses of vision and hearing become dominant. Nevertheless, it is important to promote all the senses, and encourage children to taste different foods, smell many different smells and develop their awareness of different textures.

Play

We all like to play. Adults play games, exercise, dance, explore creative activities, go on holiday, visit museums and art galleries, and indulge in passive activities, such as watching television, going to the cinema and theatre, listening to music and reading. All these activities adults find stimulating and enhance their enjoyment of life.

Children need the same opportunities, and you will be experienced in offering play activities to the children in your care. For them, stimulating play is vital as it is mainly by play that children learn.

For children, passive play such as watching videos is not as valuable as active play in which they participate. That is not to say that there is no place for television, but the child learns more if she watches with an adult, who helps to interpret what is happening.

Children's play reflects intellectual ability and development and has been called 'children's work'. It is an integral part of the daily life and the promotion of all-round development. Through play, the child experiences life and learns to understand the world and her place in it. Play can be social, when children interact with each other; some researchers look on play as a process of socialisation.

The baby plays from birth, the first 'toy' being the mother's breast. From this stage, play develops through several stages: solitary, parallel (playing alongside another child or adult), associative play with other children to co-operative play, involving planning and games with complicated rules.

There are many different types of play, indoor and out, structured and spontaneous. These include:

- child centred play, where the child chooses the activity
- imitative play, where the young child copies what the adult is doing
- domestic play, such as pretending to make cups of tea and sweeping the floor
- messy play
- play with natural materials, such as sand, water and mud
- imaginative play, which involves creative thought
- repetitive play, where the child feels the need to repeat an activity over and over again, until she feels satisfied
- creative play including art work and model-making
- vigorous physical play, usually taking place outside
- organised games, which include ring games and board games, and which often have rules.

Adults should avoid intervening too frequently and attempting to impose too rigid a structure on children's play. By interaction with the children, the adult can enrich the play, as long as this is done sensitively, based on observation and assessment of the child's need.

Activities with children

However familiar you are with providing play opportunities for the children in your care, you will need to remember that all activities should promote the children's all-round development.

Through your knowledge of the children and of the norms of development, you will be able to plan your activities with the children's needs in mind. This will help you to be aware of what is happening and when you need to step in to move the play forward. There will be many occasions when you feel that unstructured and spontaneous activities will be fun for all concerned and allow children to use their imagination. There are very few activities that do not have some value. The important point is that you are aware of the value of the activities you are planning and preparing.

Play and activities should start from birth and this stage is discussed in Chapter 6. It is not always possible to provide an activity in which all children within a wide age-range can participate. You might have to wait until the younger children are napping before offering a more complex activity to the older children.

Let older children help you with routine domestic activities. Laying the table, preparing food, sorting the clean washing, and putting away the shopping all require mathematical skills, concentration and a good vocabulary, and is part of their social development. Growing independence gives children self-esteem and confidence, all of which aid learning in other areas.

MESSY PLAY

Some activities provided for children are not adult-directed. You will just need to provide the materials and observe how the children use them, without expecting any end-product. You have to be very tolerant of mess if you allow messy play to take place inside your home, but it is possible to do most of the activities outside on a fine day.

Messy play, such as playing with cooked spaghetti mixed with liquid detergent and colouring, or experimenting with cornflour and water which becomes solid in your hand but liquid on a hard flat surface, is enjoyable for all children, but particularly so for the youngest ones. A large sheet of paper can be attached to a wall or to a fence in the garden, and paint in squeezy bottles can be squirted at it. Finger painting comes into this category: paints and paste are mixed together, and patterns made in the mixture with the fingers. Older children might like to print their creations.

Messy play is one of the best activities for intellectual development, as children use their imagination and creativity in planning and producing this work. Their concentration span is often extended in well-thought-out and enjoyable activities. Different materials encourage exploration and experimentation and this, in turn, leads to an understanding of design and technology. Mathematical and scientific concepts may be explored. Patterns may lead to an understanding of spatial relationships.

NATURAL MATERIALS

Water

Water is an indestructible material and children can bang and splash without harm. Playing with water, as with messy play, allows for many mathematical and scientific concepts to be learnt. Some children will enjoy using the equipment provided and finding out about floating and sinking, while others might enjoy playing with water on its own, finding it a soothing and relaxing experience. Playing with water links home with the childminder's home, as children are used to playing in their bath or at their parents' sink. Children learn that water comes in many forms – as snow, rain, steam and ice – and is essential for life.

Sand

You are unlikely to provide sand indoors in your home and, although some childminders have sandpits in their gardens, it is generally less familiar to children than water. Dry sand is relaxing and therapeutic to play with. A great deal can be learnt with the use of various tools. It is not suitable for very young children, unless closely supervised, as they tend to throw it around and get it in their eyes and hair as well as eat it. Wet sand is suitable for all age-groups. It can be used as a modelling material, and can be combined with blocks and cars and other small toys to stimulate the imagination. It will lend itself to many mathematical, scientific and technological experiments. Making patterns and marks in sand is linked to early literacy.

Mud

Once children are mobile, most of them find out about mud quite quickly, and should be allowed to play with it outside freely if suitably dressed and fully immunised. You will need to check that the garden is free from pesticides. Childminders should check their records to make sure children are protected against tetanus. It is one of the most enjoyable of natural materials for young children and is free and readily available in every garden. Mud can be mixed

with water to give enjoyable sensory experiences, and can be seen to dry out to revert to dry soil. Small animals found in the mud give interest and pleasure to children, who often need to be persuaded to return them to their natural habitat.

Modelling materials
Plasticine, dough and clay are all used for modelling. It is unlikely that you will use clay in your home, even outside, as it is extremely messy and needs close supervision.

Plasticine
This useful manufactured material is good for developing manipulative skills, and for making models with older children. It is much cleaner and less messy than other malleable materials and is often familiar to children from their play at home. It can get hard very easily and needs storing in a warm environment.

Dough
Dough can be made in many ways and presented to children in a range of colours, and the children will enjoy participating in the mixing. By adding other ingredients, apart from the essential flour and water, different kinds of elasticity can be achieved. Salt should always be added as a preservative, and it will also ensure that children do not eat it. Dough should appear attractive, have enough elasticity without sticking to surfaces or fingers, and should last for at least a week in a sealed plastic container, kept in a cool place. Playing with dough is a relaxing, soothing social activity, and is one often chosen by children when settling in a new environment. Conversations when playing with dough often stimulate a shy child to take part, as the experience helps relaxation.

Activity
Experiment with different dough recipes using various flours, ingredients and colours. Make a note of the recipe you find most successful.
   You might like to involve the children in making dough with you.

Cooking
From a very young age, children enjoy watching and helping adults prepare and cook food. Children learn about food hygiene and balanced meals, how to make choices in the supermarkets for taste and value, and where different foods come from.

   It is possible today to buy foods from all around the world, and by using recipes from various countries children learn about a range of cultures in a most enjoyable way. Children and parents who were not born in this country feel valued and at home when an important part of their culture is recognised.

   'Cooking' covers a wide range of activities, from making a sandwich to producing a complicated meal. It is important that the children do as much as possible for themselves, being involved from the preparation stage through to sharing the end-product. By helping to plan the activity, children gain shopping skills, such as making lists, choosing ingredients and handling money. Listening to and following instructions aids concentration. Cooking enforces a range of mathematical, scientific and technological concepts. It promotes an understanding of nutritional principles, home safety and hygiene. Recipes and labelling make links with reading and writing as does the recognition of different scripts if the food is labelled in various languages. Knowledge of foods from many cultures will be gained, and children from the age of six years will begin to follow recipes from a book.

Imaginary play

Imaginary play grows out of imitative play. Babies from a very early age imitate adults in games of 'peek-a-boo', waving goodbye and copying actions. Later, children do not need a direct role model in front of them, but will start to use their memory, pouring out imaginary cups of tea for all and sundry, and pretending to eat non-existent food.

At around two years old, children start to take on roles. One will be the 'mummy' and another the 'daddy', and this will gradually extend to include the baby, the big sister, the childminder, and even a visiting aunt. As children become older, role play will be extended to other people familiar in their lives or from books, such as the nurse, and the firefighter. The provision of dressing-up clothes often stimulates the imagination of the children. It is best to provide clothes that can be used in many different ways.

Activity
Make a cloak from a piece of material gathered at one end with elastic. Do you think boys and girls would play with it in the same way? Describe the different types of play.

Although discouraged in most homes and pre-school establishments, and to the despair of many parents, childminders and teachers, children do have imaginary shoot-outs, but they do not need toy guns, as toy bricks will do just as well. But it is from this ability to symbolise inanimate objects that the readiness for reading grows, as a child starts to understand that those inky blobs on a page stand for real words in a story.

For some children, acting out a role can be a release of emotions through pretending to be someone else. A child who is constantly listening to adults quarrelling may find it helpful to pretend to be one of those adults, and have some say of her own. This type of play can give you an insight into possible difficulties at home, but caution must be exercised, as the child could be acting out what she has seen on the television the night before.

A child waiting to go into hospital will find it very useful to be a make-believe patient, as a way of expressing emotions and fears. Some children, who may be withdrawn or shy, may still have difficulty in expressing their emotions. Puppets or a toy telephone can be a great help here, as the child uses them to voice

hidden feelings. Ready-made puppets should be introduced cautiously, as small children can be fearful of a toy that seems to have a life of its own.

As children are small, vulnerable people, they enjoy acting out roles of super-heroes. It makes them feel empowered and strong, and is a boost to their self-esteem.

Children play with dolls in different ways at each stage of their development. Once babies start to walk, they will use the doll as any other inanimate object, just holding onto it anywhere (usually the feet) and dragging it after them. At about two years, some children will start to cuddle the doll, treating it more as a baby, particularly if there has been a recent birth in the family. This doll might come in for some very hard knocks! A little later on, children enjoy bathing dolls, dressing (but mainly undressing) them and taking them out for walks in a pushchair. At about six years, groups of children might play with several dolls, having pretend tea parties or schoolroom lessons. Many girls start to collect dolls, such as Barbie, and there is often rivalry in the collecting of their clothes and artifacts. Some boys might have dolls, such as Action Man, but rarely collect them in the same way. Graded dolls and dolls' clothes help children understand concepts of small, medium and large

Small scale models of people, animals, vehicles, dolls' houses, and items of domestic equipment are often used in imaginary play. They are familiar to the children, and the play allows them to relax, and extend and develop their language.

Activity
Describe what equipment you might provide to encourage creativity in children.

Domestic play, such as making pretend cups of tea or using a broom, is a link with home, and very comforting to the insecure child, or a child experiencing a new situation. You may see children using stereotypes in their role play, copying situations observed in their environment. You will have to challenge this behaviour in a sensitive way if negative attitudes are displayed.

Imaginary play allows boys to take on and dress up in perceived female roles such as the mother or the ballerina, while girls can be fathers and firefighters. It presents opportunities for children to direct and organise activities, promotes creativity, and may lead to writing imaginative stories. Imaginary play allows children to express and release positive and negative emotions. It gives confidence, and allows self-esteem to develop.

Painting and drawing

All children should be offered frequent opportunities to paint and draw when they feel inclined. When children are very young, before fluent speech has developed, spontaneous drawing and painting is a most valuable means of expression. This is very much reduced if adults insist on questioning children about their paintings, suggest additions to the work, and want captions for every painting or drawing.

Adults interpreting children's paintings are quite often wrong. Children love to do all-dark, one-colour paintings at some stage in their development – this does not mean that something terrible has happened to them that they wish to forget! Understanding what stage of development children might have reached through interpreting their paintings is interesting, and there are many books on this subject.

Painting, in particular, often allows children to express emotions that they find difficult to put into words. Painting and drawing encourages imagination and creativity, and lends itself to pattern creation. The exploration of materials, textures and techniques expands knowledge of colour and shapes. It helps children to understand spatial relationships and composition. Symbolic blobs might lead to the foundation of reading and writing.

Bricks, blocks and construction sets

A bag of bricks is the most versatile piece of equipment that any child can have access to from the age of one year onwards. Blocks can be hard and made out of wood or plastic, or they can be soft and manufactured from rubber, cotton or foam, and they can be brightly coloured or in natural wood – but they are all construction toys and are there to build with.

At first, children will play on their own, building a tower of bricks, and enjoying knocking it down again. This leads on to four-year-olds planning small and large constructions together, playing co-operatively and imaginatively.

There are very many types of construction sets on the market, the best known being Lego. Most children will be familiar with Lego from home, and it is probably the most versatile of the construction toys. Younger children will find Duplo (the large scale version) easier to put together. Children from five years upwards, enjoy Meccano, the wooden and the plastic types being easier to manage than the metal, which is more sophisticated.

Building with bricks is a first-hand experience of three-dimensional objects and spatial relationships and encourages creative thought and problem solving.

Puzzles and simple games

Jigsaw puzzles are familiar to all young children, and create an excellent home–childminder link, as children feel relaxed and safe doing jigsaws. They are essentially a solitary experience, although children may do the large floor puzzles with other children.

Jigsaws range from very simple inset boards for the youngest children, to very intricate puzzles for adults. Sometimes children will choose easy puzzles when they are feeling the need for reassurance, and at other times will enjoy the challenge of more demanding jigsaws. It is important that no pieces are missing, particularly for the younger children, as this spoils the pleasure of completing a task satisfactorily.

Board games, similarly, come in varying degrees of difficulty. Most are not suitable for the under-fours as the children will not have yet gained the concept of taking turns and may get upset at having to wait, and spoil the game for others. Most games are a variation of Ludo or Snakes and Ladders.

Matching games, such as Picture Lotto and Connect, help children to see similarities and differences, and to match like with like. This is a pre-reading skill and can be played by one child alone, or with a group of children.

Card games, such as Snap, Go Fish, Pairs or Sevens, are enjoyed by children of four years upwards. Snap or Pairs cards can be made quite easily, using pictures or photographs familiar in the children's cultural background.

Doing jigsaw puzzles also helps children to find similarities and differences and so are valuable early reading activities. Card games encourage memory and quickness of thought. Concentration, logical thought, reasoning and perseverance are necessary for all these activities.

Activities that aid manipulative skills

Children enjoy threading beads and cotton reels, and again these are graded in order of difficulty, the younger children finding the larger beads the easiest. Pegboards and mosaic pieces help children to make patterns, as do sewing cards, where children are asked to thread in and out of holes with a lace or a threaded needle.

Books and stories

Enjoyment of books and stories usually starts in the home and will continue with you. Before a child is a year old, she enjoys looking at pictures or photographs while being cuddled by an adult. Nurturing this love of books is probably the key factor in the later acquisition of reading skills.

Young children, in particular, derive great pleasure in being told stories. These can be personalised, either being tales from the storyteller's past, or stories where the listener becomes the centre of the tale. Being told or read a story is delightful and relaxing. Many parents read to their child just before settling her down to sleep, and she will enjoy the attention of a loved adult. You may wish to read to a child before she takes a nap.

Poetry for older children will enrich their vocabulary and let them know that it is acceptable to express emotions. This may encourage older children to write their own poems. For younger children, humorous verse is a good introduction. Repetitive rhyming is most helpful to children with limited language skills. For all children, it can, like books, open up a world of fantasy and imagination.

Being able to read gives a child independence. Empathising with a character in a book allows a child to understand her own feelings. On a one-to-one basis, reading with an adult is a nurturing experience, giving feelings of love and security. Being able to read gives a child self-esteem and a sense of achievement. Books and stories encourage concentration, extend the child's knowledge of the world and aid imagination.

Activity

Look at the range of books you have at home.
1 How many represent girls in strong roles? How many represent minority ethnic groups in strong and positive roles? How many show disabled people in active roles?
2 Which books are the most popular with children? Why do you think this is?

1 Books should always be available to the children and, ideally, an adult should always be there to read to them if required. Children enjoy reading on the floor. Books should be accessible to children. They should be kept in good condition, and children taught at a young age to treat them with respect. Children who damage books should be encouraged to help in the repair.

2 A comprehensive range of books needs to be available. The books should reflect our multi-cultural society, with stories from countries around the world and some books in the home languages of the children in your care. Great care must be taken to avoid stereotyping when choosing books, whether it is in the area of race, religion, class, age, disability or gender. Positive images reflecting the diversity of culture and family patterns need to be included, together with stories portraying children with disabilities and girls in strong roles.

3 Children identify with characters in books, and you should be aware of the needs of all the children in your care in order to help them make sense of their feelings and to promote self-esteem and feelings of worth.

4 Remember the value of telling stories, as well as reading books. This is particularly valuable for the younger children

5 The appropriateness of the book or story needs thinking about. The youngest children will be content with stories about familiar events, such as shopping and bedtime, and some simple tales that are happily resolved about other children and animals. As children's experience of stories is extended, longer books about imaginary events can be read, but always be aware of not frightening the children. Young children's imagination is very vivid, and fairy stories can be terrifying, as they often deal with tales of rejection, death and separation. Ogres and witches should be left for an older age-group, and even then not all children feel comfortable with fantasy tales, as they may still have difficulty in discriminating fact from fiction. The way that you read stories has a good deal of bearing on how much the children will enjoy them. You should choose stories you enjoy reading and telling, and you will need to be familiar with the story you are going to read.

6 Children want the same stories time and time again, but occasionally you need to introduce new stories.

7 Some books have many words in them that are unfamiliar to the children. It is not a good idea to change the words into more familiar ones as you go along. This is disrespectful to the writer, and it deprives the children of learning new words. If the language is so difficult that the children become bored, re-introduce the book another time.

8 Allow some time for relaxed discussion at the end of the story. Children do not always want to talk about the book, so do not force them to do so. Sometimes children want to participate throughout the reading or telling of the story. It depends on your personal preference as to whether you let them do this or wait until the end of the story session. Usually the youngest children cannot wait until the end if they have something to say!

9 Reading sessions are sometimes held in local libraries. Older children should be encouraged to join the library, and the younger ones should become familiar with the building.

10 Books should represent the whole spectrum of society, not just the ideal nuclear family with no financial problems.

11 When buying new books, or borrowing books from the library, care must be taken to make sure that none of them contain elements that could offend adults or distress children, by displaying offensive attitudes. Show children that you enjoy books, as it is by your example that they will learn to value and appreciate books and stories.

12 Books are an ideal way of presenting positive images of children from many varied ethnic groups. By giving all children insights into different cultures with their own traditional stories and into varied child-rearing practices, they will learn to value and respect people for what they are, and to challenge stereotypical attitudes. Check the illustrations for stereotypes of black people, women and minority ethnic groups. Make sure that children with disabilities are not depicted as being weak and needy. Girls should be depicted in strong roles, not as dependent, passive onlookers.

13 Books are available from the library to help children who are having to deal with problems in their private lives, such as hospitalisation, parental separation, bereavement and so on.

Playing outside

Nearly every activity that takes place in the house can equally well be taken outside if the weather permits. Some activities can only take place outside, and it is to these that this section refers.

A safe outside-play area is a bonus for young children, to exercise and let off steam, to practise their developing physical skills and to build self-confidence. Exercise in the fresh air promotes good health. A safe outdoor play area allows children freedom to investigate and explore their environment with little adult restriction. Very young children, who are not used to playing outside, and live in a flat, may find the garden intimidating and overwhelming at first, but when their self-confidence has developed will soon enjoy being outside.

You will need to be outside with the children and make sure it is safe. What is provided will influence the quality of the play. Traditional games may be organised, either by the children, or by you, such as What's the Time, Mr Wolf?, Hide and Seek, Simon Says and Ring-O'-Roses.

Playing outside releases surplus energy and is a licence to make more noise. It stimulates the appetite, aids digestion and circulation, promotes sleep, and gives resistance to infection. It promotes a healthy skin, as well as developing muscle tone, manipulative skills, balance and control. Children develop skills, such as stopping and starting, running, hopping, digging, planting, skipping, climbing, pedalling, swinging, steering and crawling through and under equipment. Children share and collaborate, take responsibility for sharing space, and gain understanding of the rules governing outside play and games. They learn respect for living things.

The garden provides a stimulus for all the senses and an opportunity for a range of imaginary play experiences. Children must be dressed according to the weather, protected against the sun as well as the rain.

Activity
If you do not have access to a garden, how would you ensure that the children
that you mind get enough fresh air and exercise?

The early years curriculum

The curriculum can be described as the experiences, opportunities and activities that you offer children in your care to help them to learn and develop. Some of these activities you will prepare and plan. Other opportunities for learning will occur unexpectedly and your skill will be needed to make the best use of them.

For young children, the Foundation Stage of the Curriculum relates to Early Learning Goals. The Goals are arranged into six areas of learning:

■ personal, social and emotional development
■ communication, language and literacy
■ mathematical development
■ knowledge and understanding of the world
■ physical development
■ creative development.

The Foundation Stage is for children from 3 until the end of the reception year. The Early Learning Goals set out what most children should be able to do by the end of the Foundation Stage. Each set of Goals has a set of *stepping stones*, which lead up to the Goals and describe what children of 3, 4 and 5 might be expected to do. Childminders will find the stepping stones a useful guide to providing appropriate activities for children.

Detailed information is available in *Curriculum Guidance for the Foundation Stage*, which is available free from the Qualifications and Curriculum Authority (QCA) – phone 01787 884444 and quote reference QCA/00/587.

Children learn from everything they do. Any activity will offer an opportunity to learn across a range of learning outcomes. Some childminders might feel anxious about being asked to provide a curriculum for the children in their care, but the curriculum is only the sum of the total experiences of the child. Everything you do with the child will contribute to the learning outcomes, whether it is:

■ preparing and sitting down to eat a leisurely meal with the children
■ involving them in domestic tasks, such as clearing up, shopping and gardening
■ going for a walk in the park
■ all the play activities you plan, inside and out-of-doors
■ any routine carried out by you and the children, that you are describing and talking about with them.

NCMA suggest that all activities and experiences for children should be appropriate for their stage of development and should use as a starting point the child's current stage of development based on what the child can already do and has achieved so far, and the child's interests and preferences. Children develop at different rates and it is not helpful to compare children with one another. The learning outcomes should not be seen as the ultimate and only goals for five-year-olds. Many children of this age are capable of much more and of much wider learning. NCMA suggest promoting children's learning and development by the use of the 'seven Cs' (see page 59).

From September 1998, registered childminders working in NCMA approved childminding networks, who have been accredited as promoting learning outcomes, will be eligible to receive funding through an early years development plan.

All research has shown that close partnership between teachers, carers and parents encourages children's learning and that this has remained the same in every piece of educational research.

GOOD PRACTICE IN SUPPORTING CHILDREN'S LEARNING

1 Ensure that children feel secure and valued, promoting their self-esteem and self-confidence.
2 Make learning a pleasure and give all children a sense of achievement.
3 Provide parents with a statement of aims, objectives and curriculum.
4 Liaise with other professionals, such as the staff at the school the child will attend.
5 Encourage children to think and talk about what they are learning.
6 Help children to develop self-control and independence.
7 Plan activities and experiences for children, based on their achievements so far, and their interests and abilities.
8 Give children many hands-on experiences and clear explanations.
9 Make sure children have the time to play and talk.

10 Intervene only when appropriate.
11 Assess and record children's progress, and share this with the parents.
12 Seek additional support if specific needs emerge.
13 Create a safe and healthy environment, in which space, facilities and equipment support learning.
14 Reflect on your own training needs.

(From The Schools Curriculum and Assessment Authority)

Children's development and learning

The Seven Cs

Confidence
Children who feel capable and valued by other people have the confidence to reach out into the environment and to other children and adults, and learn from exploration and discovery. A child in a secure situation in which she receives individual attention and loving care will develop self-esteem and be able to tackle new ideas and experiences. When she has opportunities to try out new skills and take new responsibilities, her confidence grows, and she is ready to move on to more new learning.

Communication
From her earliest hours, a baby is learning to give and receive communication – at first non-verbally, later with words. She develops understanding of language and the body language of facial expressions, gestures and tone of voice long before she produces her own earliest words. The toddler's frustrations diminish as she is more able to tell adults what she wants and to understand what they expect of her. The pre-school child wants explanations, and learning the words for the way she feels (sad, happy, cross) helps her deal with her feelings when they are so strong they threaten to overwhelm her. The foundation of communication skills is essential for later learning to read and write.

Co-ordination
As a child progresses from crawling to staggering to toddling to running, jumping and climbing, she is gaining control of her limbs and developing skills of directing the use of her body. The baby placing objects in a container (and taking them out again), the toddler wielding a stubby crayon, and the pre-schooler busy with scissors and threading beads are all learning to make their hands and fingers work as they want and as their eyes direct. Later, writing will depend on those skills.

Concentration
A child who is interested in and enjoying an activity so much that she becomes absorbed in it and spends a length of time focusing on it, is acquiring habits which will underlie all her later learning. She is learning to stay 'on task' – to concentrate on the matter in hand. The nature and activity and its end product are less important then her pleasure in doing something which holds her attention. Quiet time and space, and an activity which is based on what excites a child's interest enable her to lose herself in her play.

Competence
Learning the skills to be a self-reliant human being begin early – walking, feeding and dressing yourself, going to the toilet and washing. Children need practice and praise for the progress they make.

Co-operation
Learning to live and work alongside other people starts early. Babies enjoy playing 'give and take' games; toddlers like to 'help' grown-ups and be thanked; pre-schoolers play elaborate games of make believe with each taking a role. Sharing is a hard thing to learn, and taking turns is even harder. Children need opportunities to tackle these difficult social skills and become aware of the feelings and rights of others. They may need help to cope with the strongest feelings their efforts may produce.

Creativity
Play activities enable children to experiment with making and seeing how various materials behave and can be used (technology). Making up stories and playing games of make-believe are ways of exploring 'what if?' ideas. Children who will be adults in the twenty-first century need to learn to solve problems and become imaginative thinkers.

Reproduced by kind permission of the National Childminding Association

5 UNDERSTANDING CHILDREN'S BEHAVIOUR

> **This chapter includes:**
> - Factors that influence behaviour
> - Common causes of challenging behaviour
> - Your role in managing behaviour
> - Managing unwanted behaviour
> - How to manage separation
> - Issues that cause conflict
> - The smacking debate

Behaviour is the way in which a person conducts himself in relation to other people. It is the response to an action. If we want to teach children to behave in a sociably acceptable way, we have to devise guidelines for ourselves in the way we carry this out. We need to be very clear about our aims and objectives, and be consistent in the way we manage children's behaviour.

Behaviour is learnt through the child observing the people closest to him and the way they react to him, both verbally and non-verbally. Rewards and punishments shape behaviour. The reward may just be praise and encouragement, and the punishment a disapproving look, but it will have an effect.

Knowledge of the normal development of children will help you to understand what behaviour is appropriate at what age and stage of development. For example, a toddler is not expected to be completely toilet trained, but regularly wetting and soiling pants would be worrying behaviour in a five-year-old.

The children you mind will come from various backgrounds, perhaps from a variety of cultures, with parents who may well have different expectations of their children's behaviour. For example, some parents might explain in great detail to the child what he is doing wrong, while others might be more of the 'do as I say, not as I do' school. Some parents might have different gender expectations, allowing boys to be more vigorous and active, and expect girls to adopt more passive pursuits.

CASE STUDY

Berenice minds two children and has two of her own. She was asked to look after a six-year-old, Clive, during the school holidays. She found him to be a delightful child, always happy and helpful, but his habit of never saying 'please' and 'thank you' drove her to distraction. It was clear that this was not expected of him at home.

1 What action should Berenice take?

2 Should she insist that Clive says 'please' and 'thank you'?

Once you have established your own way of managing children's behaviour, and found that it works, you will need to discuss this with the parents and make sure they are in agreement with your methods.

Factors that influence behaviour

Most of the factors that influence behaviour are family-based. This is because behaviour is learnt initially in the family, and the earliest experiences have the greatest effect. These factors include:

- birth order
- siblings
- expectations of the parents
- cultural child-rearing practices
- influence of the extended family
- opportunities for play within the family home
- abuse and neglect
- gender stereotyping.

Outside events that affect the whole family may also influence behaviour. These might include:

- unemployment/work pattern of parent(s)
- moving house
- divorce and separation
- adapting to a re-constituted family
- death and grieving for people and pets
- disability within the family.

Other factors include:

- the personality of the child
- the school
- the peer group
- the media
- having a disability
- experiencing discrimination.

Common causes of challenging behaviour

Some forms of behaviour are so common that one might be concerned if a child did not at some time display one or more of them. Some of these behaviours are due to frustrated emotional needs.

EMOTIONAL CAUSES

Attention-seeking behaviour is one of the most common forms of challenging behaviour. Children need to be reassured that they are loved and cared for, and if they are not given attention, they will seek it by being aggressive, angry, rude, swearing, showing off, dominating conversations, and other negative behaviours.

Cecelia, an experienced minder, has been asked by social services to care for a four-year-old boy, Edward, whose parents have recently separated. This is the third week she has been looking after him, and she is finding it very difficult to manage his constant attention-seeking behaviour. He is defiant and disobedient, frequently upsets the other children, swears and refuses to join in any planned activities.

1 Why might he be behaving like this?
2 How would you approach the parents?
3 How would you help Edward?
4 How would you minimise the effect on the other children?

Temper tantrums

About fifty per cent of two-year-olds have tantrums on a regular basis, usually in the presence of their parents or minder, and very seldom when on their own or when at school or playgroup. The tantrum comes about because the child feels frustrated and needs to get attention. Tantrums can be quite disturbing to observe, and need to be dealt with in the same way by you and the parents. If you see one coming, it is often possible to distract or divert the child, and by leaving the room you remove the main focus of the anger. If it is already too late, or you are in a public area and unable to walk away, you will need to hold and hug the child until the tantrum is over. The child will be frightened and needs reassurance.

When the tantrum is over, cuddling the child and talking about feelings in a positive way should discourage further tantrums. It is positively harmful to smack or handle a child roughly during a tantrum, and even more dangerous to

shake him. Equally, giving in to the child and allowing him to manipulate you will increase the frequency of the tantrums. Always report back to parents if the child has had a severe tantrum, and if this behaviour is becoming problematic ask the parents to inform you if it is happening at home, so that you both can follow the same consistent approach.

Jealousy
It is an unusual household that never quarrels, and most children will fight from time to time. A new baby will sometimes arouse deep feelings of jealousy from a displaced older child, and this may be shown by aggressive behaviour to the younger children that you mind. Often, rivalry is expressed by quarrelling over toys and attention. In general, children can sort out most of these rows for themselves and unless they are doing serious damage to each other, it is often better to just let them get on with it.

CASE STUDY

Siobhan, a newly registered minder, with a two-year-old of her own, agreed to care for a four-month-old baby. She was upset when, during the first week, she walked into the room to find her own child pinching the baby, and telling her to send it away.

1 Is this normal behaviour?

2 How might she have prepared her own child for the baby coming?

3 How should she respond to the situation?

Comfort behaviour
There are many forms of comfort behaviour, some more embarrassing than others. No one minds if a child drags a soft toy everywhere with him, but masturbating in public is not so acceptable. Sucking thumbs, dummies, and pieces of material are all objects that children use to comfort themselves. They may become reliant on them at particular times of the day, usually at nap time and when confronted by a new or distressing situation. Not all children feel the need for a comfort object, but if a child has a comfort habit you will have to tolerate it in the same way as the parents. It would be most upsetting for the child to have the object or the habit taken away suddenly and he will give it up in his own good time.

Other children might show their need for love and reassurance by displaying anxiety or fear, and/or withdrawn behaviour, finding it difficult to express their feelings in the usual attention-seeking ways. Children need approval from adults, so as to gain confidence that they are valued. If this is not forthcoming, their self-esteem will be low, and they will find it difficult to learn and achieve.

PHYSICAL CAUSES

Sometimes problematic behaviour has a physical cause. Lack of sleep can lead to irritability. Hunger can cause some children to lose concentration and become aggressive because their blood sugar level drops. Infection, particularly in the incubation period, can cause changes in behaviour patterns.

GROWING INDEPENDENCE

There are some types of behaviour that can be challenging that are inevitable, as they are part of the child's development.

Curiosity and exploration

As a baby becomes a toddler you will not have a cupboard that remains unexplored, or a meal that is peaceful and does not have a messy end as the toddler seeks to feed himself and enjoy the texture as well as the taste of food. Safety factors and constant vigilance are of increasing importance as the child's curiosity knows no bounds.

Toilet training

There is much written about the best way to satisfactorily toilet train a child, and there are many myths around as to the time it takes and the best way to go about it. Encourage the parents not to get into any competition with any of their friends, and it is important that you both share the same ideas and go about the process in the same way. There is no point in you leaving the nappy off and offering the child the pot at regular intervals if the parents decide not to do this at weekends. The child will just get confused. Whatever regime you choose, you must make sure that you do not adopt a punitive approach to any occasional accident, and you should show pleasure in any initial success.

Activity
Remembering all the children you have cared for, including your own:
1 At what ages did they become reliably dry and clean?
2 Was there a gender difference?
3 Was there a variation in methods used?
4 Did any parent ever suggest a regime that you felt uncomfortable with?
5 How did you manage this situation?

Dressing and undressing
Some children would always rather you dressed them than have to bother for themselves, but the majority express their independence at a young age, first by undressing and then by starting to dress themselves. It can be difficult to encourage children to dress themselves when you are in a hurry to get them ready to go out. Some children are more reluctant to dress themselves than others, but at some point they have to learn for themselves or be shown up when they start school or go to stay with a friend. You and the parents will have to agree at the pace you expect and the encouragement that you give.

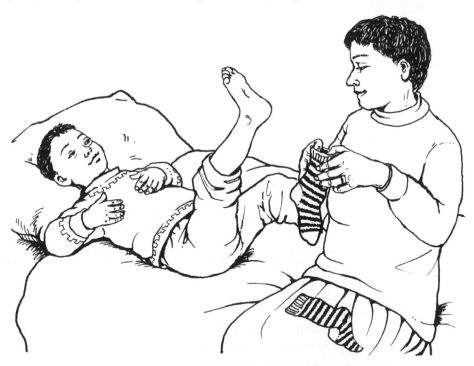

BOREDOM

Children need stimulation and the opportunity to play and learn about the world around them. If they are restricted and frustrated, this will lead to boredom, perhaps resulting in attention-seeking behaviour.

If you have received some training, you will have learnt about the skill of recording careful and objective observations (see Chapter 14). If you are worried about any aspect of a child's behaviour, you might complete an event sample or a time sample. An event sample will show how many times in the day or week the worrying behaviour occurs, whether or not it is provoked and if it takes place at a particular time of day. A time sample will monitor a child's behaviour at regular intervals throughout the day, demonstrating, for example, how often and to whom a withdrawn child makes an approach.

Your role in managing behaviour

Your role with all the children, including your own, is to:
- be fair
- be consistent
- have as few rules as possible
- set clearly defined boundaries, helping them to understand how far they can go and what behaviour is not acceptable
- understand what behaviour is appropriate for each age group
- have realistic expectations
- give brief explanations as to why you do not accept certain behaviours
- maintain communication and discussion with the parents
- prepare children to play a valuable role in society
- understand cultural variations, and different expectations that some families might have.

GOOD PRACTICE IN INFLUENCING BEHAVIOUR

1 Show approval when children behave as you wish. Give rewards of hugs, smiles, praise, time to talk and play, and attention.
2 Praise children to their parents and other people.
3 Help children by offering positive choices. For example, say 'Let's tidy up' rather than 'Don't make a mess'.
4 Give the child plenty of warning when it is time to tidy up.
5 Explain why you expect certain behaviours.

6 Avoid creating confrontations and battles. Do not over-react to minor matters.
7 Give children a chance to work out minor disputes. Do not intervene too soon.
8 Be firm and do not give into whining or tantrums.
9 Be a good role model. Behave in the way you wish the children to behave.

Managing unwanted behaviour

When children are cared for by more than one person, they will sometimes attempt to play one adult off against another. This can be a particular problem when children are being collected at the end of the day. It is helpful for parents and childminders to agree on a strategy so that this does not become a time of conflict. Consistency of care and methods of discipline help the child to know what is expected and acceptable. All children need to understand boundaries set by their parents and childminders, as to what behaviour might be tolerated. As children grow older the rules may change, but consistency is still the key for managing behaviour. Disagreements can cause a great deal of friction, and it is worth spending some time, when you first meet the parents, agreeing what is acceptable behaviour, and how this will be achieved.

Behaviour is not acceptable if it:
■ is dangerous, hurtful or offensive to someone else
■ is dangerous to the child himself
■ will make the child unwelcome or unacceptable to other people
■ damages other people's property.

Activity
You overhear a four-year-old child in your care making a hurtful racist remark to a younger child.
1 What is your immediate reaction?
2 How might you involve the parents?
3 What steps might you take to alter such behaviour?
4 How would you support the younger child?

Acceptable behaviour will be encouraged by you and the parents by:
■ talking freely and frequently about the children
■ discussing which rules are more flexible than others
■ not allowing a child to manipulate either of you, by playing one off against the other
■ treating each child as an individual. One of the children might dissolve into tears from a cross look, while another might find even a stern telling-off quite amusing
■ remembering that rules should change as children become more mature, and are able to understand the effects of their behaviour.

MODIFYING BEHAVIOUR

Behaviour modification is the name given to techniques used to influence and change children's behaviour. It works by promoting and rewarding positive aspects of children's behaviour and by ignoring and discouraging negative aspects. There is a spectrum of behaviour modification techniques, from the practice of firmly holding children with autism so as to force interaction upon them, to the frequent giving of praise and encouragement for 'good' behaviour.

Research done at the University of Wales, in Bangor, in 1998, looked at a way of encouraging children to eat fruit and vegetables. More than 200 children between the ages of two and seven were shown videos outlining the adventures of some street-wise children called Food Dudes who are locked in combat with General Junk and his Junk Food Junta. He is trying to take over the world by tricking children into eating unhealthy food, but the Food Dudes eat fruit and vegetables to keep their 'life force' strong, enabling them to outwit the baddies.

At the end of the film, our heroes encourage children everywhere to join the fight, and stickers and other small rewards are offered to those who eat fruit and vegetables. The results were quite amazing. The researchers had not been expecting a behaviour change that was quite so marked. Schools and nurseries showing the video had made fruit and vegetables available in the few weeks before the video was shown. After the video had been viewed, fruit and vegetable consumption rose from thirty-five to seventy per cent. Home-based studies of children known to be faddy eaters showed that fruit consumption leapt from four to one hundred per cent after viewing the video. This improvement in eating habits continued, and the children were eating at a similar level six months later.

GOOD PRACTICE IN MANAGING UNWANTED BEHAVIOUR

1 Distract the child by providing more attractive alternatives.
2 Remove the child from the situation. Do not humiliate him or shut him away on his own.
3 If a child is having a tantrum, restrain him gently until he calms down, and then cuddle him and offer reassurance.
4 Ignore swear words.
5 When you are saying 'No', make sure your whole body shows that you mean it.
6 If there is danger, grab the child and say 'No'!
7 Do not reward unacceptable behaviour with your attention.
8 Do not argue with a child in a tantrum.
9 Show disapproval, and make it clear that the behaviour is not acceptable.
10 Make it clear that it is the behaviour that is not wanted, rather than the child.
11 If the child is old enough to understand, explain why the behaviour is unacceptable.
12 Limit punishments, but any sanctions used must be immediate and appropriate.
13 Never smack, shake, bite or humiliate a child.
14 After any incident, show affection, and offer cuddles.
15 Stay calm and in control of yourself.

How to manage separation

It is normal behaviour for children to be upset when they are first left by their parents, but in most cases this is of very short duration, and after an initial protest, the children will soon settle with you. If the children are old enough, you will probably have encouraged the parents to prepare them well in advance. If they are very small, it will be more difficult for them to understand, and you may find they take longer to accept the situation.

If the children are upset when the parents are leaving, the best way to handle it is to ask the parents to leave as quickly as possible, as hanging around and inquiring if they are 'all right now' will only prolong the distress. On the other hand, if the parents sneak out without saying goodbye, this may make the children feel insecure, as they will never be sure when the parents are suddenly going to disappear. Stress the importance of collecting the child on time so that he knows, for example, that his parents will be there by the time he is having his tea

Issues that cause conflict

We all want children to eat well, go to bed on time, and live in peace with their siblings and peers, but mealtimes, nap times and sharing toys and space can all cause conflict and ignite challenging behaviour. Occasionally, childminders and parents can have conflicting views about managing these situations.

MEALTIMES

Because we invest a great deal of love and thought in what we provide for children to eat, we may take the rejection of such food personally, and react to food refusal. This reaction and over-anxiety on the behalf of the adult gives the child power, and may encourage later food disorders.

Sensible rules as to when and where food is eaten need to be kept by both you and the parents. Agreement about the type of food provided, how it is cooked and presented, the size of the portion, second helpings, and the time allowed to eat the food all have to be sorted out when you first meet the parents, and updated as the child develops.

REST TIME

If a child has a regular rest time, and the parents want you to keep to this, you will need to discuss it with them. The difficulties are:
- the child may have different rest needs when with you compared to his needs at home
- it is more convenient for you if the children can all nap at the same time, but this may not be possible to achieve

- a child who becomes very tired and fractious needs a nap, even if the parents request that this does not take place
- a child might not want to rest, but the parents wish him to, so that they can enjoy his company in the evening
- rest needs change as the child grows older.

SWEARING

Children are excellent mimics, and enjoy new words. They get a great deal of pleasure in repeating words that get a response. The best way to deal with swearing is to ignore it.

CASE STUDY

Rani has been childminding for one year. She has just taken on Christopher, aged four, who has started swearing. Rani and her husband never swear, and were appalled to hear some of the words Christopher said. They were concerned that the other children might start to copy Christopher. Rani spoke to Christopher's mother who maintains that she never swears either, but that at the judo class that he attends weekly two of the older boys use bad language.

1 How should Rani react to Christopher's swearing in the short term?
2 How might she advise the parents?
3 How can she protect the other children?

MASTURBATION

Some children masturbate as a comfort habit, particularly when bored, watching television or settling to sleep. The best advice is to ignore it, particularly in the younger child. Older children will soon learn from their peers that masturbating in public is unacceptable.

When children's behaviour causes concern, the question you need to ask is whether this is a normal stage in their development, or if there is a more serious problem. Most problems sort themselves out in time, and the quarrelsome child becomes charming and manageable. If this is not the case, you may have to encourage the parents to seek other professional help.

Activity
1   How can you help children to safely resolve conflicts themselves?
2   At what stage do you find yourself intervening?

The smacking debate

Smacking is seen as a negative way of dealing with behaviour problems, as the main thing the child learns is that larger people can hurt them, and when they grow up they will be able to hurt smaller people. It seldom resolves the problem. Sir William Utting (author of the report on children and violence, 1995) puts it succinctly. 'Hitting people is wrong. Hitting children teaches them that violence is the most effective means of getting your own way. We must develop a culture which disapproves of all forms of violence. All the lessons of my working life point to the fact that violence breeds misery. It does not resolve it'.

If parents smack their children (and the UK is one of the last European countries where it is legal to do so) it may be harder for you to correct their behaviour by other means.

In 1995, a High Court judgement upheld the right of a childminder to smack a child with the permission of the child's parent, challenging the status of guidance and local authority registration requirements. Despite this, it is still regarded as bad practice to resort to corporal punishment. The majority of local authorities require a 'no smacking' policy from their registered minders.

Activity
Explain why childminders should never use physical punishment.

As a professional person looking after other people's children, it is never correct to administer physical punishment whether the parents request it or not. A light slap is one end of the continuum of beating a child and causing injury, and there would never be any reason why a childminder should hit a child. In your working career you may come across parents who choose to use physical chastisement to discipline their children. You must use your judgement as to when you feel it is necessary to intervene. Parents sometimes need help in understanding there are alternative modes of control. This is explored more fully in Chapter 11.

Activity

How might you manage the following situations?

1 An older child deliberately provoking his younger brother into losing his temper and throwing food onto the floor.
2 A three-year-old refusing to rest, although obviously very tired.
3 A three-year-old refusing to put on his coat to go outside in very cold weather.
4 A six-year-old taunting and teasing children from a different culture.
5 A child demanding sweets in a supermarket.
6 Three children quarrelling and fighting in a car.
7 Seeing a mother hit her child as she walks along the road.

If you have minded a child from babyhood, it is unlikely that you will experience too many difficulties in managing his behaviour. It may be more challenging to start to mind an older child, who you do not know so well. With very few exceptions, all children respond to affectionate care in a secure consistent environment, where it is obvious that their interests are paramount.

6 CARING FOR BABIES AND TODDLERS

This chapter includes:
- Understanding the additional demands of babies and toddlers
- Partnership with parents
- Routines
- The development of the small baby and the need for stimulation
- Encouraging development in the toddler

Some childminders adore babies, and this may be one of the reasons they become childminders. Their own family may be growing up, having another baby of their own may not be an option and minding babies is something they enjoy and are competent at, so they can provide the consistent care and stimulation that all babies need. Other childminders will see babies as too much of a responsibility and too time consuming.

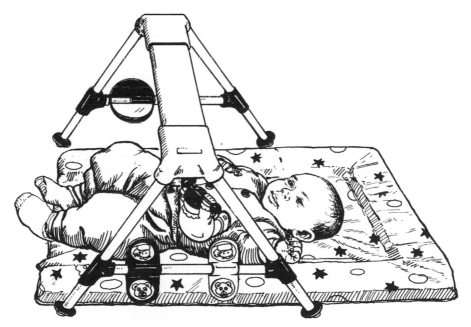

Understanding the additional demands of babies and toddlers

Babies are attractive and provide their carers with constant rewards. A baby who is loved and given as much attention as she demands will reciprocate with smiles and cuddles. Caring for babies takes much time and energy. Routines have to be established, such as feeding, winding, rest times, play times and changing and disposing of nappies. If the baby is prone to colic she will be difficult to settle, and you may have to walk around with her while you are managing your other commitments. Every time you leave the house, you will need to take a great deal of equipment with you, such as nappies, food, toys, and clothes. Small babies are very vulnerable to infection, and in addition to sterilising any feeding equipment, you will need to be extremely vigilant in preventing cross-infection.

A calm and equitable temperament helps when looking after very small babies, as they can be trying. Caring for a baby who continually cries for no apparent reason can be an upsetting and frustrating experience if all your efforts to pacify her are fruitless. If you find you are reaching the end of your tether, as an experienced childminder you will know to place the baby somewhere safe, and to remove yourself from the situation until you feel able to cope once more.

As the child matures and becomes mobile, you will have to provide close supervision throughout the day. As the child explores her environment, you will have to make sure she is safe, and try to protect your belongings and those of the older children. A toddler is very messy, with her food and with play materials, and it requires patience to allow her to explore.

SETTLING THE BABY AND THE TODDLER INTO YOUR HOME

A baby will show her personality from the start. She may be placid or excitable, easy or difficult to feed or to settle for sleep, need constant attention or be content on her own, she may cry rarely or a great deal or may display a mixture of all of these behaviours.

Some babies appear not to mind who handles and cares for them and will welcome new people and new experiences. This makes it easier for the parent to share the care with you, knowing that the baby will be happy as long as her needs are met. Other babies are slower and more reluctant to accept change and have to be coaxed until they are more familiar with a new carer. A few babies are extremely difficult and will protest loudly at every change. Many babies will exhibit a mixture of these responses.

With a small baby, it is important that you and the mother care for the baby together for a while, so that you can be aware of the baby's fussy moods, and be shown the best way to respond to her. Small babies need warm consistent care that promotes emotional security, and encouraging the mother to spend some time in your home caring for the baby with you will reassure the mother before she returns to work.

Curiously enough, it may be easier to settle a very young baby with you than one of seven months or so. At this age, babies start to miss their mothers and become very aware of strangers, and with some babies this may continue for some time. Between seven and fifteen months, babies feel 'stranger anxiety', becoming anxious in the presence of strangers and strange places, and 'separation anxiety', not wishing to be separated from the primary caregiver.

Partnership with parents

Many parents prefer to use childminders, rather than group care, because they want consistent, individual care for their baby in a family home. You should feel pleased that they have chosen you for what could be the start of a long relationship, stretching over many years.

You will be able to appreciate how difficult it is for many parents to separate from their babies and you will need to support them by welcoming any visits or telephone calls during the day, and by working hard to establish a strong, trusting relationship.

Communication with parents is important whatever the age of the child you are minding, but if you are caring for babies and toddlers it is vital. They are unable to speak for themselves and to tell the parents what they have achieved during the day. They are also very vulnerable to infection and ill health and any changes in appetite, behaviour, excretion or sleep pattern need to be noted by both the childminder and parent, and information should be exchanged in the morning and the evening. All these events should be noted, and the parents informed at the end of the day.

Right at the start, the mother will need to tell you how she expects to feed the baby. If she is using formula milk, you will need to discuss who makes up the feeds and is responsible for sterilising equipment. If the mother is breast-feeding, she may wish to visit your home during the day to feed the baby and you may wish to store some frozen expressed breast milk for emergency use. This will keep for up to forty-eight hours in a fridge, or up to three months in a freezer. Do not use a microwave to thaw or warm milk, as it heats the milk unevenly, and it may scald the baby's mouth. As the baby matures, her feeding needs will change, and you and the mother will have to work together in introducing new tastes and foods to the baby.

You will also need to find out about the baby's preference for:

■ sleeping times and routines
■ sleeping position
■ comfort objects.

You will need to discuss what type of nappies the mother prefers, and arrangements to ensure you have a constant supply. The mother will also wish to tell you about the baby's skin care. This is particularly important if the baby is from a culture different to your own. Dry skin is common in black children and should be given special attention.

Routines

Before leaving the baby with you, the mother will have established certain routines with her baby. It is important that these are discussed, and an attempt is made to continue the established routines.

CARE OF THE SKIN

There are some very common skin conditions that are not infectious but nevertheless need careful handling. To prevent cradle cap, heat rash and nappy rash make sure that you and the mother:

- wash the baby's hair only once or twice a week and rinse it very thoroughly
- look out for any crust on the scalp, and apply olive oil to the crust, washing it off after a few hours
- do not allow the baby to become too hot by over-dressing her, or leaving her in a hot room with a great many bed coverings
- change nappies frequently and wash the baby's bottom at each change
- are aware that creams and washing powders can cause allergies
- adequately rinse terry-towelling nappies, if used
- expose the baby's skin to the air at regular intervals during the day.

BATHTIME

If you are responsible for bathing the baby, it should be an enjoyable, rewarding and relaxing time, but you need to be fully aware of the following potential safety measures:

- the bath should not be too full
- the cold tap should be run before the hot tap
- the temperature should be checked before putting the baby into the bath
- a non-slip mat should be put in the bath
- the baby should be put in at the end without the taps
- the room should not be cold
- all equipment and clothing should be gathered together before the bath
- the baby should never be left unattended in the bath.

Bathtime should be fun and an opportunity for the baby to splash, make bubbles, play with bath toys, enjoy the sensation of the warm water against her skin and the freedom of playing without clothes on. If the baby should be frightened of the water do not have a confrontation. It is better for the baby to go without bathing for a while until she is ready to enjoy it. Developing a fear of water as a baby could inhibit learning to swim at a later date.

SLEEP

First of all, you must ensure you have a cot that is exclusively for the baby, because of the risk of cross-infection, and so that the baby has access to the cot whenever she needs to sleep. Sleeping patterns vary considerably in babies. You need to ask the mother the baby's pattern, and understand the importance of allowing the baby to sleep when she wants to and not when it is most convenient for you. You will probably want to check on her once or twice during her nap. A baby-recording device is a useful investment. Other safety factors include:

- cots and prams should meet British Standard Institute safety regulations, displaying the Kite mark

- the mattress should be firm and well fitting
- pillows and duvets should not be used
- cot bumpers should be avoided
- the baby should not be put down to sleep if she is wearing anything with a string or ribbon round her neck.

You will soon know the amount of noise the baby can tolerate, and whether loud sudden noises disturb her or not. As the baby grows and matures, other routines such as tooth brushing and story-time will be established and sleep-time will be shorter.

Sudden Infant Death Syndrome (SIDS)

This is the sudden and unexpected death of an infant, usually found dead in her cot or pram with no obvious cause. It occurs in babies between the ages of one week and two years, peaking at three months and it occurs more frequently in the winter months. It has been linked with smoky environments, untreated minor ailments, over-concentrated formula feeds, and multiple births. To reduce the risk:

- always place the baby on her back in the cot or pram
- always place in the feet-to-foot position, so that the baby cannot slip down under the covers
- avoid over heating. Use blankets, not duvets, and avoid cot bumpers
- be sure to report any minor ailment to the parent when the baby is collected.

PREVENTION OF INFECTION

Small babies are very vulnerable to infection and you must be scrupulous in your personal hygiene when sterilising feeding equipment (see page 78), making up formula milk, changing and disposing of nappies and bathing baby. If you have older children in your care, they may need to be taught to always wash their hands after using the lavatory, before eating or preparing food. They should also wash before handling the baby and any cuts on their hands need to be covered.

Crowds and over-heated rooms might expose the baby to the risk of illness, whereas a brisk walk in the park will expose her only to fresh air. As the baby develops and becomes more sociable and meets more people, she will be more exposed to possible infection, but by this time her immune system is more able to cope with it.

FOOD AND NUTRITION

The giving of food and nourishment is a key factor in your relationship with the baby. Take your lead from the mother. She may have very definite ideas about how you will feed her baby and when to wean her from milk to solids and what type of foods she wishes you to offer her. The mother will be reassured by observing how you hold the baby close, maintain eye contact, talk to the baby, and in general show an understanding of how to feed and interact with a baby.

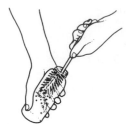

1 Wash the bottles, teats and other equipment in hot water and detergent. Use a bottle brush for the inside of bottles. **Do not rub salt on the teats**. Squeeze boiled water through the teats.

2 Rinse everything thoroughly in clean running water.

3 Fill the steriliser with clean, cold water. Add chemical solution. If in tablet form, allow to dissolve.

4 Put the bottles, teats and other equipment (nothing metal) into the water. Ensure everything is covered completely by the water, with no bubbles. If necessary, weight down. Leave for the required time according to manufacturer's instructions.

The procedure for sterilising feeding equipment

Breast-feeding

Some mothers will wish to continue to breast-feed either by expressing milk, or returning to the childminder's during the day. The desire to do this must be respected, but it can be stressful as babies do not necessarily match timetables or recognise lunch breaks. Make sure there is plenty of expressed breast milk in your freezer, to use in an emergency.

Bottle feeds

An approximate guide to calculating the amount of formula milk required by a baby is 75 ml of fully reconstituted feed for every 500 g of a baby's weight ($2\frac{1}{2}$ fluid ounces per pound body weight) in twenty-four hours. The total is divided into the number of bottles the baby is likely to take in that time. Like a breast-fed baby, the baby should be allowed to dictate her feeding requirements to allow for changes in appetite and growth.

Studies have shown that bottle-fed babies are frequently given feeds that are over- or under-concentrated, so always read and follow the instructions on the packet, as manufacturers often develop and change their products. See page 79 for steps in preparing the bottle feed.

Activity
What are the risks associated with over- or under-concentrating formula milk?

1 Check that the formula has not passed its sell-by date. Read the instructions on the tin. Ensure the tin has been kept in a cool, dry cupboard.

2 Boil some **fresh** water and allow to cool.

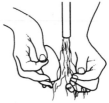

3 Wash hands and nails thoroughly.

4 Take required equipment from sterilising tank and rinse with cool, boiled water.

5 Fill bottle, or a jug if making a large quantity, to the required level with water.

6 Measure the **exact** amount of powder using the scoop provided. Level with a knife. **Do not pack down.**

7 Add the powder to the measured water in the bottle or jug.

8 Screw cap on bottle and shake, or mix well in the jug and pour into sterilised bottles.

9 If not using immediately, **cool quickly** and store in the fridge. If using immediately, test temperature on the inside of your wrist.

10 Babies will take cold milk but they prefer warm food (as from the breast). If you wish to warm the milk, place bottle in a jug of hot water. **Never keep warm for longer than 45 minutes** to reduce chances of bacteria breeding.

Note Whenever the bottle is left for short periods, or stored in the fridge, cover with the cap provided.

Preparing the bottle feed

Weaning

You will have discussed with the mother when to introduce mixed feeding and when the baby is ready to start solid foods. You will want to agree a routine with the mother so that the baby experiences continuity.

All mealtimes, especially those for a baby, should take place in a quiet calm atmosphere, and you should encourage her to enjoy new tastes without ever forcing them upon her. If the baby dislikes something on a Monday, she may well enjoy it the following Friday. It is always worthwhile reintroducing foods, as the baby's tastes become more mature.

HEALTH CHECKS

Once the mother has returned to work, it is possible that she will ask you to take the baby to the clinic for her regular developmental, hearing and health checks and for her immunisations. Written permission will be needed before the immunisations can be given, and the doctor will wish to have a full medical history, which only the parents can provide. If there are any anxieties about the baby's development or health, it is essential to encourage a parent to attend the clinic. The health visitor's name and telephone number will be recorded on the medical information chart and it may be useful to establish a relationship with her.

Illness develops faster in a baby than in an older child, and any disease can progress quickly, in some cases becoming life threatening. If you are at all worried about the baby, you should contact the parents as soon as possible at an early stage, and then, with their permission, telephone the doctor. Signs of ill-health to cause concern:

- refusal to feed over several feeds
- a rise or fall in temperature
- noisy or laboured breathing
- convulsions or fits
- excessive crying that continues despite cuddles and feeds
- a sunken or bulging anterior fontanelle (the soft spot on the crown of the head)
- a rash
- a persistent cough
- discharge from the ears, or if the baby pulls on the ears and cries
- changes in the stools or urine
- a very quiet, pale baby, difficult to rouse, and refusing to feed
- vomiting and diarrhoea
- poor muscle tension (the baby is very 'floppy').

The development of the small baby and the need for stimulation

Babies learn and develop as soon as they are born, quickly learning to recognise the smell, taste, voice, feel and face of the mother, thus using all the senses to ensure survival. In addition to love, protection, shelter and food, the baby also needs stimulation. At first the mother provides all the stimulation the baby requires through gentle handling and stroking, speaking in a soft voice and feeding. As the baby develops, the interaction between the mother or the main caregiver and the baby becomes increasingly important. As routines become established, there is time to play when feeding, bathing and changing nappies. Many babies are spending longer parts of the day awake, and you will have fun interacting and playing with her and making sure that she is not left alone or bored.

ENCOURAGING DEVELOPMENT

By six weeks, most babies are smiling, showing that they are responding to a stimulus, usually during a conversation whilst maintaining good eye contact. This is a good time to introduce mobiles and rattles. The mobiles which will interest her most will have horizontal pictures, so that she can gaze at them when lying on her back in a cot, or supported in a bouncing cradle. Bright colours add interest and some mobiles have a musical attachment.

Many toys are taken to the baby's mouth, so that she can learn with one of the most sensitive parts of her body the shape and substance of the object. This should not be discouraged, but checks must be made for safety. Everything needs to be durable, well made, non-toxic, washable, too large to swallow and with no sharp edges.

By far the most important stimulus is still the consistent contact given to the baby by parents, family and childminder. Interacting with songs and cuddles and talking to the baby will aid emotional, intellectual and language development. The first response will be facial: smiles and intense looks. Be sure to take turns and listen to the baby when she begins to vocalise. After changing the baby's nappy allow time for her to play with hands and feet unrestricted by clothing. Most babies enjoy their bathtimes, getting pleasure from the warmth of the water and the freedom to kick and splash. This aids all-round development.

At around six weeks, babies can be seen occasionally moving their hands towards objects in their field of vision and sometimes accidentally succeeding in touching them. At three months, the baby discovers her hands and begins to engage in finger play. By six months, this area of hand–eye co-ordination is usually well established and babies can reach out for a desired object and grasp it. Initially, toys such as an activity centre, which hang suspended just within the baby's reach, will help develop this skill. Play mats with a range of different sensory activities will help stimulate the baby's interest.

Increasingly, the baby's responses are no longer just reflex actions to sensory stimuli, but become selective, choosing which stimulus to react to. Lightweight rattles and toys that can be easily held in the hand help to develop hand–eye co-ordination.

Once the baby is able to sit up, supported by cushions, other toys may be offered. An exciting assortment of objects gathered together for her to explore will encourage her all-round development. Bricks can be built into towers and knocked down. Objects can be banged together. Singing to a baby comes naturally to most adults. From action songs to finger rhymes, from nursery rhymes to lullabies, the baby will get pleasure from them all and enjoy a sense of security and comfort. Singing helps babies to recognise different sounds and anticipate repetitive actions.

At this age too, the baby will start to enjoy books. Sitting with you and looking at pictures of familiar objects can start as young as six months, and will lay the foundation for a life-long enjoyment of books.

THE TREASURE BASKET

All areas of sensory development can be encouraged by the use of a treasure basket as described by Elinor Goldschmied. The baby is offered a container filled with objects made of natural materials, and chosen for their interesting shape as well as texture. About twenty items are needed to stimulate the five senses, such as a baby mirror, an orange, a fir cone, a piece of pumice, a small natural sponge, tissue paper, small cloth bags containing lavender or cloves, a brush, a piece of velvet, clothes pegs and a bunch of keys. All the equipment needs to be kept clean, and perishable objects such as fruit need to be discarded and replaced as necessary. Select items that have no sharp edges. Do not put in any items that are small enough to be inserted into noses or ears. A comfortable and safe position for the baby must be found, so that she does not topple over and become distracted. She should be allowed to explore the items on her own. You should keep an eye on her from a distance and not talk or interact with her as she plays and explores, as this will interfere with her concentration. You need to be alert to when she becomes bored, or has had enough.

Activity
Plan a treasure basket. List five items for each of the senses.

Safety factors
- all toys and equipment given to the baby should be clean and need to be washable to avoid infection.
- they should be durable to avoid accidents from broken edges and any painted items should be covered in non-toxic paint
- small babies are vulnerable to suffocation, so avoid using pillows and cushions and ensure any plastic bags are stored out of the baby's reach
- anything with strings should not be near the baby as, if the string becomes wrapped around the neck or other parts of body, the blood supply could be cut off, or the child could be hanged
- be careful with heavy toys or objects near the baby
- always use a harness when the baby is in the pram, or high-chair
- avoid small items that the baby might swallow or choke on.

Encouraging development in the toddler

Toddlers are challenging, and often the toys and activities provided by you may be used in a very different way by the child, but this is acceptable as learning is still taking place. Toddlers should be given every opportunity to explore and set their own agenda within a safe environment.

SOCIAL DEVELOPMENT

During the second year as the child begins to understand more, she has to learn how to fit happily into the household and the larger outside environment and a whole set of rules has to be learnt about acceptable behaviour. At this stage play is solitary, but the presence of a familiar adult provides reassurance and security. The toddler is not interested in playing co-operatively with other children. She has just learnt the meaning of 'mine', and the concept of sharing does not usually occur until the third year.

Taking toddlers to the park, shopping, visiting friends, parent and toddler groups, drop-in centres, the local library and visits to the clinic where other small children are likely to be found, will enlarge her social circle and allow her to play alongside other children. Provision of small scale household equipment, such as brooms, tea-sets and telephones, promotes domestic play and the beginning of role play.

PHYSICAL DEVELOPMENT

During the first year of life, the baby will have developed physical control. Some will be walking confidently by their first birthday, while others may need encouragement to get started and develop balance and co-ordination.

If you have stairs in your home, the gate may be removed on occasion, and the toddler shown how to climb up the stairs and, more importantly, how to crawl down. Strong supermarket cartons, which are sturdy and large enough for toddlers to climb in, promote skills of getting in and out of objects, co-ordination and balance.

Fine manipulative skills
During the first year, babies start to practice handling and manipulating small objects, reaching and grasping, holding and letting go, moving objects from hand to hand, passing objects, poking and pointing with one finger, and picking up objects with finger and thumb.

Equipment and activities that aid physical skills
There are many materials that will help develop manipulative skills and hand–eye co-ordination, such as bricks for building towers that can be knocked down; stacking cups and beakers; small tins and cartons that can be improvised from around the house; posting boxes; hammer sets; dolls that are easily undressed and simple inset jigsaws.

Outings to parks where the playground will have swings, seesaws, climbing frames and rocking toys are enjoyable and aid balance and co-ordination as well as strengthening arm and leg muscles.

Physical skills are encouraged by ball play, pull-along toys and small scale climbing and sliding equipment. Other toys and equipment you might find she enjoys at this age include wheeled toys to push along or sit on and move with the feet, rockers, and tunnels and boxes to climb in and out.

Playing with stacking beakers, posting boxes, barrels, bricks and small model toys will be good for her manipulative skills. Child-sized tea sets and cooking and cleaning equipment encourage her to imitate you, and this type of play is a spur for later more creative and imaginative play.

The contents of the lower kitchen cupboards, where it is sensible to store only safe sturdy equipment such as saucepans, plastic storage containers, baking tins and wooden spoons, can be played with as well as small bouncy balls, Duplo, large threading toys and screw toys. Playdough, crayons and finger-paints can be used.

INTELLECTUAL DEVELOPMENT AND COMMUNICATION

Children learn at an amazing rate, and during the first year the baby has learnt, among other things, to become mobile, to understand a great deal of what is said, to speak a few words, to identify people with whom she is in regular contact, and to recognise food she enjoys. The next year shows an acceleration of learning as the toddler becomes more proficient with language.

The toddler spends an increasingly large proportion of time in exploratory and experimental play. She will enjoy looking at books, listening to and taking part in songs and rhymes, learning that objects have names as do parts of the body, and realising that, by using language, needs are met without having to point and cry. Children's minds develop at different rates and in different ways, and they often have individual preoccupations, such as wrapping things up, making 'nests', taking toys around and around and arranging objects in straight lines over and over again.

Activity
Build up a repertoire of songs and finger-rhymes to use with babies and toddlers.

One good way of promoting language development is to sit down with a toddler with a book or a toy, and have an enjoyable conversation, making sure you take the time to listen to her responses, and to enlarge on her replies. This can be difficult in a busy childminder's household, but is rewarding for the child and for you.

EMOTIONAL DEVELOPMENT

During the first year, the baby progresses emotionally from total dependency to an understanding that there are some things she is able to do on her own, and this increases during the second year. You will need to have patience as the toddler tries to help you with her own care, or assist with the chores.

Tantrums can be caused by the toddler being bored, frustrated, hot or cold, hungry or feeling anxious. Sometimes they just cannot cope with their angry feelings. It is often possible to avoid confrontations but, if these do take place, toddlers are usually quite amenable to diversions. Some feelings are so strong and over-powering that you just have to wait until the storm has passed and then cuddle and comfort her, as she may well be frightened by the immensity of these emotions.

A great deal depends on the developing personality of the child as to how happy or sad she may be. Comfort objects may play a large part in her life and no attempt should be made to remove them. It is best to have as few rules as possible and to make sure that the environment is safe and offers security. Toddlers still need the love and support of a familiar adult and find new emotional demands difficult to deal with. You need to be aware of this when first building a relationship with a child of this age and proceed slowly and sensitively.

This is the age when toddlers really get into messy play. This allows them to express their frustrations and is relaxing and soothing. It is not always easy to organise this in the home but if it is at all possible let painting and water play take place outside. One can buy water-based paints and markers which wash out of clothing. Parents should be asked to bring children in clothing that is durable and easily washed. The garden offers opportunities for messy play, such as making mud-pies and digging for worms, and as long as she is not wearing her best clothes, she will be quite easy to clean up after a soak in the bath.

SENSORY DEVELOPMENT

Very young children learn mainly through their senses. As they grow older, learning in this way becomes less dominant. Toddlers, not yet in full command of language, use all their senses spontaneously in exploratory and experimental play. In general, toddlers will explore everything through the senses as this is instinctive, but you may need to encourage children who have some sensory impairment.

Activities

1 What materials and activities would you provide for an eighteen-month-old toddler who is visually impaired?
2 What areas of development are extended and promoted at mealtimes?
3 What particular messy play activities help promote emotional development?

Working with babies and toddlers can be challenging, but is immensely rewarding, and you may make relationships that endure for life.

7 CARING FOR THE SCHOOL-AGE CHILD

This chapter includes:
- **Growing independence**
- **Road safety**
- **Liaison with the school**
- **Bullying**
- **Holiday activities**

Childminders are frequently employed to care for children before and after school, and in the school holidays. They may be children that you have cared for as babies or toddlers, or they may be the older siblings of children you are caring for now. They may be children who have been at home with their mothers, or used other forms of daycare, and who now need looking after before and after school, as their mothers have returned to work. Some children may require more attention than others, and may take time to adjust to the childminder and new routines. With new government initiatives, it may be that more children will be requiring after-school care.

Growing independence

Once one of the children you look after starts school full-time he will have reached a stage of growing independence and his peer group will become increasingly important and dominant. Judith Harris (*The Nurture Assumption*, 1998) proposes that the peer group, together with inheritance factors, has more influence on the child than the parents. In spite of this, he will still need care and stimulation from you and an understanding of his different status.

Children have a busy day at school, and need to have their routine firmly structured. Going to bed at a reasonable time, dressing themselves as quickly and efficiently as they can manage, having time to eat a nutritious breakfast, cleaning teeth and combing hair, and being ready on time all take practice. You can play your part in preparing the child by making sure that in the holiday before school starts he can dress and undress himself and see to all his toilet needs. You can talk to him about the school day and how it will be more structured than the pre-school. Without frightening him, you could explain that the playground will be noisier than he is used to and the dining room will be larger. The lavatories may not be as hygienic as those in the pre-school or playgroup and there may not always be anyone to accompany him.

Alternatively, he could be a child new to you, whose mother has returned to work now that her son has started school. In this case, the child may need some additional care and attention at first, as he has to adjust to two new environments.

Whoever is collecting the child from school will need to make sure that he is not kept waiting. Even a few minutes wait after the other children have left can have a very negative effect on a child. After school, he will need some time to unwind and perhaps have a snack before starting his homework or attending any extra-mural activities. It needs a fair amount of self-discipline for him to ignore the younger children who may be playing outside or watching television and you may have to persuade him to stick to his routine.

When he first starts school, he may regress a little, become fussy about his food, demand help with putting on outside clothes and play with toys that are old and familiar. This is just a readjustment to having to be a 'big boy' while at school, and a perfectly normal stage of development. A full school day is physically tiring, and this might also affect his behaviour.

On some days, he may be full of news and expect your undivided attention as he relates the exciting events of the day. At other times, perhaps after a day when things have not gone so well, he may be silent and sullen, and just want to flop down on the couch and watch the television. For you, this might be quite hard to manage, as you will be nearing the end of a busy day and have less patience and energy than you might at other times.

Communicating with the parents is just as important at this age as it was with the younger children. You will need to keep up to date with the changing rules in the parent's household, in respect of the child's growing independence, so that you can offer the same consistent approach. A five-year-old might assure you that he is allowed to play outside before doing his homework, as his mother always lets him do so. This needs to be checked!

At five years of age, he begins to have his own private world separate from his family and from you. Often this leads to increasing fights and squabbles with his younger siblings and the other children that you care for. He understands that his parents and his minder do not know exactly what has been happening during the day and that it is possible to keep secrets from them. When he does wish to confide in you, he demands your undivided attention.

From about the age of eight, his growing independence should be encouraged and his carers need to let go gradually, trusting him to make his own mistakes within a framework of respect, and valuing him as a more autonomous person. This works both ways, and you will expect him to become increasingly considerate, and adhere to the rules of the house. As he grows older, rules may have to be rewritten, and agreed between the parents, the child and the childminder.

Activities

1 Describe how you give added responsibility to the older children that you mind.
2 How do you encourage school-age children to express their feelings?

You will have discussed with the child's parent the routine that is required after school, and he will be quite aware of what is expected. Children these days have very busy lives, full of extra-mural activities at the weekend, extra classes and coaching, parties and team games, Cubs and Brownies. You may be involved in taking and picking up children from these activities. There will be little time for organised activities in your home during the school year, and there is a lot to be said for identifying some time for 'free play'.

THE PEER GROUP

The child's circle of friends will become increasingly important to him and his regard for their opinion will start to displace his wish to always please you or his parents. You might be told, when you arrive to collect him, that he has been invited to his best friend's for tea that day. You will have to explain to the best friend's parent that the parents expect you to collect their child, and suggest that any social arrangements are made through the parents, giving you adequate notice.

Going out to play with friends and riding a bike around the block are often requested by children while in your home, and can be a major cause of friction. The Children Act 1989 requires children to be supervised at all times by you while in your care, and this cannot be delegated to any other adult.

EQUAL OPPORTUNITIES

School-age children become more aware of their special identity and gender, due to peer-group influence, and will need your reassurance to bolster their self-esteem. Unfortunately, you may find some of the children in your care absorbing the prejudiced attitudes of their peers at school, and you will have to be alert to this and challenge name-calling and stereotypical attitudes. You will have to make clear that this behaviour is not acceptable and if it continues you may have to discuss it with the child's parents. By always using equipment that reflects positive images of all racial groups, religions and cultures and does not discriminate on the basis of disability or gender, you will be playing your part in ensuring equality of opportunity for all.

Activity

You have recently started to mind an African-Caribbean child, aged five, after school. You set up a painting activity for him. You are surprised when you see that in the picture he has painted himself with a white skin.
1 Why do you think he has painted himself like this?
2 What immediate response would you make?
3 How might you help him improve his self-esteem?

Road safety

You will probably be involved in taking and fetching children from school, and will have to take all the children you are minding with you. If you are using the car, appropriate restraints will have to be fitted and used on every occasion. If you are walking, then you will apply the rules of road safety, teaching all the children how to cross the road safely, and following the rules yourself at all times.

There is a certain discipline the children will have to obey if they are to be totally safe when out with you. If you are caring for children of varying ages, from babies to school-age, the baby should be strapped in the harness in the pram, the toddler should wear reins, and be held firmly by you, and the older children should walk close to the pram, and never be allowed to run too far ahead. When you arrive at the school, you will have to take all the children in with you and never for one minute leave the baby in the pram unattended.

Liaison with the school

The parents will have made the initial contact with the school, met the teachers and seen the classroom. Once you start to take and collect the child from the school, you will begin to make relationships with the staff team and will be informed of any concern or achievement that has taken place during the day. The school will need to understand that the parents trust you and have given you permission to discuss their child, and convey messages back to them. Some teachers find this difficult because of the professional rules of confidentiality, and you may need to take the parents' written consent. Make sure parents receive all written and practical information given to you by the school and do not rely on the children to do so – they often forget!

Activity
How might a childminder encourage teachers to accept them as professional carers and educators?

If you are asked to help with homework, all the information the parents receive from the school about curriculum planning needs to be shared with you, so that you understand what is required. There are some practical issues, such as:
- finding a quiet place for the child to work
- agreeing with the child and the parents how much time should be given to homework
- what homework needs to be done on which night

As this will be a very busy time of day for you, it may be difficult to offer intensive one-to-one support. Encourage the parents to share the information they receive at parents' evenings with you, so that you can further help the child.

If you do not have children at school, you may not be fully aware of the changes taking place in education. The National Curriculum, introduced in 1988, has to be taught by law to all children from five to sixteen. The three core subjects are English, Mathematics and Science. Religious Education has been a compulsory requirement since 1944. Since 1998, all schools have to instigate a literacy hour every day. A numeracy hour is to be introduced in 1999.

The National Curriculum is divided into Key Stages, and children are tested at five, seven, eleven and fourteen to make sure they have attained the required targets.

Bullying

The child you are minding might be unfortunate enough to be one of the number of children who are the victims of bullying. Bullying is rare among under-fives, but can occur even though they are usually well supervised at all times. In the infant school, some forms of bullying may take place, such as name-calling, fighting, excluding a child from his peer group, sending to Coventry and racial abuse.

Dan Olweus, an expert in the prevention of bullying, defines bullying as involving:
- deliberate hostility and aggression towards the victim
- a victim who is weaker and less powerful than the bully or bullies
- an outcome which is always painful and distressing to the victim.

Bullying is the main cause for school refusal and can result in emotional scars that remain for life.

There are some behavioural indicators in children that might alert you to the fact that a child is being bullied. These indicators may be:
■ reluctance or refusal to attend school or nursery
■ saying they feel unwell in the mornings
■ coming home with torn clothes
■ hungry, having had their lunch stolen
■ withdrawal, unhappiness or showing signs of poor self-esteem
■ crying frequently
■ parents report that they have frequent nightmares
■ aggressive or starting to bully other children
■ reluctance to talk about what is happening.

Children who bully others may:
■ have low self-esteem
■ have little sense of their own worth
■ be in families where they are not encouraged to show or express their feelings
■ have experienced bullying or even abuse from others (this may still be occurring).

Childminders have a responsibility to tackle bullying alongside parents and schools. If you are caring for a child who is being bullied you will comfort and reassure the child and discuss the issue with the parents and, if the parents request it, with the school. If you discover that the child you are minding is bullying others, the strategies you might use include:

- getting the facts clear, finding out from the teachers and the child's parents what has been happening
- talking to the child with the permission of the parents, about the consequences of his actions
- discussing any problems that the child feels he has at school or at home
- building up his self-esteem and valuing his achievements
- agreeing with the child's parents on how to reward the child's good behaviour.

Activity

If you suspected that a child that you mind was being bullied at school:

1 What steps might you take to help the child in the short term?
2 How might you support the family in the long term?

CASE STUDY

Sylvia, an experienced childminder, was preparing the tea in the kitchen, when she overheard David, aged seven, being racially abusive towards Ashid, aged four. When David saw Sylvia, he stopped. Sylvia decided to ignore it for the time being, and planned to talk to David's mother about it when she came to collect him

1 Was this the right approach?
2 How could she prevent such behaviour in the future?
3 What should she do about Ashid?

Holiday activities

You may be asked to mind school-age children for all or part of the holidays. You will need to establish if and when the parents are taking them on holiday, so that you can work out a suitable programme. It will need careful planning to meet the needs of all the children of various ages in your care.

Sometimes the older children may be booked into playschemes or sports camps, and you would be looking after them at similar times as in term-time. Other children may be spending the day with you, and the activities you normally provide for the pre-school children will have to be extended, and made interesting for the older children. For example, if you have introduced a junk modelling activity, ask the older children for their ideas for a theme and allow it to continue until the project is complete. You may need to extend the range of equipment that you have available.

Most local authorities provide a range of activities and entertainment in their parks and libraries. Your newspaper will also give information as to what is available. Many museums mount special interactive exhibitions for children during the holidays. It may be useful to design a large chart, displaying details of what is available for each day as a reminder of where you might take the children. Many childminders get together in the holidays, arranging outings together and pooling resources.

8 THE SAFE ENVIRONMENT

> **This chapter includes:**
> - **Types of accidents**
> - **Checking hazards inside and outside the home**
> - **Planning in case of an emergency**
> - **Hygiene in the kitchen and bathroom**
> - **Medication**
> - **Recording accidents**

Children are the responsibility of the adults who care for them. An accident is something that happens that is not anticipated or foreseen, and may be preventable with care and thought. Sometimes accidents occur because the carer is in a hurry, is experiencing stress due to personal problems, or is feeling tired and therefore less alert.

As a childminder, you will have become aware of the need to provide a hazard-free and safe environment in your home that allows children to explore safely, and in turn aids all their areas of development and promotes independence. It is not always easy to find the balance between allowing too much independence and being over-protective. The younger the child, the more supervision is necessary. If a group of children becomes very quiet, it is always sensible to investigate!

The latest figures from the Royal Society for the Prevention of Accidents (ROSPA) and the Home Accident Surveillance System (HASS) show that the most serious accidents happen in the kitchen and on the stairs, and the largest number of accidents happen in the living room/dining room area.

Types of accidents

FALLS

Twenty children die as a result of falls each year, some from windows and balconies, the remainder mostly on stairs. Forty-two per cent of all accidents involve falls. The worst injuries occur when children fall from a great height or land on something hard, sharp or hot. Most falls result from falling between two levels, such as falling out of a pram or falling from a bed.

BURNS AND SCALDS

Seventy-one per cent of these injuries happen to children under five. Most of the scalding injuries are caused by mugs or cups of tea or coffee being knocked over.

Tea or coffee is still hot enough to scald fifteen minutes after being made and it is therefore not good practice to leave cups of coffee or tea around, or to sit children on your lap while you are drinking. Burning injuries are caused from contact with hot surfaces, such as fires or cookers, or by playing with matches.

CUTS

There has been an increase in glass-related accidents, because of the fashion for patio doors, large windows and glass table-tops. As many as five children might die in one year following an accident with glass. Accidents involving all types of glass account for nearly 40,000 injuries to children a year.

POISONING

Most poisoning accidents involve medicines, followed by household products and cosmetics. Every year, 15,000 children receive in-patient treatment and 43,000 children receive out-patient treatment.

OTHER CAUSES

Other accidents may be caused by foreign bodies in the ear or eye, choking, mainly on food, and drowning either in the bath or garden pond. An increasing number of accidents involve family pets.

One child in twelve will be treated for a home accident each year. Half the children are under four years of age. Boys are more likely to have an accident than girls. Children in lower socio-economic groups are more likely to have a fatal accident than those in higher groups. Factors, such as divorce, death in the family, chronic illness, homelessness and moving home increase the likelihood of a child having an accident, due to the stress caused to the main carer.

To prevent accidents to children, a combination of factors is required:

- improvements in the planning, design and manufacture of products to create a safer environment
- an increasing awareness of risks, hazards and safety equipment
- education and training to improve knowledge and skills.

Activity
Suffocation and choking is the third most common cause of death in young children. What steps can you take to prevent this happening to the children in your care?

A professional approach to safety might involve you in carrying out the following checks on a regular basis:

- examine each room of the house for obvious hazards
- test and maintain all safety equipment

- make sure that all the children's equipment, such as high-chairs, pushchairs and prams, are clean, have attached harnesses, and are well maintained
- make sure the garden is safe
- ensure that the car is regularly serviced, and has appropriate restraints and car seats fitted
- carry out a fire drill at least once a month, making this into a game so as not to alarm the children.

Checking hazards inside and outside the home

Keeping your home safe is not just a matter of checking for hazards, and being sure that there is nothing dangerous around. It entails constant vigilance and imagination whilst inspecting and maintaining all equipment on a daily basis. You will find yourself as a role model and educator, not only with your own children, but also with the children in your care.

GOOD PRACTICE IN PREVENTING ACCIDENTS IN THE HOME

1 Check domestic and play equipment regularly for sharp edges, splinters, and loose pieces. Do not give children under three small playthings, such as marbles or small Lego pieces.
2 Always buy toys and equipment from reputable shops. Look at the label, and check for the Kite mark.

3 Keep the following objects out of sight and out of reach of children:
   - medicines and tablets, which must be kept locked in a high cupboard
   - matches
   - sharp objects, such as knives and razor blades
   - plastic bags
   - household cleaners and chemicals
   - alcohol
   - cigarettes.
4 Ensure that safety gates for stairs or doorways are secure.
5 Never use baby walkers as there have been serious accidents when using this equipment.
6 Do not use pillows for any child under eighteen months. Use a firm mattress with no gaps between it and the cot.
7 Always supervise children in the kitchen where there are many hazards. You must be sure to:
   - turn saucepan handles away from the edge of the stove
   - keep all hot and sharp objects away from the edge of units
   - use short, coiled flexes on electrical equipment
   - have a fire blanket, and know how to use it
   - keep chest freezers locked
   - keep the doors to washing machines and tumble dryers shut
   - avoid using tablecloths that hang down
   - use a harness fitted to the high-chair and see that it is always secured.
   - always supervise children when they are eating or drinking and never leave a baby propped up with a bottle.
8 Avoid giving nuts or hard-boiled sweets to children.
9 Remove rugs from highly polished floors and try to keep floor space free of obstruction, as much as possible.
10 Make sure cords are not trailing from curtains or blinds.
11 Avoid anything around babies' necks, such as anorak strings, dummies on strings and ribbons on hats.
12 Fit child-resistant locks on all windows, keeping keys readily available in case of fire.
13 Use safety-glass or safety film for large areas of glass, and for low-level glass.
14 Highlight large glass doors with stickers.
15 Secure doors leading to cellar, balcony and any unsupervised outside area.
16 Do not leave a hot drink unattended, and never sit a child on your lap while drinking something hot.

To prevent fire:
- make sure all fires have securely fitted safety guards
- have your water heating and heating equipment regularly inspected and maintained.

In case of fire:
- have smoke alarms fitted and keep them maintained
- plan how you would escape from your home, particularly if you have sealed windows or permanently locked doors
- practice fire drill with the children regularly.

To prevent electric shocks:

- cover all power points with child-resistant socket covers
- check all flexes regularly for fraying and replace those that are worn
- never put electrical appliances in the bathroom
- make sure new electric appliances come fitted with a plug.

GOOD PRACTICE IN PREVENTING ACCIDENTS IN THE GARDEN

1 Keep garage and shed doors locked, and keep all equipment and materials locked away out of sight and out of reach of children.
2 Secure garden gates and fences so that children cannot get out and people and animals cannot get in.
3 Cover or fence-off any area or equipment containing water.
4 Cover sandpits when not in use to avoid soiling by animals.
5 Destroy poisonous plants.
6 Check all outdoor play equipment such as slides and climbing frames regularly for safety, and make sure that any new equipment is correctly installed, and that the space underneath has either mats or wood chippings to ensure a soft landing.
7 Avoid trailing clothes lines.
8 Supervise animals when children are in the garden, and put a cat-net over a baby's pram.
9 It is safer to avoid ponds and water butts in gardens, but any that you cannot remove need to be securely netted. A young child can drown in two inches of water.

Activities

1 You are caring for a six-month-old baby and an active four-year-old. Which hazards in the house and in the garden are particularly dangerous for each age group?
2 Devise a safety check list for your home and garden.

Activity

Identify indoor and outdoor plants that might be poisonous.

FURTHER AFIELD

You will be taking children out very often, going shopping, posting letters, collecting older children from school, visiting libraries and friends. You may find yourself having to manage a baby in a pushchair and an active toddler.

With very young children, it is prudent to avoid places where:

- there are very large open spaces and a child might wander off
- there is a lot of traffic and pollution
- animal droppings are not cleared up promptly

- there is a great deal of litter dropped, such as in some markets
- the children have to be quiet and keep still for a long time
- it is difficult to supervise more than one child safely, such as in a playground with swings, high obstacle courses and slides, and unsupervised water play
- there are sandpits that are not covered at night to prevent animals from fouling them.

It is a good idea to take a small emergency First Aid kit on any outing. It is never too early to start teaching children basic rules of safety, and making sure that they know their address and home telephone number. When in parks and on beaches, always identify a highly visible point, such as a café, where children should go if they become temporarily detached.

GOOD PRACTICE IN PREVENTING ACCIDENTS WHEN TAKING THE CHILDREN OUT

1. Maintain prams and pushchairs in good working order and check brakes regularly.
2. Fit harnesses to prams and pushchairs and always use them.
3. Be a good role model when crossing the road, teaching children road safety from an early age. Always use zebra or pelican crossings if available. Make sure children are holding your hand, or the pram.
4. Never push the pram or other conveyance into the road first, so as to stop the traffic.
5. Be alert when in shopping centres and other busy areas. Use personal restraints, such as harnesses or reins.´
6. When in a park, use the 'children only' areas and exercise constant supervision in the playground.

7   If you are taking children further afield, you will need to plan the trip carefully and well in advance. Consultation with parents is essential, and you will need to make sure you have their written permission. Do double check that your insurance covers all the activities you are planning.

8   Children should never be left alone outside shops or schools. Prams must either be taken into shops with you, or you must carry the baby.

Activity
1   Plan a picnic in your local park, with children aged one, three and six.
2   What would it be essential to have with you so as to make sure the children were protected and you are prepared for any emergency?

Always be alert to danger, and aware that children are small vulnerable beings. A knowledge of children's development should allow you to anticipate some potential hazards and risks, and understanding your children's personality will help you to predict how they will react to situations. Part of your role is to teach children about dangers, and how to protect themselves.

GOOD PRACTICE WHEN USING THE CAR

You might find yourself using your car to transport the children from place to place. There are certain checks you need to make, and rules to establish.

1   Check that your car insurance is valid for business purposes and fully comprehensive.
2   All adults in the car must wear seat belts in the front and in the back.
3   All children in the car should be secured in child restraints appropriate to the size of the child, with the younger children in the back.
4   Make sure that child-locks are activated when you have the children with you.
5   Do not allow the family pet in the car when you are transporting children.
6   All child restraints should be professionally fitted.
7   Never allow the children to stand up on the seats, between the front seats, or travel in the back section of an estate or hatchback.
8   Make sure that children alight onto the pavement, and not the road.
9   Make sure that all the children are properly secured in the car before you get in. If you are carrying a number of children, count them, to make sure you have not inadvertently left one behind!
10 Be a careful and alert driver, a good example to the children.

CASE STUDY

In the Easter holidays, Anita, a newly registered childminder, took her two children and the two she minded to the zoo with her friend Jessie, who has three children of her own. They had to take two cars. All the children were playing up, wanting to sit in particular seats, next to friends. When they met up at the ticket office, Anita was horrified to find that her son, Jamie, who is seven, was not with them. Anita thought he had gone with Jessie, and she thought he was with Anita.

The day was ruined, as they all had to return home and find Jamie in tears in the back garden.

1 What could Anita have done to prevent this situation happening?

2 How would you have dealt with Jamie?

Planning in case of an emergency

There are many types of emergencies that might arise during the day and you need to be prepared. Each child should have an individual record form (see page 103).

As you complete this form with the parents it will be an opportunity to discuss how you handle any crisis. For example, if a child is prone to asthma, some parents might wish the child to be taken straight to hospital and meet you there, while others might like to come to you from work.

There might be other emergencies where you are unable to look after the children. You will need to think about back-up help, someone who would take over at short notice. Reassure the parents that the children will never be left with anyone who is not a registered childminder, except in a real emergency where there was not any choice. You need to have access to a telephone, together with a list of essential telephone numbers. If you do not have one at home, do you know where the nearest public telephone is? Do you always have coins or a phone-card available?

The 'House information' table on page 104 may be useful to someone who takes over from you and is not as familiar as you are with the house.

FIRST AID

It is sensible to enrol on a First Aid course, if you do not already hold the certificate. It may be a requirement by some local authorities prior to registration. Courses should be taught by those with expertise, such as the St John Ambulance or the British Red Cross or a trainer approved by NCMA. All First Aid certificates need to be up-dated regularly. First Aid is the immediate action taken to treat a person who has been injured or has suddenly become ill. Knowing what to do can save life and prevent further injury, but it is important to know your limits and do only what you are competent to do. Urgent care requires you to:

■ remove the victim from the source of danger
■ check breathing and give artificial respiration if necessary
■ control bleeding
■ place the child in the recovery position if she is unconscious
■ call for help, giving accurate information, and keeping any substance that might be relevant to diagnosing the condition.

Many hospitals now offer two-hour resuscitation sessions, which you might like

CHILD RECORD FORM
To be completed by the parent/guardian/carer and given to the childminder.
Please read notes for guidance on the cover of this pad.

CHILD'S NAME (1)_____

DATE OF BIRTH _____

HOME ADDRESS _____

_____ TELEPHONE NUMBER _____

DETAILS OF PARENTS/GUARDIANS/CARERS
PARENT'S/GUARDIAN'S/CARER'S NAME ....
PLACE OF WORK ....
TELEPHONE NUMBER ....

PARENT'S/GUARDIAN'S/CARER'S NAME ....
PLACE OF WORK ....
TELEPHONE NUMBER ....

EMERGENCY CONTACT (other than parent/guardian/carer)
_____

NAME OF PERSON WHO WILL USUALLY COLLECT CHILD (2)
_____

OTHER PERSON(S) WHO MAY COLLECT CHILD
_____

CHILD'S DOCTOR
NAME AND ADDRESS ....
....
TELEPHONE NUMBER ....
IMMUNISATIONS / VACCINATIONS Has the child been fully immunised against:
Diphtheria ☐   Whooping Cough ☐   Tetanus ☐   Polio ☐
Measles ☐   Mumps ☐   Rubella ☐   Hib Meningitis ☐

HEALTH CLINIC
_____

HEALTH VISITOR
_____

ALLERGIES/ SPECIAL DIET/ HEALTH PROBLEMS/ CHILDHOOD ILLNESSES (3)
_____

LANGUAGE SPOKEN AT HOME (4) _____

ANYTHING ELSE YOUR CHILDMINDER SHOULD KNOW ABOUT YOUR CHILD
e.g. fears, dislikes, comfort items, special words (5)
_____

Parents should notify the childminder of any changes to these details immediately. Details
of any accidents which occur while the child is in the care of the childminder should be
recorded in the Accident/Medication Record Book and signed by the Parent/Guardian/Carer.

NATIONAL CHILDMINDING ASSOCIATION 8 Masons Hill, Bromley, Kent, BR2 9EY.
Telephone: 0181 464 6164 Fax: 0181 290 6834

Reproduced by kind permission of the National Childminding Association

This sample form is for illustrative purposes only. Copies of the form can be obtained from NCMA.

HOUSE INFORMATION

Your stand-in carer has been informed: how to secure the house (doors, windows, shutters)	Tick for Yes ❏
how to set the alarm	❏
where to find a spare set of keys	❏
Where to find the:	
fire extinguisher	....
torch	....
candles	....
fuse box	....
First Aid kit	....
Emergency telephone numbers:	
Gas	....
Electricity	....
Water	....
Vet	....
Local authority	....
Arrangements for disposal of rubbish	....
How to use domestic equipment:	
Washing machine	....
Drier	....
Dishwasher	....
Microwave	....
Cooker	....
Central heating	....
Other essential information	....

This page may be photocopied. © Stanley Thornes (Publishers) Ltd

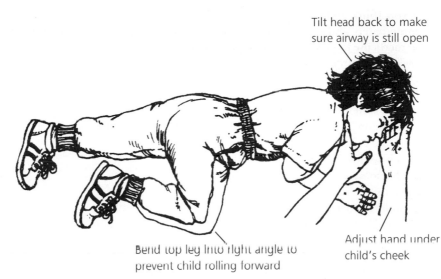

Tilt head back to make sure airway is still open

Bend top leg into right angle to prevent child rolling forward

Adjust hand under child's cheek

The recovery position

to attend, prior to taking a full First Aid course. NCMA recommends that the full range of emergency action skills requires at least a twelve-hour course.

Many accidents cause shock in children, and you will need to recognise the signs, which are:

- pale, cold, sweaty skin
- rapid pulse, becoming weaker
- shallow, fast breathing
- restlessness, yawning and sighing
- thirst
- loss of consciousness.

If you think one of the children is suffering from shock, you should summon medical aid.

Anaphylactic shock

This is a generalised allergic reaction that may occur a few minutes after:

- eating a particular food, such as peanuts
- being stung by an insect or a sea creature
- the injection of a particular drug.

This is a rare occurrence, but one where a knowledge of First Aid is essential. The air passages become constricted and swelling of the face and neck increases the risk of suffocation. The signs are:

- anxiety
- red blotchy skin
- swelling of face and neck
- puffy eyes
- wheezing
- a fast pulse
- difficulty in breathing.

If you think a child might be suffering from anaphylactic shock, you must act immediately and call an ambulance. If the child has a known allergy, there may be medicine to take in case of an attack. Give this as soon as the attack starts, following the directions carefully. Keep calm and reassure the child, putting her in a position that relieves her breathing difficulty.

Concussion
Concussion is not always easy to recognise. After a bump to the head, a child might be concussed if there is:
■ a brief loss of consciousness
■ dizziness
■ nausea
■ mild headache
■ loss of memory of events immediately preceding the accident.
An unconscious child who is breathing and has a pulse should be put into the recovery position to keep the airway clear by preventing choking on the tongue or vomit. Check for breathing and pulse until medical aid arrives.

Your First Aid box should contain:
■ cotton wool
■ prepared bandages in several sizes
■ gauze squares in several sizes
■ a triangular bandage
■ crêpe bandages in several sizes and lengths
■ tubular gauze with applicator
■ surgical spirit
■ plasters in several sizes
■ surgical tape
■ disposable plastic gloves
■ safety pins
■ small mirror
■ tweezers
■ scissors
■ calamine lotion
■ thermometer, preferably a fever strip that can be applied to a child's forehead.
You should check with your registration officer, as he or she may have a list of approved items. These lists can vary considerably.

We have suggested a basic kit, but you would need to discuss with the parents any possible allergies to plasters. You will probably keep medication available to treat your own family. You should not prescribe these medicines for other children you are looking after.

Hygiene in the kitchen and bathroom

It is particularly important for childminders to have high standards of personal hygiene, as you will have to carry out intimate tasks for the children, as well as teaching them the rules of hygiene.

Infection is spread by touch, food and water, animals, droplets in the air and through cuts and grazes. All children are vulnerable to infection and it is important that you understand how disease is transmitted in order to minimise children's exposure to bacterial, fungal and viral infections. The rooms that harbour most germs are the kitchen and the bathroom and, as you will be having other children using these, they need to be scrupulously clean.

GOOD PRACTICE IN THE PREVENTION OF INFECTION

1 Make sure that you and the children wash your hands after using the lavatory, handling animals and their equipment, coughing or sneezing, and before eating. In addition, you need to wash thoroughly after changing nappies, wiping noses, wiping bottoms and handling raw food.
2 Keep the kitchen work-surfaces, utensils and implements clean.
3 Always keep food covered that is left out on the work-surface.
4 Never re-freeze food that has already been defrosted.
5 Never store raw meat alongside other food. Keep it well wrapped at the bottom of the refrigerator.
6 Do not allow the refrigerator to become over-crowded, as this will impede the circulation of air.
7 Never eat meat and fish that has been refrigerated for more than three days.
8 Make sure the refrigerator is no more than 5 degrees centigrade, and the freezer set at minus 18 degrees centigrade to prevent bacteria multiplying.
9 Sterilise feeding bottles and teats for as long as they are used, as milk is an excellent medium for bacteria.
10 Keep rubbish bins covered and scrupulously clean.
11 Keep animals out of the kitchen.

Activities
1 Suggest two hygiene routines that will help to prevent infection.
2 Describe how you dispose of waste products and soiled items hygienically and safely.

Someone in your family, or one of the children you look after, may be suffering from:
- impetigo (a highly infectious skin disease)
- cold sores
- fungal skin infections such as ringworm
- conjunctivitis.

These are all contagious and easily transmitted by touch and other parents should be notified.

Keeping a clean home will prevent germs from multiplying. The use of soap and water, fresh air and sunlight will destroy many germs. Chemical disinfectants, such as carbolic or strong bleach, will destroy germs but are potentially harmful to children and pets, and need to be locked away after use. Antiseptics are weak disinfectants that prevent the growth of organisms but do not destroy them. They can be equally dangerous to children.

Those keeping any kind of pet should know about its food and habits, and how to care for it.

GOOD PRACTICE IN CARING FOR PETS

1 Children should be taught the importance of looking after animals, feeding them and cleaning out cages.
2 They must be told the importance of washing hands after handling a pet or cleaning a cage.
3 Children should be discouraged from kissing pets or letting pets lick their faces.
4 Sick animals must always be seen by a vet.
5 Disinfectant should be used to wash floors soiled with animal excreta.
6 Animals' foods and plates should be kept and washed separately from those used by humans.
7 Puppies and kittens should be wormed when very young, and before this, children should not handle them. They should be wormed again at regular intervals.
8 No family should have a pet that is not tolerant of young children.
9 All animals need space and exercise and a person who is devoted to their care.

Activity
Investigate two diseases that are associated with pets.
What action would you take to ensure that the children you mind are not put at risk?

Medication

Some children require routine medication for a chronic condition. For example, a child might suffer from asthma, and would need some form of inhaler to prevent attacks, as well as a medicine to have at hand if she should become ill. For your own protection, you should have written permission from the parents before administering any routine drugs asking them to complete the following form 'Permission to administer medicine/treatment'.

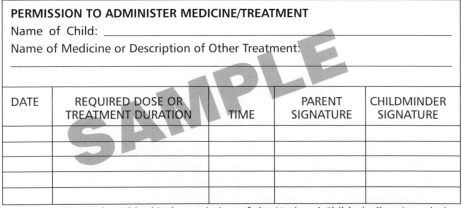

PERMISSION TO ADMINISTER MEDICINE/TREATMENT				
Name of Child: _____				
Name of Medicine or Description of Other Treatment:				
_____				
DATE	REQUIRED DOSE OR TREATMENT DURATION	TIME	PARENT SIGNATURE	CHILDMINDER SIGNATURE

Reproduced by kind permission of the National Childminding Association

This sample form is for illustrative purposes only. Copies of the form can be obtained from NCMA.

All medicines should be stored in the original container and be properly labelled. They must be in a secure place, out of the reach of children. Most medicines should be kept in a cool, dry environment, and out of sunlight. Many medicines need refrigeration and should be kept in a secure box, separate from food, and labelled 'medicines'. You should not prescribe medication yourself, not even paracetamol for a raised temperature. If you become concerned, you should follow the instructions on the child's personal record form (see page 103).

Recording accidents

If a child has an accident while in your care, it must be recorded in some detail. Fill in an accident record book sheet (see below) carefully and, after informing the parents, ask them to sign to confirm that they have been informed.

ACCIDENT RECORD	
Name and Age of Child:	Date and time of incident:
Description of Circumstances Leading to the Incident	
Record of Injury and Action Taken	
Childminder Signature:	Parent Signature:
Date:	Date:

Reproduced by kind permission of the National Childminding Association

This sample form is for illustrative purposes only. Copies of the form can be obtained from NCMA.

Every accident, however slight, should be recorded in the accident book, as some seemingly minor accidents can result in more serious concerns, and accurate recording of information can be vital. The accident book may also show regularly occurring hazards.

Every parent wants their child to be safe and healthy at all times. This does not happen just by chance, and it takes a great deal of effort to make sure that there are no hazards in your home and garden. Children need to be protected against infection and appropriate care should be taken to minimise accidents and illness. You and the parents will share the same objectives.

9 *CHILDREN WITH DISABILITIES*

> ## This chapter includes:
> - **Defining disability**
> - **Deciding to mind a child with a disability**
> - **The needs of other children**
> - **Planning suitable activities**
> - **The needs of parents**
> - **Children with HIV**

During your career as a childminder, you may be asked to care for a child with an obvious condition, such as Down's syndrome or cerebral palsy. On the other hand, during the time you are minding the child, it might come to light that he has a specific impairment, such as a hearing loss.

All children have the same needs: to be loved, valued, feel secure and protected, to receive routine physical care and to have enough stimulation to achieve their potential. Children with disabilities may have additional needs and require extra help, but the important thing to remember is that you view the child as a person in his own right, and not see just the impairment. Impairment becomes disability only if the environment is not adjusted to enable the child to function effectively, for example the majority of people with sight impairment are not disabled.

Defining disability

Up to twenty per cent of children are estimated to have a disability of some kind. This includes children with:
- physical impairments
- sensory impairments affecting sight, speech or hearing
- a range of learning difficulties
- medical conditions, such as asthma, diabetes, sickle cell, epilepsy, eczema or thalassaemia
- a need for special diets, such as milk-free, nut-free, gluten-free or sugar-free
- behavioural and emotional difficulties, including hyperactivity
- HIV positive status
- a combination of any of the above.

Deciding to mind a child with a disability

If you are considering minding a disabled child, there are skills, attitudes and knowledge that you may need to have. These include:

- being of a calm and patient disposition
- having a good sense of humour
- being physically strong, as you may have to lift a child, or manage a child having a fit
- having a firm, consistent approach, as you would with all the children
- having knowledge from the parents, as well as doing your own research, about the possible effects of the impairment
- being responsible for administering medication, as instructed by the parents
- being willing to undertake a short course of specialised training, if available
- being prepared to research and contact organisations
- being willing and competent to carry out necessary therapies
- being competent in using any necessary aids
- being willing to liaise with specialists, therapists and support groups
- being optimistic about the child's physical and intellectual potential
- seeing the child rather than the impairment
- being aware of the financial implications, as your income may be reduced. The number of children you are able to mind may be less, as you will have to give more time to a child with a disability, and there may be no enhanced payment from the local authority.

Part of the process in deciding your suitability for minding a disabled child is to consider whether:

- you are being realistic – you may need a good deal of strength and stamina, both pysically and emotionally
- you have adequate experience in caring for children with disabilities, and for those without disabilities
- you have experience of this child's impairment
- you have knowledge of appropriate language when referring to or discussing the impairment
- whether you have sufficient space in your home for additional equipment, such as wheelchairs or large pushchairs
- whether you are willing to learn about therapies, such as physiotherapy and speech therapy
- you have knowledge of the aids and the maintenance that might be needed
- you are aware of the length of time the child is to spend with you, as consistent care is so important
- you are willing to learn about any programmes he might be following and to undertake such programmes
- you have ideas for encouraging his development
- you have observation skills and can maintain written records
- you are aware of the child's specific needs and are willing to provide appropriate care
- you have adequate communication skills with the child, parents, and outside agencies.

Some common worries, apart from a general fear of the unknown, may include:

- mealtimes
- how to give enough time to all the children in your care

- how to communicate with the child
- coping with an incontinent child
- lifting the child in a skilled way
- dealing with unfamiliar patterns of behaviour
- managing a child with epilepsy
- the possible additional wear and tear on the home.

Having a sympathetic nature is not enough. You must be sure not to over-protect the child, see that he is encouraged to reach his full potential and be ready to support him in integrating himself with friends and family. You may find yourself having to challenge the negative and discriminatory attitudes of adults and children. Your assertiveness techniques (see Chapter 13) will be invaluable here!

CASE STUDY

Clara minds Sally, aged three and a half, who has Down's syndrome, and Richard, aged four. They play well together and enjoy all their activities. Richard is caring towards Sally and helps her to complete puzzles. He sometimes shows her books. Clara has recorded observations of the two children playing well together.

Usually it is Richard's mother who collects Richard, and Clara has noticed that she seldom pays any attention to Sally. Clara is astonished one day when Richard's father tells her that Richard is sometimes distressed and, when questioned, states that he doesn't like Sally because she looks funny.

1 What immediate response should Clara make?
2 How should she use her observations?
3 How should she plan to work with the parents?

Parents of children with disabilities may need a great deal of support themselves, and you may have to set aside some time in offering them a listening ear and allowing them to express their anxieties to you. Most conditions have support and information groups, and the parents will most likely be aware of these. Any information they have should be communicated to you.

The needs of other children

Apart from the child with the disability, it may be that you will be minding other children as well as your own children, and perhaps a sibling of the disabled child. The National Children's Home report in 1995 showed that ninety-eight per cent of 360,000 children with disabilities live with their families, and eighty per cent of these families have more than one child. It has sometimes been found that the needs of the other children in a domestic setting are not always met, as carers have to spend so much time with the one child.

Other children may experience:
- anxiety, leading to disturbed sleep
- resentment and jealousy
- fear of 'catching' the condition

- teasing and isolation at school
- emotional swings, from being loving and protective, to disturbed behaviour such as regression or attention-seeking.

Other children are very aware of how much time and focus is given to the needs of the child with the disability, and need some special time to talk about how they feel. You will need to:

- find time to give them individual attention every day
- reassure them that they are loved and valued
- be honest with them, and give them information appropriate to their level of understanding
- encourage them to care for the child with the disability as part of the routine of the day, talking to him and playing simple games.

CASE STUDY

Lauren cares for two children, Andrew, four, and Whitney, two, and has two school-age children of her own, twins Patricia and Henry aged six. Andrew is new to the family and is very demanding. He is with Lauren two days a week to give his mother a break. He is hyperactive, has little speech, is frequently aggressive, particularly towards Henry, and takes up much of Lauren's time, but lately he has been showing some improvement and his mother says Andrew is much better behaved at home than he used to be.

Lauren has noticed that Henry avoids Andrew, refusing to sit at the table with him and spends most of the afternoon when Andrew is there in his room. Lauren is distressed to be told by Henry's teacher that he frequently confides in her that he dislikes Andrew and is frightened of him.

1 How might Lauren help Henry?
2 Should Lauren discuss the situation with Andrew's mother?
3 Should Lauren's husband be involved?

Planning suitable activities

All children learn through play and are naturally curious. Some children with disabilities may need more help and encouragement to become involved in play. It is important to have realistic expectations of the abilities of all the children in your care, but in particular it would not be good practice to expect a child with a disability to succeed at something that his impairment makes impossible. For example, to expect a hyperactive child to sit at a table concentrating on an intricate task for more than five minutes would be unrealistic. On the other hand, do not fall into the trap of expecting too little. A child with a physical impairment is likely to be just as intelligent as any other child – think of Stephen Hawking!

Your observation skills will be a key factor in deciding what to offer individual children. In assessing their needs, you will be able to plan a programme of activities to promote their development. All children need a great deal of

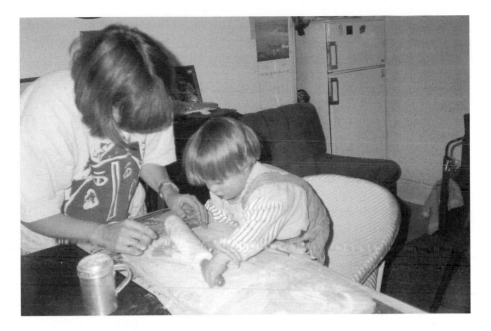

praise and encouragement in order to succeed and feel confident. For some children, breaking down a task into small steps may be necessary to help them succeed.

PROMOTING THE CHILD'S SELF-IMAGE

All parents hope for confident, well-adjusted children who feel good about themselves and become independent, autonomous members of society. This is harder for children with a disability, and they very quickly learn to compare themselves with other children as there are so many activities from which they are cut off and excluded. Any activities that you plan should be accessible to all the children you are minding, at individual levels of achievement. No child should be made to feel that he cannot join in because of his particular disability.

To foster a disabled child's self-esteem you will need to:

■ handle his physical needs with sensitivity
■ praise any achievement, however small
■ offer choices where possible, and allow the child to make decisions
■ be positive and not under-estimate his ability
■ be sensitive to his body language (this may be his main form of communication)
■ break down all planned activities into small steps, so that he can achieve
■ if just looking after the one child, find a suitable group of children, where he has the opportunity to develop his social skills and make friends
■ always use positive language and challenge any inappropriate language or behaviour from other adults or children
■ encourage any sign of independence, and do not over-protect the child.

The needs of parents

Parents are likely to experience many negative feelings about their children's situation, such as:

■ confusion (how can I cope with this?)
■ anger (why me?)
■ guilt (it's my fault, where did I go wrong?)
■ grieving (for the able-bodied child that might have been)
■ blaming (partner, in-laws)
■ shame (attitudes of neighbours, friends and even family)
■ fear (about the future)
■ rejection (of the child).

Parents may also experience denial and disbelief, especially if they secretly feel that they have contributed in some way. Bringing up a child with a disability can be a tremendous strain on the marriage or partnership, and can be a contributory factor to marital breakdown. Some parents experience increasing isolation from their neighbours and family.

By emphasising the child's positive aspects and achievements, you can go a long way to supporting and reassuring the parents as someone outside the family who values their child. There are many people who have surmounted difficulties to achieve a great deal in later life, writing books, running support groups, being ministers in government and becoming the number one scientist in the country.

Children with HIV (human immune deficiency virus)

It is possible that you may be minding a child who is HIV positive and you may or may not be aware of this. Many children who are HIV positive remain well and healthy, displaying no symptoms of AIDS (acquired immune deficiency syndrome). Children with an impaired immunity system may have a greater risk of catching infections and may also experience severe complications from common childhood infections, such as measles and chickenpox.

HIV has been isolated in many body fluids. Sufficient amounts of the virus to cause infection have been found in:

- blood and blood products
- semen
- vaginal and cervical secretions
- amniotic fluid (the fluid that surrounds the baby in the uterus)
- breast milk.

It is not thought the virus can be passed on through:

- saliva
- sweat
- tears
- urine
- faeces.

The virus is extremely fragile, and is unable to survive long outside the body. It cannot be carried through the air. It is destroyed by heat, light, bleach and detergents. The main routes of transmission are through sexual contact, blood to blood through sharing needles and syringes, and mother to baby. There is no known case of HIV being transmitted in any childcare setting. Most pathogens, such as hepatitis B are much more infectious than the HIV virus.

Good hygiene practice plays an important part in providing a safe and caring environment for children. All children, including your own, should be treated as if they were HIV positive, and this will ensure good practice and equal treatment for all.

In addition to the good hygiene practices pointed out in Chapter 8, you should always:

- wash blood, faeces and urine off your skin with warm, preferably hot, soap and water
- regularly clean and disinfect floors, equipment, toys and cups
- clean up any spilt blood or faeces with a bleach solution (one part household bleach to ten parts water)
- cover any open wounds on your skin or on a child's skin
- wear disposable gloves when dealing with faeces, urine or blood if you have cuts on your hands
- rinse with running water for several minutes if blood is splashed on your face or in your eyes
- soak any blooded clothes, or implements used for First Aid in a one to ten bleach solution for five to ten minutes

- wipe the nappy changing pad with a one to ten bleach solution after each use
- double wrap all waste that contains body fluids, and put in plastic sacks.

There is no obligation for the parents to tell you that they, or their child, are HIV positive. Adults and children can become infected in different ways and it is important not to make assumptions about how a child might become infected. If a parent does confide in you, you must respect this confidence and tell no one. Many people will not be as knowledgeable as you and may feel their children to be at risk.

THE SICK CHILD

This chapter includes:
- **Caring for children who are unwell**
- **Infection**
- **Minor ailments**
- **Infestations**
- **Chronic medical conditions**

To make sure that the children in your care are healthy, you will be working in partnership with their parents. A childminder can be regarded to some extent as a health educator who wishes to promote the health of children by understanding health issues and setting a good example. You will understand the importance of routine health surveillance and screening programmes, and encourage parents to participate.

Caring for children who are unwell

Sick babies and children need to be with their main carer if possible, and you will certainly wish to avoid the risk of cross-infection, but there may be times when you find yourself caring for a child who is sick.

If the child's temperature suddenly rises, it is important to take action so as to prevent a convulsion. The child needs to get rid of excess heat, so keep the room cool and airy, remove excess clothing and bedding, and give frequent drinks of water. Sponging with lukewarm water may help to reduce the temperature. You may have discussed the possibility of this situation with the parents, and have their written permission to administer paracetamol.

GIVING MEDICATION

You should never administer medication to a child unless you have the written permission of the parents. With any prescribed medicine it is essential to know:
- when to take it, and for how long
- what the medicine should do
- how long it will take to work, and how you can tell it is working
- what to do if it does not seem to be working
- what to do if you forget a dose
- what are the possible side-effects.

Most medicines for children are in liquid form. Shake the bottle thoroughly before giving a dose. Tablets are more concentrated than liquid medicines, and may need to be crushed to a powder. Slow-release and coated tablets must be swallowed whole. Eye, ear and nose drops are designed to coat the affected surface.

When giving medicine, it is a good idea to sit the child on your lap and have a towel and damp cloth handy in case of spills. Measure the medicine into a non-spill tube spoon. Gradually tip the medicine into the back of the cheek. Chase it down with a favourite drink. Never mix medicines into a drink or bottle.

As soon as you have given the medication, record it on the child's chart, with the date and time and amount. You must do this, even if you have been unsuccessful in administering the full amount, indicating the difficulty. All medicines should be stored in the original container and be properly labelled. They must be kept in a secure place, out of the reach of children. Most medicines should be kept in cool, dry conditions and out of sunlight. Medicines needing refrigeration should be kept in a secure plastic box separate from food, and labelled with the child's name.

If one of the children in your care suddenly becomes unwell, you will need to contact the parents and care for the child until the parents can take the child home. You should have discussed with the parents how you would cope in such an eventuality, and you may have been given their written permission to give proprietary medication if necessary. When you contact them you should offer accurate information. You can help parents by remaining calm, and reassuring them that appropriate action has been taken, as you will appreciate how concerned they are. When they collect the child, you may find you can offer some support and practical help and advice.

The parents' willingness or not to return from work, or stay at home when their child is ill can cause conflict. At the time of signing the original contract, it is helpful if you make it clear that:

- the terms of registration do not allow childminders to care for children who have an infectious illness
- their own home environment is more suitable for children who are unwell
- parents should be available in case of illness
- you will act responsibly, and not exclude children unnecessarily, but the decision lies with you
- if the parents' employment means that access and availability is difficult, a plan should be devised for alternative care
- that you cannot authorise treatment.

It may be necessary to inform the parents of other children that one of the children in your care has an infection or infestation, so that they can take steps to protect their own child's health and well-being. Confidentiality is important, but it may be quite obvious to the other parents who the child is. As a professional person you will divulge only what is necessary.

Activity
How do you inform parents if one of the children you mind has an infectious illness?

Infection

Infection is the most common cause of illness in young children and, if frequent, can cause developmental delay and slow down growth. As a childminder it is important that you know the different types of infection, how they are communicated to others, and how to prevent the spread of infection.

Infection can range from the common cold to meningitis and as you gain experience you will find it easier to diagnose the symptoms of the illness. If you are in charge of a child who suddenly becomes ill you must contact the parents and if you have any serious concerns you must seek medical advice. You should encourage parents to participate in immunisation programmes so as to reduce incidence of childhood diseases, which can be very dangerous.

In addition to the common childhood complaints there is one other infection that you must be aware of. Meningitis can develop within hours into a life-threatening illness. The signs and symptoms are variable, which makes both the viral and the bacterial forms of this infection so difficult to diagnose. If the child has a raised temperature combined with a severe headache, vomiting, painful neck, confusion, dislike of light, irritability or a purplish rash which does not disappear when you press the skin with a glass tumbler, you should seek urgent medical attention and contact the parents urgently.

Infection results from invasion of the body by pathogenic (disease causing) organisms. The main organisms are:

- bacteria
- viruses
- fungi
- protozoa.

To grow and multiply, these organisms need moisture, warmth, food and time. Once in the body they multiply rapidly: this is called the incubation period. Although children are infectious during the incubation period, they only begin to display signs and symptoms and feel unwell at the end of this time.

Infection is spread by:

- droplets: sneezing and coughing
- touch: contact with people or equipment
- eating or drinking infected food and water
- through cuts and grazes on the body.

GOOD PRACTICE IN PREVENTING CROSS-INFECTION

1 Wash hands before handling and eating food.
2 Wash hands after using the lavatory.
3 Well ventilate rooms, avoiding over-crowding.
4 Wash and disinfect toys and equipment regularly.
5 Discourage parents from bringing in unwell children to your home.
6 Clean the lavatory and bathroom daily.
7 Clean up all spills immediately.
8 Use disposable gloves for First Aid, cleaning up body fluids and changing nappies.

9 Provide regular trips out of doors.

10 Keep pets clean and healthy.

11 Use paper tissues for wiping noses and disposing of them at once in a covered bin.

12 Select, store and prepare food carefully.

13 Clear the table immediately after meals, not allowing food to be left about.

The quarantine period is the time a person with an infection is capable of transmitting that infection to another person. Hygiene, isolation and exclusion, and immunisation all play an important part in preventing the spread of infection.

Minor ailments

You need to be clear in your own mind whether you will exclude children with some minor ailments and to discuss it with the parents at your first meeting. See 'Signs of good and poor health' on page 123. You need to consider the risk of cross-infection even with minor ailments, for the sake of the minded child, your own family and yourself. If you become unwell, your services are no longer available to the family.

UPPER RESPIRATORY TRACT INFECTIONS

The areas of the mouth, nose and throat are the first to be attacked by viruses as they are breathed in. Children are very prone to colds as they are frequently in contact with new organisms and have yet to build up their own immune systems. The main sign of a cold is a runny nose. The discharge is thin at first, becoming thicker after a day or two. The nose can feel blocked, and the child may wish to pick and scratch it. The lining of the nose is more fragile, and will bleed easily. Caring for the child will consist of offering plenty of fluids, checking to see whether the child has a fever, teaching the child to use disposable tissues and to blow her own nose, and keeping her warm within a well-ventilated room.

A cough can be caused by direct infection of the throat or by nasal mucus dripping from the back of the nose. Coughs cause anxiety but serve a purpose in pushing back infected mucus that threatens the lungs. A cough indicates a more serious illness when it presents with other symptoms such as:

- difficulty in breathing
- pallor or blueness
- thick sticky mucus coming from the lungs
- traces of blood
- choking
- vomiting.

The parents should be encouraged to seek medical advice.

A sore throat may develop on its own, or be accompanied by a cold, and many only last a day or two. It is often present in childhood infections. If a child refuses to drink, has swollen pus-covered tonsils, has a high temperature or is

SIGNS OF GOOD AND POOR HEALTH

Signs of good health

- appearance of well-being and contentment
- showing signs of growing
- independence
- no obvious signs and symptoms of illness
- alert and energetic
- responsive to others
- good appetite
- sleeps well
- not too fat or too thin
- good muscle tone and posture
- good colour
- healthy skin and hair
- good teeth
- milestones within normal limits
- normal stools and urine

Promotion of health

- good diet
- protection
- security
- stimulation
- health surveillance
- immunisation
- routine physical care
- safe environment
- consistency of care
- rest, exercise, sleep

Signs of poor health

- signs of injury and/or neglect
- rashes, spots or sores
- abnormal stools or urine
- unresponsive to others
- quiet and lethargic
- fretful
- complains of feeling unwell or pain
- poor appetite
- sleeps badly
- raised temperature
- frequent worrying behaviour
- under or over weight
- poor posture/muscle tone
- dry spotty skin
- unhealthy hair or scalp
- poor colour
- tooth decay
- expected milestones not achieved
- regression

Action if child is unwell

- observation
- partnership with parents
- prompt diagnosis
- loving care
- fluids
- care of skin
- therapy
  - diet
  - physiotherapy
  - play therapy
  - speech therapy
  - occupational therapy
- medication
- rest and sleep

drowsy or dizzy, the parent should be contacted and the GP consulted by the parents.

LOWER RESPIRATORY TRACT INFECTIONS

Infections that spread into the lung tissue are more serious than upper respiratory tract infections. Croup occurs in children between the ages of six months and four years. The child is usually hoarse, with a barking cough, may have some difficulty in breathing, and will appear distressed. A doctor should see all children with croup.

RASHES

Rashes are a sign that the child's body is reacting to an irritation or infection of some type. Refer to page 125 for descriptions of common rashes. As long as there are no other symptoms, a rash on its own is rarely a sign of serious illness and usually disappears as quickly as it comes. How a rash looks is generally less important than where it is on the body. There are three main types of rash.

- The rash may be all over the body accompanied by other symptoms, such as a cold and a raised temperature. This usually indicates a viral infection.
- The rash may be all over the body with no signs of ill health. This rash will often irritate the child and is an allergic reaction to something. It needs to be discussed with the parents, as, if the cause is discovered, it can be eliminated. The child may need to be referred to the GP.
- The rash may be on only one part of the body: for example, nappy rash and cradle cap. Where it is sited will often suggest the cause of the rash. If it does not heal within a few days, encourage the parents to seek GP advice.

STOMACH ACHES AND PAINS

Stomach aches are a symptom of an upset somewhere in the body, not necessarily the abdomen. Children with tonsillitis, urinary tract infection or middle ear infection may well complain of stomach ache. Stomach aches may have different causes, from mere over-eating to more serious conditions such as appendicitis. In most cases there is nothing to worry about, but on rare occasions it is the first sign of a real emergency, so it is best to play safe.

In children, the pain is generally caused by an infection, an inflammation or a change in the activity of the bowel. Many school children complain of stomach ache in response to stress. It may not have a physical cause, but the pain is real, as the disturbed central nervous system which controls the contractions of the stomach and intestines intensifies the contractions. The pain can be so severe the child cannot eat or drink.

You should contact the parents if:

- the child cannot be comforted, and is refusing food and drink
- there is any swelling, or she refuses to let you touch where it hurts
- she vomits, but the pain continues

RASHES	
Condition	**Description of rash**
Hand, foot and mouth disease	A sparse rash of greyish white, tiny blisters with a red halo. It is seen inside the mouth, on the tongue and on the palms of the hands and the soles of the feet. It lasts 3 to 5 days and then fades rapidly. Occasionally it spreads to the buttocks.
Cold sores	Sore, painful blisters near the lips and nose that crust after 2–3 days.
Impetigo	Starts as a small blister generally near the mouth and nose as this part is more vulnerable to infection. Number and size increase, the surface of the skin breaks down, leaving a raw, moist surface that becomes a thick, yellow crust over a reddened, sore area.
Nettle rash	Pale, swollen patches and spots with a red border.
Scabies	Raised, blistery spots and raised, red, discrete spots, generally with scratch marks as it is intensely irritating. Greyish ridges of scabies mite tracks may be seen. Generally between fingers, inside wrists, under the arms, waist and groin.
Eczema	Dry skin, patches of red skin often with small, blistery spots. Inflamed by scratching. Starts on face or skin creases. May become sore or weepy.
Rubella (German measles)	Pale pink spots that start on face and spread to chest and back, perhaps the limbs. On 2nd or 3rd day they become an overall flush. Can last between a few hours and up to 5 days.
Measles	A blotchy rash of dark red spots that spreads from behind the ears to the face, body and limbs over 3 to 4 days. Up to 2–3 days koplik spots (small white spots) can be seen on the inside of the cheeks at the back of the mouth. Rash fades after 4 days.
Scarlet fever	Small spots of intense red colour that are rough to the touch. It begins with the face and spreads to the neck and chest and then the limbs over 4–5 days. It leaves a pale patch around the mouth.
Chickenpox	3 stages: 1) raised, red, discrete rash of tiny pimples starting on chest and face 2) spots develop into blisters 3) after 2–3 days the fluid in the blister becomes cloudy and yellow. It will then form a crust which is intensely irritating. By the third day it will spread to the limbs. In severe cases it can be found on the mucous membrane of the body orifices.
Seborrhoeic eczema	Inflamed, scaly rash behind ears or neck. Associated with cradle cap. Does not irritate.
Heat rash	Small, irritating blisters or pimples on the chest, neck or groin.

- she vomits greenish, yellow matter
- she has crying spasms, turns pale and vomits
- there are other signs of illness, such as raised temperature or diarrhoea
- she is lethargic
- the pain is mild, but it is mentioned repeatedly over several days.

The child's behaviour is the best guide to the seriousness of the stomach ache. Cuddle and reassure the child. Give her small sips of plain water to drink. Encourage her to rest on a sofa or a bed. She may prefer to lie against a pillow. Have a bowl ready in case she vomits. Warmth may help, so you could offer a well-covered hot-water-bottle. It is best not to offer anything to eat. If the pain is severe or continues for more than 20 minutes, contact the parents.

VOMITING

Hold the child's head over a bowl, while supporting the upper body with your free hand. Be reassuring.

After the vomiting, wipe the face with a sponge or cloth wrung out in tepid water. Encourage the child to sip a drink of water slowly to replace fluid loss, and remove the taste from the mouth. Try to get her to lie quietly on a bed or sofa, keeping the bowl handy. A small baby who vomits can dehydrate quickly, so ask the parents to consult a doctor.

EAR INFECTIONS

Earache can follow a cold, flu or a throat infection, or develop by itself. The child may have a raised temperature, complain of pain, refuse to drink, and may be seen rubbing or pulling her ear. Encourage the parents to seek medical advice as soon as possible.

STOOLS AND URINE

As a childminder, you are frequently wiping bottoms and emptying potties. The table below will help you to identify any concerns that should be communicated to the parent.

STOOLS AND URINE	
Condition	**Description of stool**
Underfeeding in a baby	Small, frequent, green stools
Diarrhoea	Frequent, loose watery stools. May contain blood or mucus
Straining	Bright red blood may be seen on the stool
Taking iron medicine	Very dark stools
Bleeding in upper intestine (rare)	Very dark stools
Cystic fibrosis	Large, watery, foul-smelling stools
Constipation	Hard, dry stools, difficult to pass. Hard, dry pellets in a baby
Jaundice	Very pale stool
Inability to digest fats	Large, pale, fatty stool
Threadworms	Worms that look like threads of cotton 1–2 cms. Seen in stool
Normal stool	Soft, clay-like, easy to pass
	Description of urine
Normal	Pale, straw-coloured, no smell
Child lacking fluid	Very dark fluid
Jaundice	Very dark fluid
Urinary tract infection	Frequent passing of small amounts. May smell fishy and child may complain of pain
Diabetes	Frequent passing of urine containing sugar

A minor illness is becoming serious if the child:
- has a fit
- has a temperature and a stiff neck
- has a temperature and a severe headache
- has a temperature and photophobia (dislike of light)
- has a headache and sickness and dizziness
- is drowsy
- is becoming dehydrated
- becomes quiet or limp
- is in pain

- loses consciousness
- has difficulty breathing
- develops noisy breathing
- begins to turn blue.

You should immediately seek medical attention as a matter of urgency for any child in your care presenting any of these signs and symptoms.

Infestations

Infestations are caused by animal parasites that live on and obtain their food from humans. All children are likely to be affected at some time.

HEAD LICE

Head lice are small insects which live in human hair, close to the scalp where they can bite the skin and feed on the blood. Many children are infested by coming into contact with children who are already carrying head lice, and lice show no preference between clean and unwashed hair. The lice lay eggs, called nits, close to the scalp and cement the eggs firmly to the hair. You may think the child has dandruff, but if you try to dislodge it you will find the nits are firmly fixed. The first indicator of head lice is the child scratching her head and complaining of irritation.

Tell all the parents immediately, and suggest they seek advice from the local chemist. Many people now are unhappy with the chemical shampoos and treatments. The current method recommended by many schools is to apply a conditioner to the child's head, and use a nit comb to remove the nits and lice. Regular brushing and combing will discourage lice.

THREADWORMS

Threadworms are small white worms that live in the bowel. They resemble small pieces of white cotton. They can often be seen in the stools. They come out of the bowel at night to lay their eggs around the anus. This causes severe irritation and the child will scratch herself. If the fingers are then placed in the mouth, the cycle of infestation will continue.

Constant sleep disruption will cause the child to become drowsy during the day and lack concentration. Inform the parents of the child, so that they can seek medical advice, as the whole family will have to be treated. Apply the rules of personal hygiene stringently encouraging careful hand-washing, disinfect the potty each time the child uses it, and be alert to the signs in other children.

FLEAS

Fleas are small insects that jump from host to host and feed on blood. Fortunately, human fleas are rare in the UK but many children are sensitive to fleas that live on cats and dogs. If bitten by a flea it will leave a red mark that irritates and swells. Pets need to be treated regularly to avoid this problem.

RINGWORM

Ringworm is a fungus infection of different types that may affect the skin or nails. It is seen as a red circle with a white scaly centre. It spreads in increasing circles whilst healing in the centre. The active edge is raised into small bumps. On the scalp it will result in bald patches. It causes much irritation. The parents must seek medical advice.

SCABIES

Scabies is a skin infestation caused by the scabies mite, which burrows under the skin, causing severe irritation. The mites feed on the skin and lay their eggs. Characteristic lines may be seen on the skin. The child will scratch causing redness and infection. The mites can crawl from one person to another. The child must be seen by a doctor who will prescribe a lotion to kill the mites and eggs.

TICKS

Ticks live on animals and feed on blood. They are often found on deer. Although rare in this country, if children have been to an area where deer roam, they are at risk from tick bites. These are very dangerous as, if untreated, they can cause Lyme's disease. The symptoms are like a bad dose of flu, but can result in brain damage. Children should be examined for tick bites whilst being bathed, and, if found, medical attention should be sought immediately by the parents.

Chronic medical conditions

Many children now spend nearly half their waking hours in the care of a childminder. About ten to fifteen per cent will have a known medical condition that may affect their physical health, their ability to learn, their relationships and their emotional well-being. It is important for you to have some knowledge and understanding of these conditions and how it may affect a particular child. At the initial meeting with the parents, you will need to establish:

- how the child is affected by the illness
- whether there are any significant signs and symptoms you should look for
- what actions you should take if any problems arise whilst the child is in your care
- precise instructions and written permission to administer any medication or therapy required by the child
- knowledge of any side-effects of medication
- whether there are any physical restrictions placed on the child.

You will, of course, have an emergency contact number for the parents.

WORKING WITH PARENTS

Minding a child with a chronic medical condition has additional rewards, such as the feeling of satisfaction, the use of all your skills, and the self-esteem you will gain from meeting the challenge. If you decide to care for a child with a chronic illness, it is important that you reach this decision after discussing the following points with the parents:

■ the cause (where known) and the effect of the condition
■ details of all routine medication and therapy required by the child
■ possible side-effects of any medication and therapy
■ any possible emergency that may arise, and your ability to manage the situation
■ possible hospital appointments and admissions
■ the need for any special equipment.

You would need to assess how much support the parents might demand of you and whether you are willing to take on this responsibility, which will take up your time and energy. You should also consider the effect on and the reactions of other children in your care, and the impact on your own family. It might be wise to suggest a probationary period, when you can assess how everyone is coping.

For any child that you mind with a chronic medical condition you must:

■ have full knowledge of the condition and its effect on the child
■ liaise closely with the parents
■ be very familiar with any treatments and medication.

DIABETES

Diabetes is an endocrine disorder where the pancreas gland fails to produce the insulin that controls the amount of sugar or glucose released into the bloodstream. The high level of blood glucose is too much for the kidneys to cope with, and it is discharged in the urine. Signs of diabetes include:

■ excessive thirst
■ frequent passing of urine
■ loss of weight in children.

Children may complain of headache and abdominal pain, and may vomit. Sugar will be found in blood and urine samples. Most children with diabetes require insulin by injection. Each child will have her own diet plan providing a balanced diet, controlling the intake of carbohydrate. Exercise burns calories, so you may need to offer a sensible snack after any vigorous activity. Normal growth is an indication of good diabetic control.

If you care for a child with diabetes you must:

■ make sure the child is wearing a diabetic identity disc
■ provide meals promptly
■ teach other children in your care about diabetes
■ help the child to behave as normally as possible
■ be very clear about emergency procedures
■ understand hypoglycaemia (a drop in blood sugar which may lead to a

seizure or the child becoming comatose). Always have an emergency supply of glucose in the house

■ understand hyperglycaemia (a rise in blood sugar, which may mean that the child needs insulin).

ASTHMA

This is an increasingly common, distressing condition, where the muscle walls of the lungs constrict. Excess mucus is produced that blocks the already narrowed passages. Breathing becomes difficult, the child will wheeze and cough, and may choke. It is often associated with allergic conditions such as eczema and hayfever. It may be triggered by exercise, viral infections, smoke, pollen, fur, house dust mites, yeast, dairy food, anxiety and stress.

It is treated by medication, both preventative and curative. Inhalers and nebulisers are often used to administer the medication. Physiotherapy and a well-balanced diet may also form part of the treatment.

If you are caring for a child with asthma you must:

■ know the individual triggers
■ be very familiar with the medication used by the child, and know how to keep inhalers and nebulisers clean
■ encourage normal activities
■ observe for any chest infections
■ be fully aware of emergency procedures.

Reducing allergens in your home
■ damp dust all surfaces regularly
■ put soft toys in the freezer for 24 hours twice a month, and then wash at 60 degrees centigrade or above to kill the mites
■ invest in a high filtration vacuum cleaner
■ regularly air the house and keep the house well ventilated
■ replace upholstered furniture with leather, wood, plastic or cane
■ wash cushions once a month, and never use feather-filled ones
■ choose short-pile carpets or wooden or tiled floors
■ avoid carpets in kitchens or bathrooms, where they can become damp
■ dry all clothing out of doors when the weather is good
■ use bleach to kill any fungus present in the bathroom
■ have heaters and central heating serviced regularly
■ take advice about plants and trees in the garden
■ avoid compost heaps.

If you are asked to take a child with asthma, and you have a pet, you should discuss this with the parent.

ECZEMA

Children with eczema usually have a very dry skin that becomes inflamed and cracked, making the skin vulnerable to infection. It causes intense irritation and

can be very painful. The irritation is made worse when the child is warm, and this can disrupt sleep, leading to tiredness, irritability and lack of concentration. There are times when the skin flares up and is badly affected, and other times when it is completely clear. It can be triggered by infection, irritants such as soap and washing powder, environmental factors, certain foods, exercise and anxiety, medication and handling pets.

If you care for a child with eczema you must:

- know the triggers that cause the allergy
- understand the special attention you may need to give the skin
- keep the child cool when she is showing signs of irritation
- limit messy play if the eczema on the hands is infected. An older child might be willing to wear gloves
- discourage petting strange animals
- teach the other children about the condition, stressing that it is not contagious.

EPILEPSY

There are many different types of epilepsy. Grand mal (tonic/clonic seizure) produces a typical fit, with loss of consciousness, convulsive movements and frothing at the mouth. Petit mal (absences) is less dramatic, and may go unnoticed. The child may look as if she is day-dreaming. There is no cure, but modern treatment reduces and prevents frequency of fits.

Children with epilepsy need a normal environment, but if you care for a child with epilepsy you must:

- be alert to the signs of an epileptic fit and how to respond
- make sure the child is wearing a medical identity disc

- not leave the child alone for long periods of time
- restrict television viewing, as flickering lights can sometimes result in a fit
- observe the child closely if she is unwell
- teach the other children about epilepsy
- supervise very closely if the child is swimming or cycling.

BLOOD DISORDERS

Haemophilia is an inherited blood disorder where excessive bleeding results after even a minor injury, often causing bleeding into the joints and a great deal of pain.

Sickle cell is a chronic genetic condition, commonly found in people of African-Caribbean and African descent, and sometimes in people from the Middle East, India and Pakistan. Abnormal haemoglobin is produced, assuming a sickle cell shape that is not full oxygenated. It is an extremely painful, distressing condition.

Thalassaemia is a general term for a number of genetic blood disorders in which there is insufficient haemoglobin. It is found in children whose families came from the southern Mediterranean and the Middle East.

If you are caring for a child with an inherited blood disorder you must:
- try to avoid over-protecting the child, but be aware of hazards
- be aware of the child's need to attend hospital regularly
- understand any possible side-effects, which might include lack of concentration, pain, infection, anaemia, fear of rough and tumble play and dehydration
- be aware of emergency procedures.

CYSTIC FIBROSIS

This is an inherited disorder, found mainly in children of North European descent. It produces problems in the lungs and digestive system. Over-production of sticky mucus secretions clog the lungs and block the pancreatic ducts, preventing the flow of enzymes needed for digestion of food. The severity of symptoms will vary, but can include repeated chest infections, failure to thrive, and large watery foul-smelling stools that are difficult to flush away. A sweat test will show a high concentration of salt.

This is a life-threatening condition, but the prognosis has much improved over the last few years. Treatment includes:

- antibiotics
- physiotherapy
- a high-calorie diet
- additional vitamins
- immunisation.

If you are caring for a child with cystic fibrosis you must:

- try to avoid contact with infectious children
- observe closely for signs of infection
- encourage the child to develop as normally as possible, including her in all activities
- supervise the child at mealtimes, with regard to medication, and encourage her to eat well
- understand that physiotherapy may be painful and distressing
- try to boost the child's self-confidence, as she may be shorter and lighter than average
- be aware of the child's need to attend hospital on a regular basis.

COELIAC DISEASE

This is caused by an inability to digest gluten, found widely in various cereal products. It is diagnosed when the baby is weaned from a milk to a mixed-feeding diet. The baby may begin to refuse food, fail to thrive, become lethargic, irritable and listless, pass abnormal stools, may vomit and look malnourished. The only treatment available is a gluten-free diet. All foods containing wheat and rye flour, oat and barley products must be excluded. Rice and maize products are acceptable. This diet must be maintained throughout life. Many products in the supermarket indicate if they are gluten-free.

If you are caring for a child with coeliac disease, you will have to liaise closely with the parents, particularly concerning the child's diet.

PHENYLKETONURIA

This is a genetically inherited disease, causing an excess of phenylalanine (an essential amino acid), which cannot be broken down and absorbed by the body. It accumulates in the bloodstream, causing brain damage and learning delay. All new-born babies are screened for this disorder. Treatment is dietary and life-long and it is a very restricted diet. Children will have routine blood tests.

If you care for a child with phenylketonuria you will have to liaise very closely with parents and be extremely knowledgeable about the diet.

Activity

A little boy of three that you look after is constantly thirsty, needs to empty his bladder often, and does not appear to be thriving.

1 Why might this be?
2 What steps would you take?

Ninety per cent of children are healthy most of the time. Nevertheless, it is prudent to be able to recognise illness, however minor, so that steps can be taken to prevent cross-infection, to relieve symptoms and to ensure that the child receives the care she needs.

11 *CHILD PROTECTION*

> ## This chapter includes:
> ■ **The role of the childminder**
> ■ **Definitions of abuse and neglect**
> ■ **Statistics**
> ■ **Recognition of abuse and neglect**
> ■ **Referral and investigation**
> ■ **Factors which contribute to abuse and neglect**
> ■ **How to protect yourself from allegations of abuse**
> ■ **Helping children to protect themselves**
> ■ **Caring for children who have been abused**
> ■ **Maintaining relationships with the parents**

You have made your house and garden a safe place, prepared safety plans for when you take the children out of your house, and made sure that there are no avoidable health hazards due to poor hygiene. But there are other dangers in the environment. These days, there is a great deal in the media about abused and neglected children and, while we must be careful not to over-protect our children, we must always be alert to the dangers surrounding them.

The role of the childminder

The whole of society has an obligation to protect children. You, as a childminder, need to explain to the parents when making initial arrangements that you have a duty to report any suspicious incidents as well as accidents. You should emphasise that the welfare of the child is always your first responsibility. It is often difficult to be a 'whistle-blower' when you have a relationship with the parents. Common reasons given for not taking action are:
■ disbelief
■ fear of being seen as interfering
■ fear of becoming involved in a difficult or distressing situation
■ friendship and loyalty to parents
■ fear that a family will be split up and the children taken away.
There is no doubt that you will feel conflict, as your professional approach to confidentiality will be at odds with the need to report your concerns so as to protect the child.

Very few children are removed from the family. Decisions are taken in the best interest of the child, and the usual policy of local authorities is to try to help and advise families in order to ensure the child's safety within the family. For childminders, there is also the fear of making a costly mistake, losing a child and income, and risking future livelihood by losing the trust of local parents.

As a childminder you have a professional responsibility to protect children and to help stop any abuse that you think may be taking place. Make sure that you:

- do not ignore possible signs of abuse and be sure to express your concerns
- listen to children if they state someone is upsetting or hurting them
- do not assume someone else will take action to help the child.

If you are concerned about a child, his parents may be the first people to talk to, as you may feel this is only fair and a continuation of your partnership arrangements. If there is a satisfactory explanation, it will avoid unnecessary investigations. On the other hand, before you do that, consider the possibility that you may be deceived by the parents, and only too ready to accept their explanation. You may be vulnerable if the parents accuse you to protect themselves or evidence may disappear as the parents are given time to prepare a plausible story.

If you feel a child is at risk you should contact your registration officer or refer to the guidelines you will have been given by the local authority. You might also consider talking to NCMA, the NSPCC, or your local health visitor if you are unsure of the appropriate action to take.

Definitions of abuse and neglect

Child abuse is sometimes difficult to define, but a clear understanding is necessary so that you may act with confidence when working with children. There are some commonly accepted definitions of child abuse, but local authorities may differ in their definitions. The broad categories are neglect, physical abuse and injury, emotional abuse and sexual abuse, but all these categories overlap and interconnect.

Defining childhood abuse is not an exact concept. The point at which a child generates sufficient concern to be deemed in need of protection can be subjective. For example, when does smacking become hitting? When does demonstrative affection become a sexual assault?

DEFINITIONS

Physical abuse and injury
The intentional, non-accidental use of physical force and violence, which results in hurting, injuring or killing a child. It includes poisoning.

Physical neglect
The failure by the parents/carers to feed, shelter, keep safe, keep clean and provide medical care for a child.

Educational neglect
Failing to meet the child's need for stimulation by not providing any opportunities for play and education to encourage language and intellectual development.

Emotional neglect
Withdrawing or not providing love, affection and emotional consistency for the child, and not providing an environment of warmth, interest and care.

Sexual abuse
'The involvement of dependent, developmentally immature children and adolescents in sexual activities they do not fully comprehend, are unable to give informed consent to and that violate the sexual taboos of family roles' (Schecter and Roberge, 1976).

Emotional abuse
The exposure of children to constant criticism and hostility, always linked to emotional neglect.

Failure to thrive
The failure of a baby or child to achieve his expected weight or height with no obvious medical or physical cause. It is often associated with a negative relationship with the parent/carer.

Organised abuse
Sexual abuse, and perhaps physical injury, with a number of perpetrators and a number of children. There is an element of deliberate planning.

Munchausen syndrome by proxy
A psychological condition, where the parent/carer fabricates a child's illness, seeking different medical opinions and inducing symptoms in the child to deceive the doctors.

Statistics

The NSPCC estimate that 150 to 200 children die each year in England and Wales following incidents of abuse or neglect. Thousands more suffer emotional and psychological problems because of ill treatment by their parents or those looking after them. More than 20,000 children a year tell ChildLine they have been physically or sexually abused. Figures published by the Department of Health for the year ending 31 March 1996 revealed that there were approximately 32,000 children on the child protection register in England.

There have been several studies that show, where there is domestic violence, the children also are often physically assaulted and often also sexually abused. See, also, the Gulbenkian Foundation report on page 139.

Most abuse is perpetrated by people known to the child, close family or family friends. The media has aroused people's anxieties about stranger abuse, yet the amount of abuse by strangers is a tiny percentage. Abuse happens in all socio-economic groups, and across all cultural, religious and ethnic groups. Both boys and girls are abused by both men and women.

The extent of violence involving children

Children are far more often victims of violence than perpetrators of violence, and certain groups of children, including disabled children and some ethnic groups, are particularly at risk. One of the most disturbing social statistics is that the risk of homicide for babies

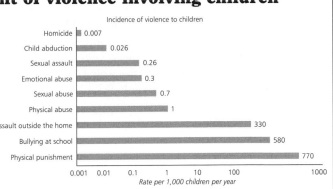

Incidence of violence to children

	Rate per 1,000 children per year
Homicide	0.007
Child abduction	0.026
Sexual assault	0.26
Emotional abuse	0.3
Sexual abuse	0.7
Physical abuse	1
Assault outside the home	330
Bullying at school	580
Physical punishment	770

under the age of one is almost four times as great as for any other age group. There is increasing knowledge of and sensitivity to violence to children – in particular to sexual abuse and to bullying and other violence in institutions; it is not possible to tell whether the incidence of these forms of violence has increased or become more visible. There are problems about building any accurate picture of violence to children within families, but the most recent UK research shows that a substantial minority of children suffer severe physical punishment; most children are hit by their parents, up to a third of younger children more than once a week.

Only a very small proportion of children – mostly male but with an increasing minority of young women – get involved in committing violent offences. Very roughly, four per 1,000 young people aged between 10 and 18 are cautioned or convicted for offences involving violence against the person.

In terms of trends it appears that children's involvement in some but not all crimes of violence in the UK has increased over the last decade. But in comparison with the USA, overall levels of interpersonal violence in the UK are very low, and there is recent evidence that in comparison with some European countries, levels of self-reported violence by children in the UK are also low.

A Gulbenkian Foundation report

Recognition of abuse and neglect

As a person who cares for children in a professional manner, you need to be able to recognise the signs of abuse and neglect. Whatever sort of relationship you may have made with the family, your first duty is to the child. This is laid down in the Children Act 1989: 'the welfare of the child is paramount'. The following indicators should ring alarm bells:

- all bruises on the head or face of a small baby
- bruises on the cheeks of a toddler
- bald patches on the head
- cigarette burns
- two black eyes
- any neck injury
- finger tip bruising
- bruises on genitalia
- adult bite marks
- scratches
- scalds on the child's feet and legs, caused by 'dunking' in very hot water
- splash burns
- babies unable to move any limb
- bruises on soft tissue
- injury to ear lobes
- bruising of lips, gums or a torn frenulum (the piece of tissue that attaches the lips to the gums).

SHAKING BABIES AND CHILDREN

Shaking a child can cause serious injury, even death, and many people are ignorant of the effects of such shaking. Violent shaking of a young baby has the same effect on the baby's brain as dropping him directly onto a concrete floor. A baby's head is large compared to the rest of his body and the neck muscles are not yet strong enough to support it. Shaking the head with great force will cause tiny blood vessels to tear and bleed inside the brain. This can lead to loss of vision and hearing, fits, brain damage or death. Shaking can also cause serious harm to older children. Signs to cause concern would be a baby arriving at your home, looking lethargic, with poor muscle tone, miserable, not interested in feeding and unable to settle. This may also indicate an onset of infection, but you should immediately contact the parents and seek medical advice.

> **Activity**
> It can happen that child abuse is not deliberate cruelty but something that happens when an adult loses control. Do you think that an adult who deliberately abuses children is more at fault than an adult who loses control? Discuss this with other childminders.

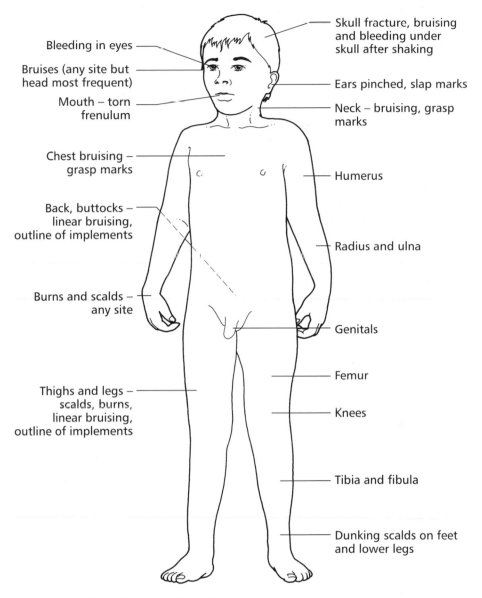

Bleeding in eyes

Bruises (any site but head most frequent)

Mouth – torn frenulum

Chest bruising – grasp marks

Back, buttocks – linear bruising, outline of implements

Burns and scalds – any site

Thighs and legs – scalds, burns, linear bruising, outline of implements

Skull fracture, bruising and bleeding under skull after shaking

Ears pinched, slap marks

Neck – bruising, grasp marks

Humerus

Radius and ulna

Genitals

Femur

Knees

Tibia and fibula

Dunking scalds on feet and lower legs

The principal sites of non-accidental injuries

Most children will suffer accidental injuries. Deciding what is accidental and what has been inflicted upon a child can be a very difficult process, testing the skills of experienced paediatricians. See diagram above for the principal sites of non-accidental injuries. Many signs that might lead you to think that abuse has taken place, might be explained. For example, bald patches might occur if a child frequently pulls and twists his hair as a comfort habit. It is your responsibility to be alert to any unexplained or suspicious injury, making sure you record your concerns, and discussing it with your registration officer or NCMA adviser.

CASE STUDY

Simone, a ten-month-old child of an African-Caribbean father and an English mother, was left with Jessie, a childminder. Jessie identified what she thought were bruises on Simone's buttocks. That evening, when she questioned the mother, she was reassured that the marks were Mongolian blue spot – an area of natural hyperpigmentation that occurs in many African, African-Caribbean and Asian babies at birth.

1 How would Jessie confirm this information?

2 Can you think of any other signs that might be open to the wrong interpretation?

SEXUAL ABUSE

Sexual abuse ranges from showing pornographic materials or inappropriate touching to penetration, rape and incest. It is found in all cultures, all classes and in all religious groups. It may involve very young babies. It often begins gradually and increases over a period of time. Children are trusting and dependent, wanting to please and gain love and approval.

The majority of abused children know the perpetrator who is often a member of the family, a close family friend or someone in a position of trust. It rarely involves the use of physical force and there are usually no physical signs, but if you did see bruising in the genital area, bloodstains, torn underclothing or vaginal discharge, you would be immediately alerted and take steps to protect the child.

CHANGES IN BEHAVIOUR

Abuse and neglect may cause a change of behaviour that will vary a great deal according to the age of the child. You may see the child:

- withdraw from physical contact
- be wary of forming close relationships with adults and other children
- show apprehension when children cry
- appear to be frightened of the parent/carer
- display a lack of spontaneity and become wary of adult's reactions to him
- display self-destructive behaviour such as hair pulling and head banging
- display aggression
- begin to over-eat or to refuse food.

Some areas of abuse are more difficult to recognise than physical abuse and neglect. For example, emotional abuse, such as shutting a child in a cupboard as punishment or constantly belittling and undermining the child in everything he does, can be almost as damaging as physical abuse. An indication that this is going on may appear in the behaviour of the child who may show:

- fear of new situations
- comfort-seeking behaviour, such as thumb-sucking, excessive masturbation and rocking to and fro
- speech disorders, such as stammering and stuttering
- delay in all-round development
- extremes of passivity and aggression
- low self-esteem and lack of confidence
- nightmares and changes in sleep patterns
- wetting and soiling after the child has become clean and dry
- temper tantrums which are not age-appropriate
- inability to concentrate for more than a few minutes.

SIGNS OF SEXUAL ABUSE

Many of the changes in behaviour would be similar to those described above, but in addition the child might:

- behave in a way sexually inappropriate to his age, particularly when involved in imaginary play
- produce drawings of sex organs and use sexual language
- display insecurity and cling to trusted adults
- act in a placatory or flirtatious way, or in an inappropriately mature manner.

Changes in behaviour are not necessarily due to abuse or neglect. Children go through many difficult stages in their normal development. It is only when there are a cluster of behavioural changes that you should begin to consider the possibility of abuse.

SIGNS OF NEGLECT

A child who is underweight, may be small for his age, with poor muscle tone and a dry wrinkled skin may be suffering from neglect. On arrival he may immediately demand food, displaying an enormous appetite during the day. If his personal hygiene needs are not being met, he may appear dirty and uncared for, smell of urine, have unbrushed hair and teeth, and wearing inappropriate dirty clothing.

The younger child may suffer from severe persistent nappy rash and/or cradle cap. He may appear constantly tired or lethargic, with frequent colds and coughs, stomach upsets and rashes and the parents may appear reluctant to seek any medical help. You may find the child frequently arrives and is collected late. You may notice that the parents fail to express any affection or display warmth and interest in the child, but seem to have unrealistic expectations of his behaviour and capabilities.

Activity
List the ways in which you recognise distress in children.

DISCLOSURE

If you find yourself in a position where the older child is disclosing abuse to you, you need to respond in a way that will not further harm the child. Listen carefully and patiently, without asking leading questions: that is, without putting words into the child's mouth, or making them give the response you want them to. You should:

- attempt to make the child feel secure and safe when disclosing to you
- reassure the child, stating that you are pleased to have been told and that you believe him
- never look shocked or disbelieving
- never express criticism of the perpetrator
- never promise to take an action, which you may not be able to carry out
- reassure the child that he is not to blame for the abuse
- explain that in order to help him, you will have to tell other people what is happening
- keep calm
- resist pressing for information or questioning the child, as other agencies will have to interview him
- make an immediate timed, dated and signed record of the conversation.

RECORD KEEPING

As soon as you suspect that a child may have been abused, you need to be meticulous in your record keeping. Keeping the NCMA accident book, existing injuries record (below) and filling in a record of concerns (see pages 145 and 146) may be helpful in any future investigation of suspected abuse.

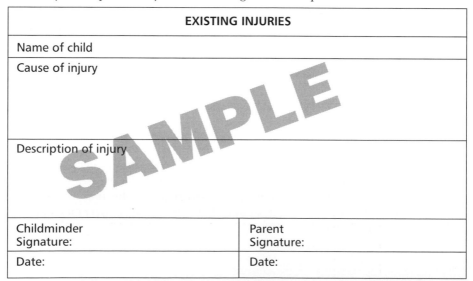

EXISTING INJURIES	
Name of child	
Cause of injury	
Description of injury	
Childminder Signature:	Parent Signature:
Date:	Date:

Reproduced by kind permission of the National Childminding Association

This sample form is for illustrative purposes only. Copies of the form can be obtained from NCMA.

RECORD OF CONCERNS

Name

Date of birth

Start date

Date Time	Incident	Physical injury	Non attendance	Conversation	Behaviour causing concern	Action	Signature

This page may be photocopied. © Stanley Thornes (Publishers) Ltd

RECORD OF CONCERNS

| Name | Gillian B | | Date of birth | 3.2.97 | | Start date | 2.1.99 |

Date Time	Incident	Physical injury	Non attendance	Conversation	Behaviour causing concern	Action	Signature
30.3.99		Bruises seen on both arms		G says she fell off bike		This chart started	CM
6.4.99 9.30am 12.15pm	G very hungry asked for food 9.30am 3 helpings at lunch					Noted	CM
11.4.99 21.4.99			Did not attend	Mother states child unwell. Did not see GP			CM
24.4.99				Avoided contact with me & other children all day	Quiet, withdrawn, passive	Observe next week	CM
30.4.99	Mother collects child, smells of drink					Discuss with NCMA	CM
1.5.99		Small burn on leg?		No response from child	Found crying in sitting room	NCMA Soc. services Reg. Officer	CM
6.5.99			Did not attend			To contact soc. services	CM

Timing, dating and signing all noted incidents is essential as they may be required at a child protection conference, and may also protect you from allegations of abuse. All records should be factual and accurate, and you should be scrupulous in leaving out your own feelings and in being objective. These notes and records should be made within 24 hours of the incident or conversation if they are to be legally admissible. They should be kept in a secure, locked place where they are not accessible to anyone else.

Referral and investigation

Once you have reported your concerns to social services, it becomes known as a referral and an investigation will be made in order to establish the truth of the allegation, to make a record of the allegation and to assess the current risk to the child. See page 148 for the procedure for investigating a case. Social services will also decide whether protection procedures should be put in place. If you have not made the referral, but an investigation has been started on, say, the referral from a neighbour of the family, you will still be involved as the person outside the family who sees the most of the child.

Following the investigation, if there is no cause for concern, the person with parental responsibility for the child and the referrer are informed in writing. If there are grounds for concern, there will be a formal child protection conference. This conference is not called to apportion blame but to exchange information, decide on the level of risk and whether the child needs to be placed on the register. The conference will make some forward thinking decisions for the benefit of the family and the protection of the child. Conferences require a number of different agencies to be present before decisions can be made. Specialists may also be called to give advice.

As a childminder, you may be required to attend a child protection conference to present observations you have made of the child or assessment of any recent changes in his behaviour. You will not be asked for opinions but only for objective evidence, and this is where your observations and record keeping will be most valuable. You should be sent an agenda in advance and a checklist of basic information about the conference. Parents and carers will be invited to attend the conference for at least part of the time and be given the opportunity to express their views. This can be a stressful experience, but you may find support from your registration officer or from your local NCMA organiser. NCMA may be able to offer you support in preparing for and attending a child protection conference.

If the conference decides the child is suffering or is likely to suffer significant harm, the conference will register the child under one or several categories of abuse or neglect. It will appoint and name a key worker and recommend a core group of professionals to be involved in a child protection plan. A review date will be set.

In very serious cases the child protection conference may recommend that court proceedings are taken, and the courts will decide the future of the child. You may find yourself called as a witness. This is not a pleasant experience and

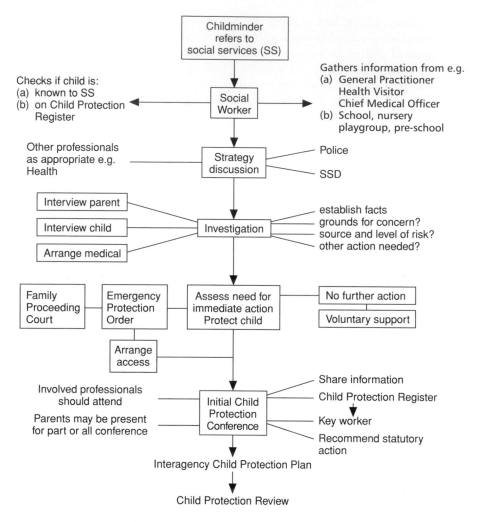

An outline procedure for investigating a case of possible child abuse

you may feel anxious and worried about the event. You may be given support by social services and NCMA.

Activity

You have attended a child protection conference because a child you mind has been sexually abused by a family friend. As part of the child protection plan, you have been asked to monitor the child's behaviour and emotional development and keep detailed records.

1 How might you begin this task?
2 How might you seek the co-operation of the parent?
3 What additional support might you offer the parent?

Factors which contribute to abuse and neglect

There have been many theories put forward over the last fifty years as to why some children are abused or neglected. These include:

- separation of mother and baby at birth, preventing bonding
- maternal deprivation
- inequalities in society
- a patriarchal society
- scapegoating of some children within the family.

Activity
Identify any theories you may have heard which try to explain poor parenting.

Current thought is that the reasons for child abuse must be looked at as a combination of social, psychological, economic and environmental factors. Abuse is found across a wider range of people than any one theory would have us believe. The table, 'What places children at risk of child abuse' on page 150 shows some of the conditions and developmental stages of small children that may trigger abuse.

Activity
Sally is two-and-a-half, and has been minded by you for six months. The family is affluent, living in a large detached house. Sally's father is frequently away from home, and Sally is usually collected by her mother, Jane. It has been difficult to establish a relationship with Jane. She seems to have very little time for or patience with Sally, often describing her in a disparaging manner. Sally is becoming quieter and more withdrawn, and on one occasion said she had been shut in a cupboard for a long time. When Jane arrives to collect her that day, she looks tearful, upset and smells of drink. Sally runs and clings to Jane who pushes her away.
1 What factors might cause you concern?
2 How might her mother's rejection affect Sally's emotional development?
3 What are Sally's needs and what are the family's needs?
4 What might you do to help Sally and her family?

How to protect yourself from allegations of abuse

When working as a childminder you need to be aware that you are in a vulnerable situation. There have been some cases of childminders, or members of their family, being accused of abuse so make sure your behaviour is professional at all times and open to scrutiny. There are steps you can take to prevent yourself or your family being unjustly accused of abuse. These include:

WHAT PLACES CHILDREN 'AT RISK' OF CHILD ABUSE?

The 'seven deadly sins' – conditions and developmental stages that may trigger physical abuse of small children

Condition/trigger	Description	Age of most danger	Common abuse injuries associated	Advice for stopping/preventing abuse
Colic	All babies show some 'fussy' crying that is inconsolable. About one baby in ten will cry like this frequently and persistently in ways parents find impossible to stop, and for long periods.	1–3 months and then stops	Internal bruising in head, grab-mark bruises, broken arms, legs and ribs	1 Check for any medical causes and then reassure parents this is normal and will stop at about three months or before. 2 Help them to learn soothing techniques and give permission for them meeting *their* needs for sleep and time away from the baby.
Habitual night crying	Some babies develop a habit of waking in the night even after they no longer need a feed. They get to enjoy the extra attention /or find it difficult to sleep without parental care.	4 months – 2 to 3 years	Injuries as above	1 Stop naps during the day, move cot to baby's own room and make bedtime calm. 2 Make 'check-up' visits short, boring and at long intervals. 3 Give more attention and stimulation during the day.
Clinginess and separation anxiety	At about six months a baby comes to depend upon his/her main caregiver(s) for security and will show clinginess and anxiety when separated. Some parents do not understand and see this as the child being spoiled.	6 months – 3 to 4 years	Spanking and slapping injuries. Emotional cruelty e.g. locking up	1 Explain that this stage is normal and necessary for healthy development. 2 Help parents to make separation easier for child – by rehearsal, making it gradual etc. 3 Make sure child is always left with somebody they know, like and trust.
Curiosity and exploration	Children as they develop mentally and physically increasingly explore their surroundings as they become more mobile. Unchecked they can expose themselves to danger. Some parents expect them to follow adult rules and punish them for damaging property or making messes.	1–3 years old	Too little control – burns, poisonings etc. Too much control – bruised from spanking and rough grabbing	1 Explain that exploration and curiosity are natural and necessary parts of growing up. 2 Safety-proof the home and draw up rules for protection, develop firm but non-abusive strategies for managing behaviour. 3 Provide an environment that allows plenty of opportunities to explore.
Disobedience and negativism	As children begin to develop a sense of independence, they often test this out by being disobedient and negative. Parents may feel feel very threatened by this disobedience.	1½–3 years	Slaps and punches to body and head. Cruel emotional punishment may include locking up, taunting, etc.	1 Explain the phase is normal however irritating. 2 Go for minimal rules and non-confrontation. 3 Offer child choices where possible but don't bargain where there is no choice.
Fussy eating	Because growth slows down, a child's appetite falls off somewhere between months and two years. Refusing to eat may become a child's way of self-assertion.	1½–3 years	Slap and pinch marks on face and injuries to mouth from force feeding. Children may choke or suffocate.	1 Explain that it is usual to eat less at this age and reassure that the child is fit and well. 2 Cut down on snacks and drinking too much milk. 3 Take the 'heat' out of mealtimes.
Wetting and soiling	Children gain control over their bladders and bowels only gradually. Parents may expect to toilet train too soon or see wetting and soiling as deliberate disobedience.	1–3 years	Bruises, burns and scalds around bottom and genital areas.	1 Advise parents to wait until child is ready for toilet training. 2 Don't attempt to train child at times of stress. 3 Be sympathetic about 'accidents'. They are very seldom deliberate.

- making sure your record keeping is up to date: registers, observations, accident and incident report forms should be written up daily and kept in a safe place
- making a note of when another adult witnesses an accident to one of the children
- reporting your suspicions or concerns about a child to your registration officer and keeping a written record
- joining NCMA and any local support group
- keeping the child's parents informed of any incidents, accidents or events concerning the child that have occurred during the day
- completing the existing injuries form to record any injury, however minor, sustained by a child when not in your care
- ensuring the children are well supervised at all times, and not leaving them in the care of unauthorised people, even a member of your family
- telling the child's parents if a child behaves in a sexually inappropriate manner towards you, recording the incident and making sure your under-eights adviser or a NCMA representative, knows about it
- encouraging independence in children, and not carrying out intimate tasks that they are quite capable of doing for themselves
- not asking children to keep secrets
- while managing children's challenging behaviour, never involving rough handling of a child
- never shaking, hitting or smacking a child in your care, even if the child's parents want to give their permission
- not shouting or using a sarcastic approach with children
- using appropriate language in front of children
- while responding to children's emotional needs, never forcing kisses and cuddles on children who do not wish it
- taking advantage of any child protection training courses.

You need to make sure that no one in your household behaves in a threatening or inappropriate manner towards the children in your care.

If a complaint is made against you or a member of your family, you will feel distressed and most unhappy. Do not panic, all complaints have to be investigated. This is a legal requirement and everyone involved will be trying to reach an objective decision. Keep a record of all conversations you have, both face-to-face and on the telephone, concerning this matter. Include times, dates, places and participants. Keep copies of all correspondence. You should seek legal advice, either independently or through NCMA.

Helping children to protect themselves

Some of the children you care for will come from families who are demonstrative and show affection by frequent kissing and cuddling, while other families may be equally fond of their children but are not very outgoing with their emotions. You will need to build up a trusting relationship with each child and this will only happen with time. All children should feel they can come to you for help and protection. It is important to involve the parents in helping children to protect themselves, as the message must be consistent.

When children are mature enough, teach them:

- the difference between comfortable and uncomfortable touches
- that safety rules apply to all adults and not just strangers
- that secrets they feel uncomfortable about should be discussed with a trusted adult
- any cuddles and kisses given by an adult 'in secret' should always be disclosed
- to feel good about themselves and know they are loved and valued
- to trust, recognise and accept their own feelings
- that because their bodies belong to them, nobody has the right to touch or hurt them
- that they can say 'No' to requests that make them feel uncomfortable, even from a close relative or friend
- that they can rely on you to believe and protect them if they confide in you
- that they are not to blame if they are hurt
- that rules of good behaviour can be broken if they are in danger, and that it is perfectly all right to kick, bite, punch, scream and shout if they feel threatened
- that they must not speak to strangers however kindly they may appear, or go off with someone they do not know.

An organisation called Kidscape was founded in 1984 to enable children to learn about personal safety and teach them strategies to keep themselves safe. Kidscape produces many useful leaflets and books. The NSPCC also produces a great deal of useful material.

Caring for children who have been abused

The vast majority of children that you will be working with in your career as a childminder will come from stable, happy homes, where you will work in partnership with the parents to meet the needs of the children and promote their all-round development. There are some children who are not so fortunate and if you are caring for one of these children you will play a key role in identifying abuse, observing the child and helping him to recover from the effects of abuse and neglect.

Persistent abuse discourages children from:

- learning through play and exploration of their environment
- making trusting relationships with adults and other children
- developing language skills.

Children who have been abused may experience many different overwhelming emotions. These feelings will depend on their age and their level of experience. These emotions include:

- fear
- a sense of isolation

- anger
- depression
- guilt
- sadness
- shame
- confusion.

1 Have a good understanding of child development, and how this can be affected by abuse and neglect.
2 Display empathy and understanding.
3 Encourage trusting relationships.
4 Respond to the child's wish to be held and cuddled.
5 Be professional and do not feel threatened or distressed by the child's expression of emotions.
6 Establish and maintain a professional relationship with the parents.
7 Give extra time to the child, whenever you can, on a one-to-one basis.
8 Provide activities every day to allow emotional expression and encourage communication.
9 Understand if the child's learning or behaviour regresses.
10 Applaud success, however small.
11 Accept challenging behaviour, showing disapproval of the action rather than the child. Set limits for the child to promote security.

12 Value the views and opinions of the child, involving him in decision-making and in becoming more assertive.
13 Show the child you care for him, but resist the temptation to over-protect.
14 Always touch the child gently and be aware of any movement that the child might see as threatening.
15 Continue to observe and assess the child's needs.
16 Take advantage of any training in child protection that might be offered by the local authority.

Maintaining relationships with the parents

It is part of the professional practice of childminders to work closely with parents, communicating effectively and regularly, respecting their greater knowledge of the child and involving them in all decision-making. The Children Act 1989 emphasises the need for partnership with parents and, where possible, enhancing and not undermining the parents' role.

If you have identified abuse, try not to jump to the conclusion that the parents are the perpetrators. It could be someone in whom the parents have placed their trust, such as a family member, a babysitter or a neighbour. Be available to support the parents, listen to them with sympathy, and respect and value their views and opinions.

You will be able to advise parents if they are going through stressful times by pointing out helplines such as Parentline, and finding out if there are local support and information groups.

WORRYING FAMILY BEHAVIOUR THAT MIGHT CAUSE CONCERN

All families behave differently and some of the following factors might occur, from time to time, in families where there is no question of abuse. A number of these signs exhibited over a period of time should cause concern:

■ frequent shouting and the smacking of babies and children, often for behaviour that is developmentally normal, such as a toddler wetting his pants
■ expecting the child to be the parent, giving love and comfort to the adult
■ parental indifference to the whereabouts and safety of their children
■ barking orders at a child, without displaying patience or clear explanations of what is expected
■ never giving praise or encouragement
■ discouraging the child's natural curiosity, and not providing enough stimulation
■ seeing the normal behaviour and actions of a child as a deliberate act to upset and annoy the parents
■ knowledge of frequent rows and disagreements between the parents and other family members, perhaps leading to violence.

WORKING WITH PARENTS WHO HAVE ABUSED

You may be caring for children where abuse and neglect has been diagnosed, or social services may have requested them to be placed with you as part of a child protection plan. You should not have to take on such an arrangement if you cannot cope with it, or if you feel that social services will not give you enough information or support. Whatever the type of abuse, try to build up a friendly relationship with the child's parents. Children can quickly sense bad feeling between adults, and it will help the child's recovery to know that the adults in his life are working together.

If you find yourself in the position of working with parents who have abused you will attempt to:

■ acknowledge your feelings, and seek support from your registration officer, NCMA or the child's social worker
■ avoid colluding with the parents through fear of aggression
■ be aware of the child protection plan for this family
■ record in writing, conversations and decisions taken with the family
■ acknowledge the stress of the family.

Remind yourself you are helping to break the cycle of abuse. Try to assume a non-judgemental attitude, and refrain from questioning the parents about the abuse, or from challenging information they may give you, as this is the task of other people. Give them as much information as possible about the care of the child, listen to what they are saying and express appropriate concern and kindness, whilst remaining objective. Your behaviour towards their child will help them to realise that children respond well to love and firm consistent guidelines

If one of your parents has been accused of abuse, and this has been shown to have no foundation, you may find yourself having to rebuild your relationship, and this may prove very difficult. If you both have the welfare of the child at heart, it is achievable.

12 THE PROFESSIONAL APPROACH

> **This chapter includes:**
> - **Professionalism**
> - **Equal opportunities**
> - **Keeping up to date**

Caring for other people's children is skilled work which depends upon a sound foundation of knowledge about children and their families. Looking after other people's children is not the same as caring for your own. It is quite difficult to balance the needs of your own children and partner with any employment that you might take up outside the house. It is much more difficult if you are self-employed and caring for children in your home alongside your own children. It requires a professional approach to make it work.

Professionalism

Becoming a professional is a gradual process, and encompasses knowledge, skills, behaviour and attitudes. The NCMA concept of professionalism includes:
- working in a skilful, expert and well-organised way, reflecting on one's own practice and seeking to improve performance
- being paid for work done
- working in a detached, objective way, that keeps personal emotions and opinions separate from judgements and behaviour related to work
- working in a way which demonstrates adherence to certain principles of conduct
- being committed to work, to providing a service as agreed, even at personal inconvenience but not permitting oneself to be exploited
- expecting to take up opportunities for training and other ways of developing practice and keeping up to date, including maintaining contacts with colleagues.

Refer to Appendix C, the National Childminding Association's 'Principles of Excellence in Childminding Practice'.

CHILDMINDING GROUPS

NCMA has worked to support registered childminders for over twenty years through the development of local groups and associations. Today over 1,200 groups offer a range of support to local childminders, holding drop-in sessions, providing information to parents about childminding vacancies, and running toy libraries and equipment loan schemes.

Meeting regularly with other childminders will help you to reflect on your practice, hear the views and opinions of other childminders and prevent feelings of isolation.

KNOWLEDGE

During your preparation or induction, on-going training and perhaps undertaking the 'Developing Childminding Practice' course, you will be gaining knowledge. Using your library, reading books, NCMA publications and relevant journals, and learning through theory and observation about the all-round development of children will make you sensitive to their needs and so enable you to develop good standards of practice.

Such knowledge plays an important part in preventative work, for example identifying children who are in need of protection or need to be referred to the health services. As you grow in knowledge, you will be better able to understand children in your care, and to interpret records and observations, so that you spot problems quickly and ensure that the child receives the necessary help and support.

You will never come to the end of what you can learn about looking after children. A good indicator of a professional childminder is the willingness to update knowledge and understanding regularly by attending courses and reading professional journals. The professional childminder will always be ready to question and challenge in a thoughtful and constructive manner.

BEHAVIOUR

A professional childminder will display motivation, enthusiasm and commitment at all times, showing a positive attitude towards the work. You will become aware of your role and responsibilities, and reach a good understanding of what you can and cannot do in the family daycare setting. You will take time to review and evaluate your practice, thinking regularly about your provision and identifying strengths and weaknesses.

Completing the 'Self-appraisal' table on page 158, honestly and by yourself, might help you to appreciate your strengths and indicate areas that you might try to improve.

RELIABILITY AND COMMITMENT

Being reliable means:

- always making sure that you and your household are ready to welcome the children you mind at their expected time of arrival
- keeping to the contract you have with the parents, and putting the children's needs before your own

SELF APPRAISAL

Areas to consider	Strong	Satisfactory	Weak
Business organisation			
Relationship with parents			
Always ready for children's arrival			
Commitment to equal opportunities			
Observation skills			
Awareness of safety issues			
Provision of equipment			
Good range of activities available			
Enjoyment of reading with children			
Enjoy company of children			
Knowledge of support groups			
Interest in training			
Keeping up to date with care and education issues			
Find it easy to provide a range of nutritious meals			
Professional attitude and approach			
Able to balance the needs of all the children			
Manage time well			
Liaison with other professional workers			
Able to balance needs of family and employment			

This page may be photocopied. © Stanley Thornes (Publishers) Ltd

- giving the parents good notice if there should be a time you are unable to look after the children
- collecting school-age children in good time from school, and younger children from pre-school or playgroup.

The well-being and safety of the children in your care has to be your main concern. Be cautious about taking on too many responsibilities, or commitments where you feel you may not have the necessary knowledge or experience to carry them out successfully.

Being committed means:
- offering a professional service over a period of time
- negotiating contracts with parents, that are kept to
- being organised and business-like, maintaining well-kept records and accounts.

COMMUNICATION

You will be using three methods of communication, writing, speaking and using body language. You will need to keep written records and make written observations. From time to time you may need to write to the parents and outside agencies. If you are not confident about expressing yourself in the written word, seek support from other childminders and NCMA.

The clarity of your speech and the ways in which you talk to children, parents and other professional people, will show them that you are a caring, knowledgeable and sensitive person. You should be able to state your views and ideas clearly and concisely.

Your body language should convey that you are interested and motivated. Shrugging your shoulders and turning away is no substitute for expressing your point of view over a disagreement calmly and clearly. Maintaining eye contact with children and adults will help foster good relationships. Share your knowledge, opinions and observations in a positive way with parents while valuing their knowledge and expertise.

CONFIDENTIALITY

You will become aware of much confidential information concerning the children and their families. All information that you receive, either written or verbal, is strictly confidential. You should never share it with your family and friends. You will make it clear that you will not take part in gossiping about the children and their families with other parents. As a professional person, you will be expected to share information only with other professional colleagues if this is in the best interest of the child. Particular care should be taken in childminding groups. This issue should be discussed and the groups should have an agreed policy.

ATTACHMENT

The children will develop a close relationship with you and, while you must meet their emotional needs, you must always keep in mind that the parents are the primary caregivers. Love and affection are not finite emotions, and children are capable of relating lovingly to many adults. However close an attachment is formed, you must always bear in mind that your relationship is temporary, and that of the parents is permanent.

ATTITUDES

As a professional childminder, you will show awareness of and sympathise with the needs of children and their parents, regardless of racial origins, class, cultural background, religion, disability, gender or age. You will never display favouritism or special treatment towards some children in preference to others, but always show respect and interest in the customs, values and beliefs of all the children. This will help you to provide them with positive images of themselves and with each other.

Equal opportunities

A childminder with a professional attitude needs to recognise that no member of society should be discriminated against because of his or her race, gender, class, culture, age, religion, disability or sexual orientation. This is especially important for you working with young children since you are in a good position to influence their developing attitudes. All children will be damaged by prejudice and by bias. Those who are subjected to discrimination are made to feel ashamed and inferior and their self-esteem is damaged. Research has shown very clearly that young children do notice differences in gender and skin tone. We should show by example and by talking to children that these differences should arouse interest and enjoyment. Always answer children's questions honestly and accurately, as lack of information can lead to prejudice.

Activity
You are an experienced childminder caring for an African-Caribbean child. Your aunt, of whom you are very fond, drops in unexpectedly. She sits the child on her knee, and starts singing an unacceptable nursery rhyme.
1 What is your immediate response?
2 What range of emotions might you feel?
3 How might you discuss this issue with your aunt?
4 Should you discuss it with the child and her parents?

Children need to feel confident about themselves and to be sure they are valued. If children are not cared for with a commitment to equal opportunities, they may develop negative feelings about themselves that would lead to a lack of self-esteem and inhibit their development. We are all products of our environment and heredity. The way we have been treated by our families and by society will have a bearing on how we see others. In spite of legislation against racial, gender and disability discrimination, many people still experience negative and hurtful attitudes.

You are likely, as a childminder, to care for children from various cultural backgrounds and racial groups, with many views of the world and possibly speaking several languages. The society in which we live is multi-racial and multi-cultural, and all children need to acknowledge and learn about racial and cultural groups other than their own in a positive way. When they go to school, or out into the wider world, they will come into contact with various racial and cultural groups, and need to develop their interpersonal skills, and ability to form relationships with a wide range of people. If one particular segment of society is allowed or encouraged to feel superior because of their racial origins and cultural background, the all-round development of their children will be impaired.

GENDER

Any play opportunities that you offer the children in your care should be available to both boys and girls. You might find some parents still expecting to see girls engaged in doll play while the boys are encouraged to use the construction toys. If this happens, opportunities are being limited, and the young children are learning stereotypical expectations of gender roles. Attitudes are learnt very young in the home and from the media but you can challenge stereotypes. A stereotype is a generalisation of expected behaviour from a certain group, for example, expecting a football fan to be a lager-swilling, abusive male.

Stereotypes may be positive or negative. Either might be damaging to children as, if we label them and have certain expectations of them, we might deprive them of the opportunity to develop other skills or interests. We all have fixed ideas about certain groups. For example, if you join your local NCMA group, and prepare to attend your first meeting, you will make certain assumptions about the people you may meet there and what will happen in the group. This can be helpful and aid your settling into the group.

Activity

Think of a group that you recently joined or an occasion that you attended.
1 What assumptions did you make prior to the event?
2 Did the people you met behave in the way you expected?

The pressure later on in life for children to conform to certain behaviour is very strong, and it is most important that the children experience equal opportunities in their play at the youngest age. Denying girls the opportunity to ride bicycles may inhibit the development of their spatial awareness and delay mathematical ability. Not allowing boys to play with dolls may hold back their emotional expression, and make them fearful of appearing caring when they grow up. Boys should be allowed to cry if they are hurt, and not told to be 'brave little soldiers'. You will be seen as a role model by the children, and must try to offer and participate in all activities. If you play football in the garden, the girls should be encouraged to join in. All play materials, including books, should show men and women in a variety of different roles, such as female firefighters and male nurses.

It sometimes appears that boys seem to monopolise the attention of adults, with rough and noisy play demanding adult time. You need to be aware of this, and make sure that you value the contribution of both boys and girls. Watch your use of language with the children, make sure you sometimes comment on how caring the behaviour of one of the boys has been towards a younger child, or how well a girl has constructed a Lego building.

RACIAL ORIGIN

Britain is a multi-racial society and the children you care for may reflect this racial diversity. Even if this is not so, children need to have a good understanding of other racial groups and cultures. Your own attitude to cultures other than your own will influence the children and their families.

Racism manifests itself in various ways:
■ racism supports the idea of one superior race or culture
■ racism prevents people fulfilling their own potential because of their racial origin
■ racism creates a hostile atmosphere for people of different ethnic groups where learning cannot take place.

As a childminder you can play a key role in confronting and challenging racism. You may hear a child, or even a parent, make a racist remark or 'joke', or insult another individual. As a professional, you should challenge such remarks, making it quite clear they are unacceptable to you, and certainly should not be repeated in front of the children in your care. It is difficult to confront racism at first, whether from children or adults, and it may be helpful to discuss strategies for dealing with this issue with your training group or local childminders group.

Activity

Jonathan, aged five, who is African-Caribbean, asks a group of children at a child-minding group meeting, who are playing with blocks, if he can join in. Sarah, aged four says 'No', and makes a derogatory racist remark. You overhear this remark.
1 What do you do immediately?
2 How do you help Jonathan deal with his hurt feelings?

Children need to have a good understanding of racial and cultural groups other than their own, and this should be reflected in your home. Books should have positive images of black adults in positions of authority and of black children in active roles in the story. Your dressing-up box should contain clothes from a variety of cultures, and you should offer the children food from a variety of cultures such as pasta, pizza, rice, lentils, sweet potatoes, tropical fruits and much more.

RELIGION

You may be minding children who come from families with beliefs different from your own. Respect, tolerance, acceptance and willingness to learn from others is essential, so that you can develop awareness and sensitivity to the needs of children in your care. Knowledge of various religions, customs and festivals is important to those working with young children. You will need to discuss, with the parents, details concerning beliefs, diet, dress and festivals. All religions have many facets. Don't make assumptions that a particular family keeps strictly to orthodox practices. They may adopt a more relaxed approach to the faith.

DISABILITY

If you are asked to mind a child with a disability, you need to refer to Chapter 9. If the children you care for have the opportunity to mix with disabled children, ensure that your remarks about disability are positive, informative and correct and that the language you use is acceptable and preferred by people with disabilities. The children will come to see the disabled child as a child like them, and with your support will understand that all children should be treated fairly, and included in all activities.

ANTI-DISCRIMINATORY PRACTICE

Since the Children Act 1989, anti-discriminatory practice is required by law in all places where children are cared for. The child's religious, racial, cultural and linguistic background must be taken into account. This practice should be active in promoting positive images and reinforcing the self-esteem of all the children. Challenging bias and prejudice where it is encountered is a major responsibility for all childminders.

GOOD PRACTICE IN ANTI-DISCRIMINATORY BEHAVIOUR

1 Present positive images of all cultures, racial groups, gender, religion and disability in your home in your choice of books, your selection of equipment, and in any dressing-up clothes you may provide.
2 Present yourself as a good role model.
3 Acknowledge what you do not know, and be prepared to ask for help and advice.
4 Confront all discriminatory remarks, whether from children or from adults, or whether directed against yourself or others.
5 Answer children's questions honestly, with explanations appropriate to the child's age.
6 Make sure you pronounce and spell all the children's names correctly so as not to give offence, and understand the naming systems of many cultures and religions.
7 Make sure you know and pronounce the names of the garments the children wear.
8 Understand the varying skin- and hair-care needs of all the children.
9 Encourage children to have positive feelings about their skin tone, hair texture and facial features.
10 Make sure you provide a varied diet that will appeal to all the children in your care, and which will introduce them to a variety of interesting foods, while obeying the dietary laws of their religion.
11 Challenge stereotypes. You may be watching a television programme with the children that shows girls as passive and in an inferior role to boys. You will need to discuss this, pointing out that the females often show more leadership, and can be just as assertive as the males.
12 Prevent children developing stereotypes. There may be a programme on the television showing starving black children in Africa being given food by white

adults. You will need to point out that this is because of climatic and economic conditions, and has nothing to do with the skin tone of the children.

13 Involve all children in all activities. You may need to adjust the environment or provide special equipment if you are minding a child with a disability, so as to make sure that she can take part.

14 Encourage all children to be assertive and to stand up for themselves.

15 If modest dress is a requirement of the religion, be sensitive to the parents' wishes and do not insist that the children get undressed for any physical activity.

16 Show that you respect the child's home language by learning a few rhymes and words in this language, and keep a few books in the house if you can obtain them.

Activities

1 Consider your own feelings and views about equal opportunities. Write a short information leaflet that you might give to parents, outlining your equal opportunities policy.

2 You are preparing for your annual inspection. Describe how you provide for the religious, racial, cultural and linguistic needs of the children you mind.

CHILDREN'S RIGHTS

All children, regardless of their background, need and have the right to:

- physical care, ensuring safety, good health and nutrition
- emotional care, encompassing warm, caring, constant relationships
- intellectual stimulation, including education through play to develop language and cognitive skills to their full potential
- social relationships, developing friendships, mixing with other children and adults from many different backgrounds, and learning to value people for what they are.

GOOD PRACTICE IN MEETING CHILDREN'S NEEDS

1 Show sensitivity to and awareness of everyone's needs at all times.

2 Be aware of current welfare benefits and sources of help in the community.

3 Be aware of the financial pressures on some parents.

4 Have patience with those parents who place too much emphasis on one aspect of development, carefully explaining the all-round needs of the child, and the need to value children for what they are and not what you wish them to be.

5 Provide stimulating varied play opportunities which cater for the learning needs of all the children.

6 Show by your example the importance of a healthy nutritious diet, the prevention of infection by scrupulous hygiene routines and an awareness of preventative health care.

Record of training and attendance at courses and conferences

Date	Length of course Weeks Days Months	Funded by	Provider of training	Title	Course details	Certificate of attendance	Credit value	Comments

Keeping up to date

The longer you work as a childminder, the more you will realise how important it is that you remain in touch with recent research, publications and current good practice. Your confidence and skills will be developing and will be enriched by keeping up to date.

Being a member of NCMA will keep you in touch with current thinking and research in early years practice. NCMA publish a regular magazine, *Who Minds?*, that contains a great deal of relevant information. Useful periodicals and newspapers are:

- *Nursery World*
- *Child Education*
- The *Times Educational Supplement*
- Newspapers, such as the *Independent*, the *Guardian*, *The Times* and the *Observer*.

Check radio and television coverage for interesting and relevant programmes.

If you are attending a childminding course, you may find the college subscribes to:

- the National Children's Bureau
- Early Years Trainers Anti-Racist Network
- National Early Years Network
- Save the Children Equality Learning Centre.

These organisations all publish regular newsletters and up-to-date research and information. It is necessary to belong to a local library as that will help you gain access to new publications.

Twice a year *Nursery World* publishes a supplement, *Training Today*. This is a good indicator of the vast number of courses on offer to people who work with children. It is advisable to keep a record of any courses you attend (see page 166). This not only reminds you of when you attended, but can also be transferred to your curriculum vitae (CV), or used in your NVQ Portfolio.

13 COMMUNICATION SKILLS

> **This chapter includes:**
> - **Communicating with young children**
> - **Communicating with adults**
> - **Managing stress**
> - **Assertiveness**
> - **Managing conflict**

All living organisms communicate with each other. Human beings are unique in that they communicate with words, with gestures and with body language. They listen to each other attentively, and record their thoughts and deeds in writing. These skills are passed on from generation to generation, and affect all areas of achievement. Communication allows social and emotional relationships to flourish, allows the transmission of information and ideas and imparts the values and moral codes of society.

Lack of communication between you and the parents can lead to misunderstandings and this may affect the child you are minding. Time needs to be set aside at the beginning and at the end of the day, to discuss any problems that may have occurred, achievements that may have been demonstrated and any changes to the daily routine.

Communication is a two-way process, and efforts will have to be made on both sides. You may be a person with an informal, easy manner, and there will be no problems for you. Some people find it harder to find just the right manner.

Communicating with young children

Children learn about the world around them through the senses: touch, sight, hearing, smell and taste. The new-born baby will very quickly recognise his mother by using all his senses. Because of this, the way a stranger handles a baby immediately communicates either a feeling of security or of threat. Someone who wishes to work with young children needs to be responsive, warm and caring, and this will be shown in the way they hold and feed a baby, or bath and dress a toddler.

GOOD PRACTICE WHEN HANDLING YOUNG CHILDREN

1 Approach children calmly and quietly, using your voice to encourage co-operation.
2 Make eye-contact with children before attempting to pick them up.
3 Sit on the floor with younger children; if you tower over them they might feel threatened.

4   Changing a baby's nappy, brushing a child's hair, and helping a child to use the lavatory are all intimate activities and, preferably, should only be carried out once a good relationship has been established. This is one reason why it is so important to have a settling-in period with the parent present, for as long as it takes to establish such a relationship.

5   Children's need to be cuddled should be met. A child will feel safe and secure if his needs are met swiftly and responsively. Refusing to pick up and cuddle a child who obviously wants you to is not only bad practice, but can be harmful to the development of the child.

6   Be aware of the child's non-verbal communication.

7   Understand how body language can vary from culture to culture. For example, some children may be brought up not to make eye contact with adults, as it is thought to be disrespectful.

Activity

Sit with a friend and brush his or her hair, first roughly, not looking, as if your thoughts are elsewhere. Then repeat gently, talking softly to him or her. Change places with your friend and then discuss how you both felt.

SPEECH

You are obviously aware of the importance of spoken language, and the part it has to play in educational attainment. Children's ability to speak and understand book language is a key achievement in all areas of the school curriculum. The sooner that children become fluent in speech and develop their understanding, the better they will get on in school and with their peer group.

From the very first week of life, and some people even believe from the womb, babies respond to the voice, learning to recognise the mother and close family very quickly. Most language is learnt in the family, and as a childminder you must understand the importance of talking and listening to the children in your care. You should be aware of what a child says, taking care to speak clearly, so as to extend his vocabulary and develop his language skills. Being given time to express himself fully and to be listened to sympathetically, will promote his language development.

Children who use a different language at home to that of the childminder will have some initial difficulty in understanding all that goes on around them. To be fluent in two languages is a great advantage in later life, as it will lead to the easier learning of third and fourth languages. Children mixing with other children who speak English, will find it natural to acquire English without making special provision for this, but the frequent use of rhymes and songs will make them feel secure and relaxed as they often learn these before they have the confidence to construct sentences. Young children do need an opportunity to use their home language. This should be encouraged if at all possible. A child whose knowledge of English is only just emerging is very seldom delayed in other areas of development.

DEVELOPING LANGUAGE SKILLS

At about nine months, children gain an understanding of what adults are saying, providing they speak clearly and directly. Soon after this the first word might appear, and this is the time to start reading books and telling stories. Sitting down quietly with a child and reading a book together should now become a frequent event promoting an interest in books for life. Emphasising important every day words, such as 'drink' and 'bath' will enable him to gain a large vocabulary from an early age.

A recent seven-year study was carried out, where one group of babies was talked to frequently, emphasising with inflection and gesture the important words in the sentence. A control group, matched for socio-economic status and likely inherited ability, were not treated to the same input. When the children were seven, they were tested for reading ability and IQ. It was found that the first group was significantly in front in both attainment and intelligence. This shows how important it is to converse with babies in a meaningful way, even though you might think they do not understand.

At around two years, most children will be able to put two words together to make simple sentences. This is the time for quiet, relaxed conversations, always remembering to give the child time to answer. You should never correct or laugh at his grammatical errors, but it will help if you mirror his words, saying it correctly. For example, a child might say 'Daddy buyed me this doll', and you could reply, 'It was Daddy who bought it for you, was it?' These mistakes are made because learnt rules of grammar are being applied, and too much correction might inhibit speech.

Try not to ask children 'closed' questions, when the answer is already known (for example, 'What colour are your shoes?'. They will probably think it strange that you do not know your colours!) Questions which require only one-word answers, such as 'Yes' or 'No', do not allow children to extend their vocabulary. If they ask a question to which you do not know the answer, be honest enough to say so, and to discuss ways of discovering the answer together. Asking 'open-ended' questions, such as 'Why do you think some animals have fur?', will help him to develop language skills more quickly.

If you ask a child to carry out a task, it must be explained simply and clearly. Asking children if they would like to help clear up might justify the answer 'No'. They are not necessarily being defiant, but will respond much better if told politely to do it. Never ask them to do several things at once.

Make sure the children are given time to work out what they want to say. Do not anticipate children's speech, let them find their own words. Four-year-olds are very excited by new words, and particularly by those to which they get a reaction. If a child swears, remember this a normal stage, and the best way to stop the habit is to ignore it. Children do not invent these words, so be aware that careless speech from adults is often copied. See Appendix B (page 220) for a comprehensive explanation of the sequence of language development.

EXTENDING OPPORTUNITIES

You might read a favourite story to a child, recording your voice on a cassette. He will enjoy turning the pages of the book and matching the pictures to the story he can hear on the tape. This helps develop listening skills and manipulation skills

while encouraging early reading. You could make a simple puppet of the main character in a story that he enjoys. This will encourage him to look at the book on his own or with a friend, using the puppet to stimulate his imagination.

Some domestic activities, such as cooking and washing up together, usually generate discussion and lively conversation, which will help to extend vocabulary and mathematical and scientific terms. Shopping together will present opportunities for recognising familiar foods, and becoming aware that the symbols on the cans and packages represent the names of the foods. All outings introduce children to the wider environment, and stimulate language and the acquisition of vocabulary.

Communicating with adults

A professional childminder needs to develop skills in listening, speech, writing and being aware of her body language.

LISTENING SKILLS

When communicating, it is as important to develop your listening skills as your speech. Being a 'good' listener does not come naturally to everyone. You need to listen carefully to others, concentrate, look interested and not interrupt, never finishing sentences for the speaker.

Remember that in some circumstances you may not be listening effectively. If you are worried or upset about something, your concentration may be diverted. Other noises or movements in the room may distract you. Your feelings about the person may distort what you hear.

Activity
Tape a conversation with a friend with average to good language skills. Note how much of the conversation is initiated by you, and how much by your friend.
1   How would you rate your listening skills?
2   Did you or your friend dominate the conversation?
3   What have you learnt by doing this?

Listening is a positive activity and therefore the good listener does not relax when listening but has to monitor and analyse what is being said in order to make an appropriate response. It may be necessary to indicate to the speaker that you are listening attentively by the use of words such as 'Uhuh' and 'Mmm', which display interest and understanding. Sometimes summarising what the speaker has just said is helpful as it makes you listen carefully, lets the speaker know if the message was communicated correctly, and eliminates misunderstanding which might lead to conflict.

SPOKEN COMMUNICATION

You will be using speech in day-to-day conversations with the children, with your family, with parents and, perhaps, with other childminders. There is no better way of communicating than talking with people. This helps build relationships which the use of memos, faxes and e-mail can never do. Always speak clearly, slowly and expressively, particularly when in formal situations, or when the information you have to convey is particularly important.

Try to present one idea at a time and make sure that it is understood before continuing. The drawback to using speech as a method of communication is that you have to make a quick response which may be unconsidered and regretted later. Speech is generally not as precise as written language, and it is unlikely that you will keep a copy or record. Be aware of your listener's background, knowledge and feelings and what your ideas will mean to him or her. If you are speaking on the telephone in your professional role, speak very clearly, a little more slowly than usual and do not allow your voice to drop in tone at the end of the sentence, as this will distort the clarity of your speech.

Some people communicate better with speech than in writing but it may be the other way round. You will need both skills to be an effective childminder.

WRITING SKILLS

A professional person is presumed to be proficient in communicating information, ideas, directions and requests in writing and this will take many different forms. When writing for your own information such as a personal diary or a list of things to remember, you can record this information in whatever way is useful to you.

You may have to write items that need to be shared with other people, such as:

- observations of the children
- a diary to share with the family
- reports concerning accidents or incidents
- taking and recording telephone messages.

Other correspondence may have to be written more formally. You may find yourself writing to parents, social services, schools, or NCMA.

Whatever you are writing, remember to:

- be clear about the purpose of your correspondence
- use short sentences that convey your exact meaning
- be as neat and legible as possible, checking the spelling and grammar (you may find using a word processor helpful)
- keep a copy (use a black pen as this will photocopy well)
- date all correspondence
- be professional, sticking to the facts and being objective
- avoid jargon and terms not necessarily understood by the recipient.

BODY LANGUAGE

Your body is sending out messages at the same time as you are talking and listening. To be effective, all messages should be the same, but sometimes communication is spoilt when body language differs from what is being said.

Think about:

- posture
- eye contact
- facial expression
- energy level
- position of your feet and legs when sitting
- personal space
- touching others.

For example, while engaged in conversation with a parent, positive body language would be maintaining eye contact, smiling, and leaning towards the parent, while speaking at a moderate rate and in an assuring tone. Negative body language would be yawning, looking or turning away, going off into a daydream and missing cues.

COMMUNICATING WITH OTHER PROFESSIONALS

During your working life as a childminder, you may find yourself in occasional contact with other people from the educational, health and caring professions. You may be in regular contact with your under-eights adviser. A health visitor may visit you if you are working with young babies. You may be asked by the parents to take the children to the infant welfare clinic or health centre for developmental assessments or for immunisations. If the child needs specialist help, such as speech therapy or dental treatment you may be asked to accompany him in place of the parent. You may be involved with staff at pre-school or school. To aid communication you need to be aware of the roles and functions of these professional colleagues, and of the limits of your own role. Most professional people would prefer to see the parents accompanying a child, and it is not generally part of your role to discuss the health and development of children with other professionals.

Activities
1 How would you communicate to parents your concerns about their child's behaviour?
2 How do you encourage parents to share their concerns about their child with you?
3 What communication difficulties have you had in the past with parents? How did you cope with these situations?

Managing stress

Childminders sometimes find themselves in stressful situations. You need to recognise, understand and respond to the causes of stress so as to avoid harming your health or your ability to work in a positive way with children and their families.

CAUSES OF STRESS

Working in a close relationship with parents who may themselves be experiencing stress can generate anxiety. There are life events which can generate a great deal of stress such as divorce, separation, bereavement, unemployment, moving house and even taking on new responsibilities as a childminder. In your professional role, stress might, among other factors, result from:

- taking on too heavy a work load
- not making as much money as you need
- minding a child with disruptive and aggressive behaviour
- dissatisfaction with your job
- feeling isolated
- spending too much time on work activities
- sickness
- difficult relationships with parents
- a child in your charge who has been abused
- taking on responsibilities which are not necessarily part of your job, but which you find difficult to refuse
- getting behind with the paperwork
- being unable to collect money from some parents
- parents who fail to keep to the contract
- pressure from your family, who may feel neglected.

SIGNS OF STRESS

Signs of stress may include:
- variation in appetite
- insomnia
- tiredness or lethargy
- tearfulness
- tension headaches
- constipation or diarrhoea
- high blood pressure
- lack of concentration
- inability to decide priorities
- lack of interest in life
- feelings of inadequacy
- difficulty in making decisions

- feeling neglected, overworked, tense and anxious
- keeping up with coursework
- suppressing anger
- low libido.

Employment patterns are changing and many people are expected to contribute more and more in the workplace while job security is decreasing. This may have a knock-on effect on you, as if one of your parents becomes unemployed or redundant your services may no longer be required. Someone who is stressed may find themselves often ill, and having to take time off work. As so many people rely on your good health, your stress would affect many other people.

COPING WITH STRESS

First you have to admit and recognise that you are suffering from stress and discover how you got yourself into this situation. If it is the childminding itself that is the main cause, it may be difficult to extricate yourself because there are not many other jobs around and you have responsibilities and financial commitments. You must face up to the situation, be honest with yourself, look at alternative strategies such as working part-time, taking on an assistant, or even changing your career direction. If you cannot change the situation, look for further help. Think about the following:

- discussion with your under-eights adviser to help you change your pattern of work
- an appointment with your GP to discuss any symptoms you may have and to find out what sources of help are available
- personal counselling to help you reflect on your lifestyle and make possible changes
- courses on assertiveness, time management and relaxation techniques.

Coping strategies
- learn to say no
- learn how to express your opinions and feelings
- look for support from and offer support to other childminders
- try to relax on your days off and on holidays. Get your family to do the chores!
- manage your time more effectively, deciding what you want to achieve, and the priority, time and energy you are prepared to devote to each task
- look after yourself by eating a healthy diet and taking regular exercise
- do not rely on nicotine, alcohol, caffeine or other drugs to keep you going
- relax in a hot bath after work
- apply heat to the body using a heat pad or a hot-water-bottle. This may reduce muscular tension
- try massage, using aromatic oils
- explore techniques such as yoga or meditation to reduce the effects of stress. They may also boost your ability to avoid becoming stressed
- develop new interests and hobbies

- talk about your feelings to others and recognise your achievements
- be prepared to be flexible and do not live by rigid rules
- remember the good positive things that have happened and do not focus on failures or difficulties.

CASE STUDY

Jasmin is minding Sonia, aged two, as well as her own baby and her son Nicholas, who goes to school. Sonia's mother is a teacher in a failing school, and has recently been promoted. During the last month she has been frequently late in collecting Sonia. As well as upsetting Sonia, it has meant that Jasmin has been unable to take Nicholas to chess club and karate after school.

1 Who is under stress in this situation?
2 What does Jasmin need to achieve?
3 How should she decide her list of priorities?
4 How can she manage her time more effectively?

Assertiveness

In response to any problem, people tend to react in one of four ways:
- aggressively, hurting and upsetting other people, perhaps making them feel inferior
- being indirectly aggressive, manipulating or humiliating someone, arousing feelings of guilt
- passively, avoiding conflict and refusing to make choices, allowing other people to take advantage of them
- assertively, with a confident approach, respecting their own opinions while not belittling the other person.

Each will have a different effect on other people and we will feel differently about ourselves and the way we have behaved.

CASE STUDY

Look again at the previous case study.
1 Why do you think Jasmin has allowed this situation to develop?
2 What action should she take?

It is particularly important for a professional person to be assertive, especially a childminder who has so many demands on her time. Learning to be assertive allows you to be open in expressing your feelings and needs, and encourages you to stand up for your rights and respect the rights of others. It has nothing to do with aggression, but is a technique that allows you to relate to others in an open and honest way, discussing problems and not personalities. Your assertive behaviour should encourage others to be assertive.

Being assertive will enable you to:

- handle conflict, dealing with difficult situations where people are angry or upset
- be more confident, decisive and comfortable in your role
- communicate better, feeling able to express your views, identify problems and work together with other people in finding solutions
- reduce levels of stress
- develop professionally and personally.

Once you are clear about your expectations, they become easier to state and therefore to achieve. Once you start to assert yourself, the approach is simple. You state your needs, rights and opinions in a clear way without qualification.

GOOD PRACTICE IN BEING ASSERTIVE

1 Be natural. When asking for things or giving instructions do not apologise or justify yourself. Ask politely and keep it short and to the point.
2 Do not attempt to flatter or manipulate other people.
3 Accept it when other people say no, and do not take it personally.
4 If you say no, give a reason and do not apologise. Be calm and warm to show you are not angry or unhappy.
5 If you are interrupted, stay calm, and continue to speak until you have finished.
6 Value yourself, and remember your feelings and opinions are as valid as other people's.
7 Challenge discrimination against yourself or other people.

Activity
You have decided to mind children on a part-time basis, so as to have enough time for your family and to fit in a course of further study. The mother of one of the children has been admitted to hospital for emergency surgery and is expected to take some time to recover. The father has been to see you, pressurising you to take his child full-time for an unspecified period.
1 How do you respond?
2 How might you help the family, whilst meeting your own needs?

Managing conflict

If there are conflicts between you and one or both of the parents, the children you mind will sense the atmosphere and may become distressed. For example, you would expect the parents to pay your fees if they suddenly decided to go away on holiday, and they might feel hard done by. Whatever the reason, the only way to resolve a conflict is to communicate, and find out exactly what the problem is.

If a conflict exists, do not ignore it and hope that it will disappear on its own. Address the issue promptly but not impulsively, allowing yourself and the parent time to express views objectively and find a solution that suits both of you. You may both have to make compromises and show some flexibility. It is often useful to arrange a later date to look again at the problem, and see if your solution is working. Some tension within a relationship may be beneficial. In working together to sort out disagreements people may begin to understand themselves and others better, the decisions made are likely to be thought through more and the process may be stimulating. If conflict exists, ignoring it and refusing to discuss it can be harmful and totally disrupt your childminding practice. A knowledge of assertiveness skills will help you put your view clearly and purposefully.

Sometimes, due to a personality clash or inflexible rigid ideas, it is impossible to come to an agreement and, for the sake of the children, it is better to terminate the contract. This rarely happens, if enough time and effort have been put into the original meeting and the drawing up of the contract.

COPING WITH VIOLENT BEHAVIOUR

This is an extremely rare occurrence but if you feel threatened you should discuss it with your daycare adviser or NCMA. Do:
- remember your safety and that of the children comes first
- record all incidents and report them to social services
- express your concerns and fears
- seek support if an incident occurs
- refuse to accept verbal abuse, it can be as harmful as physical assault.

As you become more experienced, you will become more aware of your communication skills. If you feel that you need a little help, this is readily available, as your local college will run courses in all areas of communication.

14. OBSERVING AND ASSESSING CHILDREN

> ## This chapter includes:
> ■ The value of observations
> ■ How to record observations: some useful techniques
> ■ Evaluation and assessment

You are observing and assessing children in your care all the time, and have the advantage of working closely with the children you care for over a long period. In this way, you get to know them very well, but it is still of value to you and to the children to sometimes step back and watch in an objective way what the children are doing and how they are behaving.

Observing children in this manner, and recording what you observe, is an integral part of the role of any professional person who works with children.

> ## Activity
> Using a good dictionary find out what is meant by the terms 'objective', 'subjective', 'hearsay', 'value judgements', 'assumptions' and 'perceptive'. You will find these terms used when observation of children is discussed, and need to be familiar with them.

It is useful to observe children when they first come to you, and your initial snapshot observation (see page 181) should be completed by the end of the first week. In this way, you have a baseline with which to compare any future, more detailed observations and assessments.

The value of observations

Observations are valuable because they help you to:
■ understand the basic needs of children: for love, food, shelter and stimulation
■ become sensitive and perceptive in meeting these needs, and sometimes in assisting the parents in doing so. By recording objective observations, you learn in a practical way how to become aware of these needs, and how to meet them
■ share information with parents. For example, your observation of a child who is often tired, and reluctant to take part in any energetic activity, might lead you to discuss this with the child's parents. At another time, you might care

Snapshot observation

Name   Date

Date of Birth   Starting date

Age

	Describe
Home language	
Other language	
Place in family	
Physical description	
Physical skills	
Advanced in areas of development	
Social skills	
Toilet trained	
Relates to other children	
Personality	

for a child who does not want to go into the garden. Being aware of this might prompt you to discuss it with the parents, and find out the reason for her fears

- encourage the child's social development. Observing the way that the children play together, it is easy to see which children are particular friends, and which ones may need help in relating to others. Some children are more skilled at relating to adults, while others appear shy with strangers
- identify and understand changes in children's behaviour. Careful observations are useful in this case, as the change in behaviour might have a physical cause, such as the onset of illness, or it might be an emotional response to family problems or changes. You will grow to understand that all children are individuals and will behave and react differently in similar situations. For example, taking a group of children to visit a farm will be an enjoyable experience for most children, but there may be one or two who cling to you, and appear nervous in the presence of large animals
- understand what might provoke a child to behave in a particular fashion. For example, a child who is particularly fractious just before mealtimes, may not be eating enough at each meal and perhaps needs smaller more frequent meals
- understand normal development, so that if the pace of development of a child in your care is outside the normal range, either advanced or delayed, you would be able to plan a special programme for this child
- be aware of the possible hazards in your home. Linking this with your awareness of developmental stages will allow you to protect the children from danger
- be alert to signs of ill health. This could be obvious, such as a sudden skin rash, or a child who vomits, or lethargy in a child who is usually active and full of beans. It may be less obvious during the incubation period of an infectious disease, but a noted change in behaviour might cause you concern
- plan activities for the children, that are age-appropriate and will extend and promote learning and development
- provide evidence in child protection conferences, on the rare occasion that you may be requested to do so.

You know a great deal about the children you care for, possibly almost as much as you know about your own children. This knowledge needs to be objective, not based on assumptions and value judgements. If a parent tells you something about one of the children, this is interesting but in terms of objectively knowing the child, would be termed hearsay, as you have not observed the behaviour yourself, but heard about it from another person. For example, the parent may tell you that her three-year-old daughter can swim, but unless you see her do it, you have to take it on trust.

Being able to observe in an unbiased manner is not instinctive. If several people see a person being mugged, you would probably get many different versions of the incident, and many descriptions of the perpetrator. People's perceptions are coloured by their past experiences, expectations, desire to please, fears and anxieties and even last night's television viewing.

Having preconceived ideas about the character or competence of individual children may influence your assessment. Expecting a child to succeed in a task may prevent you acknowledging her failure. Knowing a child to come from an apparently happy and stable home might lead you to reject the thought that she might be at risk. You need to be honest when observing children, and not add anything that makes the observation easier to understand or more interesting.

Some of the children you care for will have been brought up differently from your own. In their family, there may be different expectations of children's behaviour. For example, some children may have been expected to take on some domestic tasks at an early age, while in other families the boys are allowed to be waited on. Some families may discourage their children from messy play, or dressing up in clothes of the opposite gender. The greater the understanding and knowledge you have of other cultures and various child-rearing practices, the less likely you are to make value judgements based on your own upbringing and background, and the more likely you are to view them as individuals.

If you have carried out an observation where you have found the behaviour of a child worrying, you will need to repeat it, as one observation will not give you the total picture.

CONFIDENTIALITY

As you observe and record children's behaviour in your observations, you may well discover and identify information concerning the child or her family. Never record anything you would be unwilling to share with her parents. Because parents play the central role in their child's life, they should have the opportunity to provide information or correct any mistaken facts. You should never share information about the child with anyone, without first seeking the parents' permission, unless you feel the child to be at risk, when you would need to contact your local social services department. This is discussed further in Chapter 11.

How to record observations: some useful techniques

The Children Act 1989 requires that all people looking after groups of children should observe children, assess their learning and development, report and record it. The Act acknowledges that it is not so easy in family day care, but refers to the importance of sharing information with parents, and of making notes rather than relying on memory. You may have kept a Baby Record Book for your own children, and are pleased now when you look at it, to see when they took their first steps and cut their first teeth. It is almost impossible to remember these important milestones without recording them, particularly if you have more than one child.

FORMAL OR INFORMAL METHODS?

Many times you will see or hear something that you wish to record quickly while it is still fresh in your mind. On other occasions you will plan to carry out a more formal observation, using an appropriate technique.

Informal methods

Always have a notebook and pen handy, to write down quickly some event you find interesting. For example, a normally shy child joining in a group game happily for the first time. Taking photographs of the children, either individually or in groups may demonstrate an aspect of behaviour or learning that you wish to record. You might have access to a camcorder, which will show children at various stages of development. All these can be shared with the parents, who will enjoy seeing how their children spend their day. It might be fun, from time to time, to record children singing individually or in a group. Although these are informal, by dating the record and naming the children, you will have a record of their development and progress that you can refer to. Records should be dated, and filed in a separate wallet for each child.

Formal methods

If you have a child in your care who is causing concern to her parents and to you, you may be involved in liaising with social workers or medical practitioners. In these cases, careful objective observations of the child are very valuable. The most common technique used is the written record (see page 185). If the concern is about the child's learning ability, you might wish to set up an activity in your house for all the children, and just closely observe the child about whom you are concerned. If at all possible, sit quietly in a corner and do not become involved with any of the children unless there is an emergency.

Your observation could record how the child you are observing manipulates the equipment you have provided, how much she talks about it, how she relates to the other children, how long she concentrates on the task, and anything else of interest. Several of these observations, carried out on a regular basis, will allow you, her parents and any other concerned adults to assess her progress.

Written record observation

All observations need to have certain information recorded, such as:

- the name of the child
- the date of the observation
- the age of the child
- where the observation took place
- the ages, number, gender and initials of the other children involved
- the presence of any other adult.

If you have a child who is disruptive or aggressive, and you want to discuss this with the parents, using an event sample (see page 186) will show the parents a record of each time this behaviour occurs. The event sample should be completed over a period of time, perhaps a week. Noting down the time of day, the duration of the event, whether the child was provoked or not, and a comment on the severity of the behaviour will demonstrate in an objective way whether or not there is a problem. It is easy to imagine one child is the cause of all disputes, and an event sample might show that this is not the case.

There may be a child in your care who is very shy, has difficulty in relating to other children and to adults, and seems isolated. Using a time sample (see page 187) is one way of trying to find out if this is really so and perhaps beginning to

Event sample

10.3.99
Gillian aged 3 years 2 months
C.M. and 3 children present

Concern:
Gillian frequently bites both
adults and children. She is
aggressive and demanding.

Day of week	No.	Duration	Provoked/Unprovoked	Comments on seriousness
Monday	1	2 secs.	U.P.	Gillian bit father as he left for work.
	2	1 min.	U.P.	Pushed Amit (1:9) over.
	3	2 secs.	U.P.	Bit Eric (2:3). Drew blood.
Tuesday	1	1/2 min.	U.P.	Hit Eric with a wooden brick. Raised a bump on Eric's head.
	2	2 secs.	P.	Bit Eric who pushed her over outside.
Wednesday	0			
Thursday	1	2 secs.	U.P.	Bit Amit. Not serious
Friday	1	10 mins.	P.	Gillian's father arrived 1/2 an hour late. Gillian had a tantrum – inconsolable. She threw furniture around and attempted to bite C.M.

Example of an event sample

Time sample

Concern: Home language:

Time	Setting	Language	Social group

identify a cause. You need to closely observe the child for a short period of time over regular intervals (say, one minute every quarter of an hour), and write down exactly what the child is doing. You might discover that she relates well to one of the children, who is quiet and caring, and goes into her shell whenever a noisy child arrives. You will need to do this sample for a whole day at least, and perhaps repeat it in a few weeks time.

Checklists are often used for assessing a child on one particular day, but can be used over a longer period. They might be used for a child about whom you feel some concern, or regularly for all the children in your care to help you plan for each child's needs. They can be specific, looking at one area of development or one type of behaviour, or more general, covering all areas. You should have a good knowledge of the child before you attempt a checklist. Results may otherwise be distorted by the impact of an unfamiliar adult.

Checklists often highlight areas of a child's development that have previously gone unnoticed. For example, a child who appears physically competent sometimes has difficulty in controlling wheeled toys. Once you are aware of this you will be able to provide practice and encouragement. Educational psychologist Hannah Mortimer has published a booklet containing twenty-one Playladders (see pages 190–191). These are checklists of young children's activities and are a method of recording a child's social development and how a child plays at present (see page 192), and they provide ideas on helping the child to reach the next stage.

Parents can be invited to share a booklet called *All About Me*, written by Professor Sheila Wolfenden and available from NCMA. This is a series of checklists (see page 193) which allows the parent/carer to note down their child's development and progress from time to time. It is not tied to any particular age group. It encourages: parents/carers to record

■ language development
■ playing and learning
■ independence
■ physical development
■ health and habits
■ social relationships and behaviour
■ emotional development.

There is an opportunity at the end of the booklet to record concerns and to plan for the future.

If you decide to pursue a course of study that includes working with children, carrying out observations using various techniques will be part of the course.

CASE STUDY

Melanie, an experienced childminder was really worried about Darren, aged two-and-a-half, who was aggressive and disruptive. He was as much work as three children! Melanie seemed to be constantly saying 'Stop it, Darren!' She spoke to his mother about his behaviour and was assured that he was an angel at home. She decided to do an event sample, to show Darren's mother in a professional way how he behaved in her home.

After keeping this record for a week, it became obvious that many of the fights were not his fault. Matthew, aged four, was found to be teasing him and calling him names. When Matthew started school the following month, Darren's behaviour improved beyond measure.

1 Why was doing the event sample good professional practice?
2 What should Melanie say to Darren's mother, without breaking the rule of confidentiality?
3 Should Melanie speak to Matthew's mother about his behaviour?
4 Why might Matthew be behaving in this way?

Evaluation and assessment

Following on from observation is the essential step of assessment, reflecting on what you have observed and considering what you now know about the child, and how that fits in with what you might have expected of the child at that stage of development. Try not to make assumptions, using words like 'I think' and 'perhaps', but only comment on what you have actually seen. Beware of making judgements based on gender, class, disability or racial stereotypes. Do not be surprised if a girl enjoys rough energetic play, and a boy wishes to spend time quietly reading on the sofa.

Remember to be objective, never repeating hearsay, or speculating and making unsupported value judgements, labelling children or being influenced by prior knowledge. Never personalise comments, for example making comparisons with your own children or the other children in your care.

Some observations may reveal to you that a course of action or a medical referral is needed. Some actions you may be able to carry out on your own. For example, if you discover that a four-year-old about to start school, is unable to use scissors in a practical way, you will be able to encourage her in learning this skill, and give her plenty of practice. On the other hand, if you suspect that a child may have a hearing impairment, it is important that you bring this to the parents' attention with the facts that you have collected from your observations, and encourage them to seek medical advice as quickly as possible.

Activities
1 How will you inform parents that you intend to record observations of their child?
2 How will you observe a child without influencing the child's behaviour?
3 What will you learn from observing children?
4 How do you use your observations to plan for the care and education of the child?

Extract from Playladders, *by Hannah Mortimer, Educational Psychologist, North Yorkshire LEA.* Playladders *can be obtained by sending a cheque for £2.00 to Hannah Mortimer, Pill Rigg, Sowerby-under-Cotcliffe, Northallerton, North Yorkshire DL6 3RH.*

PLAYLADDERS

Playladders are checklists of young children's play as they go about their activities in nursery, playgroup or at home. They are a method of observing and recording how a child plays now, and they provide ideas on how to help the child reach the next step. 'Playladders' combine the step-by-step approach developed in special education, with the practicalities of what goes on in a busy playroom.

The Playladders booklet contains 21 playladders, each one representing an activity typically available for under fives, for example: climbing frames, painting, home corner, book corner or glue table. Each activity is broken down into progressive steps and skills. The emphasis is on flexibility, and users are encouraged to adapt, modify or add to the ladders to suit the particular child, culture and setting. There are also blank playladders to build up for yourself.

Playladders were originally designed for nursery and playgroup staff who had children with special educational needs in their classes.

Playladders provide the ideas for moving one step at a time from simple to more complex play, encouraging young children in their learning.

AN EXAMPLE OF THE PLAYLADDERS IN USE

Beth was a three-year-old who had just started at her local nursery class. At first, she was very quiet and spent the entire session walking up and down the room pushing a trolley. She resisted any advances from the adults and children. We · used the Playladders to map her play; this needed a lot of help from her mother as Beth did so little for us in nursery. Together we concluded that Beth was still at an early stage in all areas of her play and social life, and that pushing a trolley was her safest option in her new and unfamiliar setting.

One of us began to befriend Beth, who gradually allowed the contact. She began to seek this helper out and would park her trolley for a moment while watching other children play, so long as the helper was nearby. She would help to clear up using her trolley and, in time, park it long enough to draw a scribble which she then carried around in it. Using the Playladders for ideas, and the trolley as a starting point, Beth gradually increased her repertoire of play and felt safe to leave her trolley and join in.

POSTSCRIPT

If you don't work in a playgroup, but in some other kind of setting, don't be tempted to dismiss this format out of hand. It can readily be adapted for other settings. For example, during the trialling of the pack, this format was developed by a junior school teacher into a complete record-keeping system for children's progress in physical education.

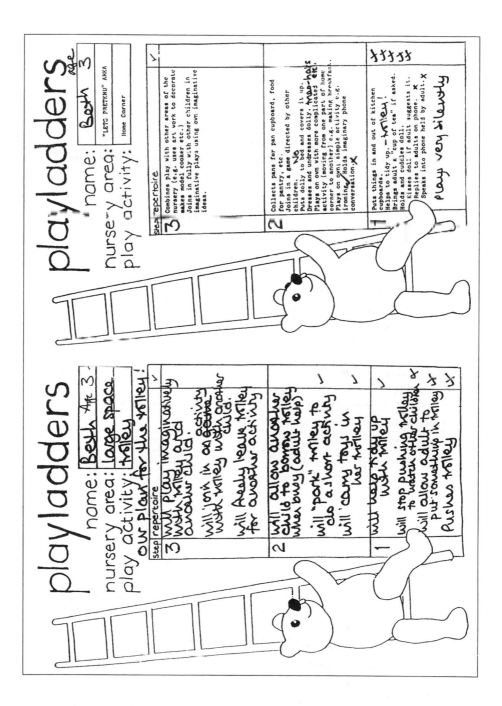

playladders age 3

name: Both

nursery area: "LETS PRETEND" AREA

play activity: Home Corner

step	repertoire	
3	Combines play with other areas of the nursery (e.g. uses art work to decorate, makes model cooker etc.) Joins in fully with other children in imaginative plays using own imaginative ideas.	✓
2	Collects pans for pan cupboard, food for pantry, etc. Joins in a game directed by other children. No. Puts dolly to bed and covers it up. May-be-hat Dresses and undresses dolly. Plays on own with more complicated etc. activity (moving from one part of home corner to another) e.g. making breakfast. Plays on own; simple activity e.g. ironing. Holds imaginary phone conversation. ✗	
1	Puts things in and out of kitchen cupboards. Helps to tidy up. – trolley! Brings adult a "cup of tea" if asked. Holds and cuddles doll. Kisses doll if adult suggests it. ✗ Replies to adults on phone. ✗ Speaks into phone held by adult. ✗	✔✔✔✔

plays very likely

playladders

name: Beth Age 3

nursery area: Large space

play activity: trolley

our plan for the trolley!

step	repertoire	
3	Will play imaginatively with trolley and another child	✓
	Will join in an activity with trolley with another child	✓
	Will easily leave trolley for another activity	✓
2	Will allow another child to borrow trolley when busy (adult help)	✓
	Will "park" trolley to do a short activity	✓
	Will carry toys in her trolley	✓
1	Will keep tidy up with trolley	✓
	Will stop pushing trolley to watch other children	✗
	Will allow adult to put something in trolley	✗
	Pushes trolley	✗

Checklist to assess children's social development

I. Individual Attributes: The child		
	Yes	No
1. Is **usually** in a positive mood		
2. Is not **excessively** dependent on the teacher, Nursery Nurse or other adults		
3. **Usually** comes to the nursery or school willingly		
4. **Usually** copes with rebuffs and reverses adequately		
5. Shows the capacity to empathise		
6. Has positive relationship with one or two peers; shows capacity to really care about them, miss them if absent, etc.		
7. Displays the capacity for humour		
8. Does not seem to be acutely or chronically lonely		
II. Social Skill Attributes: The child usually		
1. Approaches the others positively		
2. Expresses wishes and preferences clearly; gives reasons for actions and positions		
3. Asserts own rights and needs appropriately		
4. Is not easily intimidated by bullies		
5. Expresses frustration and anger effectively and without harming others or property		
6. Gains access to ongoing groups at play and work		
7. Enters ongoing discussion on the subject; makes relevant contributions to ongoing activities		
8. Takes turns fairly easily		
9. Shows an interest in others; exchanges information with and requests information from others appropriately		
10. Negotiates and compromises with others appropriately		
11. Does not draw inappropriate attention to self		
12. Accepts and enjoys peers and adults of ethnic groups other than his or her own		
13. Interacts non-verbally with other children with smiles, waves, nods, etc.		
III. Peer Relationship Attributes: The child is		
1. **Usually** accepted versus neglected or rejected by other children		
2. **Sometimes** invited by other children to join them in play, friendship, and work		

D.E. McClellan and L.G. Katz 1992

Now I can	Comments
build a bridge from three blocks ❏ yes ❏ not yet	
turn the pages of a book ❏ yes ❏ not yet	
turn taps off ❏ yes ❏ not yet	and on ❏ yes ❏ not yet
fold paper ❏ yes ❏ not yet	and fold clothes ❏ yes ❏ not yet

I am old enough now to

ride a tricycle ❏ yes ❏ not yet	ride a bike ❏ yes ❏ not yet	
unscrew tops off jars and bottles ❏ yes ❏ not yet		
thread beads ❏ yes ❏ not yet	play with Lego ❏ yes ❏ not yet	swim ❏ yes ❏ not yet
prefer using my left or right hand ❏ yes ❏ not yet		

What else can I do?

What we already do at home to help my physical development

What we can do in future to help me develop my physical skills

Checklist from Sheila Wolfendale, *All About Me* (2nd edition), NES Arnold, 1998
Reproduced by kind permission of the author and publisher

GOOD PRACTICE IN RECORDING OBSERVATIONS AND MAKING ASSESSMENTS

1 Be ready to share observations and assessments with parents.
2 Respect confidentiality.
3 Keep records in a secure place.
4 Record observations on all children in your care.
5 Never jump to conclusions.
6 Do not label children.
7 Do not generalise from one observation.
8 Do not guess why children respond in a particular way.
9 Allow for environmental and cultural differences, while all the time guarding against racist and sexist attitudes.
10 While observing a child, do not involve yourself in their activity, or influence the child's behaviour by your manner or tone of voice.
11 Write up your notes as soon as you can.
12 Use your observations for the benefit of the children and to help you develop good practice.

15 THE BUSINESS SIDE OF CHILDMINDING

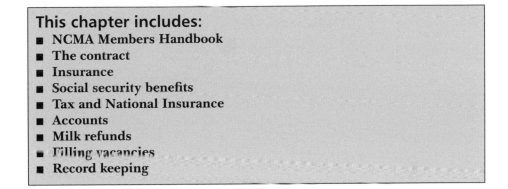

This chapter includes:
- **NCMA Members Handbook**
- **The contract**
- **Insurance**
- **Social security benefits**
- **Tax and National Insurance**
- **Accounts**
- **Milk refunds**
- **Filling vacancies**
- **Record keeping**

Becoming a childminder means that you are starting a business. You are a self-employed childcare and education provider, free to decide your own rate of fees and working conditions. For any business to be successful, it needs to be well organised, with good systems of record keeping. You need to be sure that the parents are satisfied that you are doing a good job, and that they understand and are happy with their contracts.

Being a childminder can be a stressful job, and poorly organised business methods will add to the stress. If you are well organised, you are able to concentrate on your relationships with the children and their families, and with your professional practice.

NCMA Members Handbook

One of the many advantages of joining NCMA is the quality of the support they offer in their business documentation. *The Members Handbook*, published annually in April, and available only to members of NCMA, will give you all the information you need concerning:
- fees
- expenses
- contracts and variations in arrangements
- public liability insurance
- home and car insurance
- legal advice
- legal expenses insurance
- social security benefits
- tax and National Insurance
- accounts
- milk refunds.

The contract

The contract is important to both you and the family of the child. It is not a contract of employment. You are providing childcare for a negotiated fee under an agreed set of terms and conditions. It outlines clearly in writing what is expected from you and what is expected from the parents. Using the NCMA contract will put the partnership on a professional basis and provide evidence in the event of any disagreement. This NCMA contract includes guidance notes.

It is important that an opportunity is taken to sit down with the parents and complete the contract together, so that both sides are quite clear as to their commitment. It is also an opportunity to discuss your childcare practice and to discover if the parents have any strong preferences in the way you care for and educate their children.

Once all the details have been discussed and agreed, the contract should be signed and dated by all parties. It is then a legally binding document. There should be a separate contract for each child in the family. Make a note on your calendar when the contract is due for review, and give the parents adequate notice of this date. Explain that you will review your charges at this time.

If there is to be an initial settling-in period, a temporary contract will have to be drawn up to cover that period.

CASE STUDY

Cheryl, who has just registered as a childminder, looks after two of her own children and Sam, aged three. For the first two months, Sam's mother paid her fees regularly at the start of each week. For the past two weeks, she has given continual excuses for not paying: she hasn't got her cheque book with her, she forgot to draw out cash from the machine, and so on.

Cheryl feels very anxious the weekend before the third Monday, as she has not been paid for the last two weeks. Her partner has been nagging her, saying that childminding is not a charity, and she must be more businesslike. On Monday Sam's mother says she has forgotten her cheque book and offers half a week's fee in cash.

1 What should Cheryl's immediate response be?

2 How can she prevent this happening again?

FEES

What you charge is up to you. You are embarking on a highly skilled career and should be rewarded for your expertise. There are factors that you need to take into account. For example, if you live in an area of high unemployment, the demand for your services may be limited, and you might be in competition with a number of experienced registered childminders. If you live in an area where most of the families around are dual-income, professional families, you might find your services in great demand. It is also important to realise that your household expenditure will increase.

Your social services registration officer or NCMA group may suggest the 'going rate' in your area. Other factors that might influence what you charge would be:

- your experience with babies
- your knowledge and experience of children with disabilities
- any childcare training and qualifications
- your home environment, such as plenty of space and access to a garden.

Your fees for a full-time place may be assessed on an hourly, daily or weekly rate. Children who are attending school part-time will probably have to pay full-time rates as, even though they are attending school for part of the time, they are taking up a full-time place with you. Some childminders offer a reduced rate to children from the same family, making it clear that the reduction is for the older child, so there is no confusion when he starts school. If a parent decides to keep the child at home for a half day, for whatever reason, you would still expect to be paid for that time.

After-school care is normally paid on an hourly rate for the hours care is provided. It is sometimes paid at a higher rate in order to be cost effective. Holiday care is usually paid by the hour, and is at the normal under-fives rate. You should consider the hidden costs of holiday care, such as outings, and these need to be agreed with the parents in advance.

The contract should make clear what payment you expect for:

- absences of the child
- holidays (the parents' and yours)
- illness (the child, the parents' and yours)
- older siblings
- playgroup, outings and other extras
- food, nappies etc. (whether costed into charges or charged separately)
- part-time or unsocial hours
- retainers, including holiday retainers.

The contract should also make clear when and how you will be paid by the parents. In general, it is prudent to expect payment in advance. Never allow debts to mount up, and expect payment on the day agreed.

EXPENSES

It is easy to lose track of the costs of childminding in your normal housekeeping expenditure. There are some direct expenses such as:

- food and drink
- play materials
- equipment
- safety and First Aid equipment
- insurance
- transport, either petrol or fares
- NCMA membership and publications
- courses and conferences
- stationery
- toiletries
- nappies, if these are not provided by the parent
- outings, including cost of admission to various places of interest.

There are other expenses that are indirect, such as:

- heating and lighting
- rent
- telephone
- council tax and water rates
- wear and tear on household furnishings
- cleaning.

You need to be aware of the indirect expenses, as you can claim part of your household bills against your income tax.

Activity
Calculate the cost of your provision against the above headings.
1   Does it cost you less per child if you take on more children?
2   Are there any other expenses unique to you, not covered by the above list?

Insurance

When you become a childminder, you will need to review all your insurance policies, and inform the companies of your new status.

PUBLIC LIABILITY INSURANCE

Local authorities make public liability insurance a requirement of registration, and even if this is not so NCMA strongly recommend that you obtain this cover. It insures you against legal liability arising from:

- accidental injury or death to any person, including any minded children, in your care, caused by your action or negligence
- damage caused by the children in your care to other people's property.

NCMA members can obtain this insurance from NCMA, and they will then issue you with a certificate that you can show to the parents. It cost £12 per annum in 1998 to NCMA members, but changes each year. It would be very foolish to work as a childminder without holding public liability insurance.

HOME AND CAR INSURANCE

Because you now have a business, your household and your car insurance will need to be updated. Failure to inform your insurers could invalidate any claim you might make. This is particularly important with your car insurance, if you are using the car to transport children as part of your childminding business. It has to be covered by your policy as otherwise your car insurance may not be valid if you or the children are involved in an accident.

Some insurance companies regard childminding as a high-risk operation, and have increased home insurance premiums. NCMA can put you in touch with a company with a competitive price, designed for childminders and including many extras. NCMA also offer legal expenses insurance, for the defence of any prosecution arising from normal childminding duties.

Social security benefits

These benefits are increasingly complex and subject to change. If you have been receiving benefit, and you commence working as a childminder, you will need to seek specialist advice. NCMA provides up-to-date information on this to its members.

Tax and National Insurance

In April 1996, tax self-assessment was introduced in the UK, making it a legal requirement for all self-employed people to keep accurate business records, so it has become vital that you keep clear and precise records of your income and expenses. It is unlikely that you will be expected to pay tax, as after you have claimed expenses and allowances, your net profits may be too small to attract income tax. It is important to tell the local tax office that you are now a childminder, and you may have to demonstrate that you are keeping accurate records.

The Members Handbook clearly outlines the expenses you may claim and details of the agreements NCMA have made with the Inland Revenue.

You will be liable to pay self-employed National Insurance contributions unless you claim exemption because of low earnings. You should consider carefully whether or not to make contributions, as non-payment deprives you of certain benefits, for example, sickness and maternity benefits, and retirement pension. The Contributions Agency has a pack called 'Working for Yourself'. This is a complex issue about which you might feel happier taking specialist advice.

Accounts

The book designed by NCMA, the *Childminder's Cash Book and Attendance Register* is acceptable to the Inland Revenue and the Department of Social Security as a method of recording income and expenses. It includes:

■ details of the minded children
■ the weekly attendance and record of payment, countersigned by childminder and parent
■ weekly expenditure and allowable expenses
■ monthly accounts
■ annual accounts
■ annual statement of accounts that can be presented to the Tax Office.

The use of this book, together with retaining all necessary receipts of expenditure, should allow you to complete your own tax returns each year.

Milk refunds

Childminders are entitled to claim the cost of a third of a pint of milk per child under five per day (a day being anything more than two hours a day). For a baby under a year you may instead claim for dried baby milk made up to one third of a pint as instructed on the pack. This can add up to a substantial amount of money each year, and should be claimed, or it may cease to be available. You should keep receipts as proof of purchase, and keep accurate records of children's attendance. Claim forms can be obtained from:

Welfare Food Reimbursement Unit, PO Box 1, Corby, Northants NN17 1GX (Telephone: 01536 408 008).

Filling vacancies

There are several ways of filling any vacancies: word of mouth, local group vacancy schemes, local authority lists, NCMA national resource and referral, and advertising in clinics, local shops and newspapers. In any advertisement, be wary of including your address – your telephone number should suffice. NCMA offer advice in this matter. It is important to approach this in a professional manner as first impressions count.

Record keeping

Childminders have a responsibility to know as much as possible about the children in their care. Much of this information is gathered during the first meeting with the parents. You will need to keep all the information you have about the child in a confidential file, secure from other people. The records on each child should include:

- name as shown on birth certificate
- name the child is known by
- date of birth
- address
- telephone number
- names of parents and where they can be contacted
- emergency contact name, and where he or she can be contacted
- information about the child's health
- information about any allergies
- information about the child's immunisations
- doctor's name, address and telephone number
- name and address of any person allowed to collect the child
- written permission from parents to seek medical help in the event of an emergency
- First Aid certificate
- copies of any relevant court orders.

You should also keep a record of the name and address of any person who assists you, and any person living on the premises, and be prepared to notify the local authority in writing of any changes. When one of your own children reaches the age of sixteen, you will need to notify the local authority for their records.

The other documents that you will always have to hand will include the following:

- your registration certificate from the local authority
- public liability insurance certificate
- registers of attendance, perhaps the most important document, which must always be kept up to date
- contracts between you and the parents
- forms signed by parents, giving permission to take the children on outings, and to give medication
- an accident book, recording all the accidents occurring to the children, and any First Aid given, which needs to be countersigned by the parents
- records of observations and assessments of the children
- weekly menus.

Activity
Where in your home is there a safe place to store your records, allowing easy access, while maintaining confidentiality?

In addition to the documentation you have to keep, some childminders like to keep a programme of activities carried out with the children, and have written a statement of how they implement equal opportunities. Parents should have access to all the above records concerning their child. The local authority will inform you of what they wish to be recorded, and what will be checked at annual inspections.

Although some of the documentation involved in running your business sounds daunting, it is necessary as it protects you and the children. It needs to be kept carefully and fully up to date.

16 A RETURN TO LEARNING

This chapter includes:
- **Training courses**
- **National Vocational Qualifications (NVQs)**
- **Personal management**
- **Learning techniques and working in a group**
- **Learning aids**
- **Organising your work**

These are exciting times for childminders. Your skills and experience are finally being acknowledged. You are likely to have a key role in new government initiatives. You have recognised that you wish to improve the service you offer, to extend your skills, and be ready to grasp new opportunities. You may already be familiar with adult education and training, or you may not have done any training for a long time. You have already taken one step by reading this book and most of you have taken or are taking a preparation course before becoming childminders, so you have made a good start.

Training courses

The National Childminding Association (NCMA) has worked with the Council for Awards in Children's Care and Education (CACHE) to develop the first national qualification for childminders, the CACHE Level 3 Certificate in Childminding Practice (CCP). CCP is made up of 3 units:
- Introducing Childminding Practice (ICP), a 12-hour course for people who are in the process of registering as childminders
- Developing Childminding Practice (DCP), a 60-hour course for all registered childminders
- Extending Childminding Practice (ECP), a 60-hour course for experienced childminders moving forward in their careers to become community childminders (caring for disabled children and 'children in need') or accredited childminders (providing early years education).

Each unit of this qualification is assessed through assignments. These encourage you to think about your daily work and are not formal essays.

The three units together provide the underpinning knowledge for NVQ Level 3 in Early Years Care and Education.

National Vocational Qualifications (NVQs)

These are nationally recognised qualifications that state you are competent in your chosen area of work. NVQs can be gained at various levels. Each level consists of a number of compulsory units and a number of optional units. Early Years Care and Education Level 3 is the appropriate NVQ for childminders, because you work independently without supervision. Level 2 might be more appropriate for assistants working under supervision.

An NVQ is not a course, it is an assessment of your competence. You must demonstrate your knowledge and understanding of why you work in a certain way. You will need to 'top up' your knowledge in some areas, and it may increase your confidence to attend a DCP course or seek training on particular topics.

Personal management

Before starting training you will need to consider how to manage your personal and social life, so that you are able to meet the demands placed on you. Making plans to manage your more complicated life will enable you to succeed in gaining your qualification. It is important that you attempt to discover as much as possible about the course and its requirements, prior to making any commitment. It is a good idea to meet course members who are still on the course so that you can ask questions about any elements that may be worrying you.

RELATIONSHIPS

With family and friends
Many course members have found that it is easier to be successful on an educational programme if they have the encouragement and support of their partners, the parents of the children they are minding, their own children and friends. Having found out the requirements of the course you should discuss them fully with all concerned. This way, you will be sure of help when you most need it. Other childminders can offer support and practical help. Tell them what you intend to study, and they may decide to join you.

> **Activity**
> Consider carefully who will be most affected by your new commitment and who will offer the most support.

Some course members will enjoy their studies so much that other people in their lives may feel excluded and left behind. It takes a great deal of tact to resolve this predicament. There will be help available, as tutors are familiar with this situation.

With your peer group

During the period of your course, you will be working closely with other child-minders, engaged in learning together. You will all be expected to make positive contributions to discussions, and help maintain the security and confidence of the group. You may find yourself with people from various backgrounds, ages, and varying abilities. It may take you some time to settle in your group, but you will soon relax and enjoy the company of most of the people. Communicating with everyone in the group will broaden your ideas and attitudes. You will be expected to display a professional attitude and enjoy the diversity of the group.

With tutors

Your tutor may be responsible for providing personal and group tutorial sessions. He or she will discuss your progress and personal self-development, help you to sort out any difficulties, and prepare your assessments.

All tutors will have a variety of approaches and teaching styles and you may find that you are more comfortable with some tutors than with others. All tutors come from a childminding background, or have detailed knowledge of child-minding. They will have your interests at heart, and will be anxious for you to succeed.

TIME MANAGEMENT

The key to success lies in the way you manage your time.

The professional approach

Your time-keeping will be a crucial factor in assessing your professional competence. It will be expected that you arrive punctually. You will need to have planned your journey, and allowed plenty of time to ensure that you do not let anyone down by arriving late. Your attendance record will be monitored. If being late or absent is unavoidable, you must make contact as soon as possible, explaining your predicament, and make sure that you keep in touch at regular intervals until the crisis has passed.

Organising your time when studying

This is a key factor in ensuring success. For some courses it may be expected that you will spend some of your personal time in:
- organising handouts, portfolios and files
- further reading
- writing assignments
- writing up your observations of children
- preparing individual and group presentations
- using the library
- keeping a diary.

GOOD PRACTICE IN MANAGING YOUR TIME

1. Obtain details of deadlines well in advance, and plan to finish your assignments ahead of time.
2. Keep up to date with all aspects of your work.
3. File your work regularly.
4. Your work must be planned around your other responsibilities. Try to allow time for unexpected events or illnesses.
5. Note in your diary dates of any course deadlines and avoid planning major social events at these times if possible. It may be useful to note a number of weeks ahead how much time you have left before reaching the deadline.

THE HOME LEARNING ENVIRONMENT

There will be work and studying that you need to do at home, and you will need to consider whether:
- there is a room or a space where you can work and study without being interrupted
- there is a table or desk big enough for you to spread out your work undisturbed
- you have a comfortable chair
- your environment is quiet, warm, well lit and well ventilated
- you have somewhere to keep your books, files and completed work.

If it is not ideal for you to work at home, for whatever reason, investigate the possibility of studying at a friend's house, or at your local library. Regular access to a computer would be helpful.

STRESS MANAGEMENT

In addition to the stress you may have experienced in your job as a childminder (see Chapter 13), you may find yourself under stress as a course member. The main causes may be:
- conflicting demands on your time – juggling family commitments with assignment deadlines
- difficulty with the course work and meeting professional standards
- lack of clarity about the expectations of tutors
- frequent absences from the course, leading to lack of information and inability to complete assignments
- tensions in your relationships with your peer group or tutors
- coming to terms with the course member's role
- coping with constructive criticism
- personal problems unrelated to the course.

MANAGING STRESS WHEN FOLLOWING A COURSE OF STUDY

It is important to recognise and face up to the fact that you are stressed, and you need to attempt to identify the causes. Think about the following:
- arrange to see your tutor to discuss your problems
- arrange an appointment with your GP to discuss your symptoms and see what sources of help are available
- practise your assertiveness and relaxation techniques
- look again at how you are managing your time
- look at your diet and exercise regime.

It is perfectly normal to feel stress when you are studying. You are being constantly assessed and evaluated. The course requires a strong commitment and, as you know, it is very tiring working with children.

APPEALS AND COMPLAINTS

Grievances and complaints usually occur when there has been a breakdown in communication between the course member and the tutors. This occurs rarely, but, if it does, your tutors will be as anxious as you to resolve it as quickly as possible. Courses will have grievance procedures to follow, and tutors should bring them to your attention as you start the course. For DCP courses you have rights of appeal to NCMA, the college and, in the last resort, CACHE.

Learning techniques and working in a group

You know more than you think. You will already have achieved many things in your life, not necessarily all of them academic.

To succeed on any training course, you will need to understand the variety of techniques used and the way in which different groups work. A good tutor will use a variety of approaches in most course sessions, and you will need to be adaptable and flexible so as to maximise your learning.

DISCUSSION IN GROUPS

Sometimes your tutor will introduce a topic and then expect the group to spend some time contributing their own relevant ideas and experiences. Interactive learning can be one of the best ways of understanding and learning the core elements of the course.

It is not always easy at first to have the confidence to speak within the group setting. You might be afraid that your ideas are not valid, and that the rest of the group might reject or make fun of your remarks. To benefit from group discussion you should:

- listen to other people respectfully and do not interrupt
- have pen and paper to jot down ideas as they occur to you
- indicate to the tutor that you wish to speak
- make sure your contribution is relevant to the discussion
- speak slowly and clearly
- try and avoid giving personal examples, particularly if it is going to cause you stress.

Remember that nearly everybody feels nervous at first when contributing to a classroom discussion. It becomes easier with practice. If you think that there might be an area of the course that you could find distressing, such as child protection or bereavement, be sure to mention this to your tutor in advance.

FUNCTIONING IN DIFFERENT TYPES OF GROUPS

Small groups
From time to time, your tutor may ask you to work in small groups of four or five to complete a particular task. You may be given pens and flip chart paper, and one of you may be asked to record the ideas and findings of your group.

Towards the end of the session, one of you may be asked to report back to the larger group.

Your course group

When starting the course, you may be placed in a group of approximately fifteen to twenty people. This is the size of the group for most of your course sessions. As you spend time together, you will become familiar with the group relationships and behaviour. You will no doubt make some firm friendships.

PRESENTATIONS

You may be asked, during the course to make a presentation of your work to the group, either on your own or with two or three other childminders. You will need to be clear about the purpose of the presentation, what you wish to communicate and how you are going to present the information. Remember to speak clearly, audibly and slowly enough so that the group has time to take in what you are saying. Face the group at all times, even if you are using visual aids. Remember to:

- be yourself, and find your own style
- be positive
- accept that you will be nervous beforehand and try some relaxation techniques
- concentrate on the task, remembering what you are trying to communicate
- monitor your vocal expression, thinking about volume, pitch and pace
- articulate your words more clearly for a larger audience
- avoid too many statistics. If necessary, put them in a handout and ask the tutor to photocopy it for the group
- check any visual aids such as overhead projectors beforehand
- never apologise for your presentation
- try to rehearse with friends before the actual presentation.

ROLE PLAY

While on a course, you may be asked to take on the role of another person, so that you can begin to experience the feelings and emotions that someone might feel in a certain situation. This is unlikely to occur until the group has settled and the members know each other well.

Your tutor will brief you very clearly as to what is expected of you. Sometimes, role play will be between two people, with a third one observing what is happening. The observer will then report back to the other two. On occasion, for example if you were role playing the child protection conference, a larger group would be involved, and the rest of the course group would observe. It is always important to have feedback, and for the participants to have the opportunity to state how they felt. Taking on the role of others improves your ability to see other people's points of view. This ability is called 'empathy' and is different from feeling sympathetic, as it allows you to enter into the emotions of another person. To speculate on the emotions of others and to apply them to oneself is an integral part of professional development.

EXPLORING TOGETHER

On occasion, your tutor may ask you to explore a particular topic in a spontaneous and fast fashion. This will help enrich a subject with creative, lateral and original thinking. All ideas are accepted, however wild or extravagant they may seem at first.

Someone is generally elected (the scribe) to record the ideas on a large sheet of paper, or on a board, whilst another person acts as chairperson so as to keep some order in the proceedings. Everyone in the group is expected to participate in a positive fashion. The chairperson should prevent any negative attitudes, as this will inhibit creativity. The group may decide to set a time limit. The scribe will read back the list to the group on request and at the end of the initial session.

The group will now classify the entire list, combining and improving ideas. They may discover gaps in the topic and some areas may have been oversubscribed. The tutor may now intervene, and suggest unexplored concepts. A general discussion will follow and the ideas will be evaluated in a positive way. The value of the session is that:

- it helps you to reflect on what you already know about a particular topic before taking on fresh ideas
- it allows the whole group to contribute without inhibition
- it allows free expression and spontaneity
- negativity is ruled out
- some childminders explore thoughts and ideas that they would not consider on their own
- classifying and evaluating ideas is a useful exercise in organising one's own work
- working as a group on a topic demonstrates the value of teamwork.

USING WORKSHEETS WITH VIDEOS

As a childminder, you will need knowledge and understanding of many different children, from different backgrounds, with different needs, of different ages and in different settings. Your tutor may wish you to watch a number of videos to complement your experience. This is not a passive exercise, and you will be expected to join in discussion in a critical fashion. Always note the title, date and publisher of the video, as you may wish to include it in your bibliography.

When you first start to observe children, your tutor may ask you to watch a short extract from a video, record your observations, and report to the group what you have observed. To help you become more adept at close observation of video recordings, you might find it useful to watch a relevant television documentary at home and take notes.

Learning aids

You will find many useful resources in your local library that will help you succeed on any further training you may undertake. You will need to become familiar with the facilities and be prepared to ask questions, and employ the skills of the professional staff if there is any area that is new to you.

BOOKLISTS

At the start of any course you will be given a list of books that you will find helpful to read to complete the course successfully There may be competing demands on the library stock, and you will need to reserve them as soon as you can. If you are on a DCP course discuss this with your tutor.

HANDOUTS

Frequently, your tutors will distribute handouts about various areas of the work and will either refer to them in the course group, or expect you to study them on your own. You can highlight any particular points that you or your tutor thinks to be of vital interest, and this will help you later on when you might be writing an assignment. All handouts should be dated and filed with your course material.

USING BOOKS FOR RESEARCH

As you know, all textbooks have a table of contents indicating the chapters and lists of charts and illustrations, and some will also have appendices, footnotes, bibliographies and an index. When selecting a book look at:

- the introduction or preface, which may give you some idea what the book is about and at which level it is aimed
- the contents or chapter headings, which will indicate the main topics or areas covered
- the date of publication, which will tell you how up to date the work is
- the summary or conclusions, which may give you some overview of the book
- the index, which may help you find your topic if it is not mentioned in the contents list
- the bibliography. Some books will suggest further reading, as well as resources, references or useful addresses
- the charts, diagrams, graphs and illustrations, which may be of help in your assignment.

You may not be able to find all you require on a particular topic in your local library. It is well worth enquiring if the librarians can order books for you from other libraries for a nominal fee. Consider buying books in partnership with other members of your group, and borrowing from people who have completed the course.

USING INFORMATION TECHNOLOGY

Although using a computer is not an essential part of the course, you will find a personal computer (PC) a very useful tool. If you can word-process you will soon value the acquisition of this skill. If you do not have access to a PC at home, you may be able to book sessions in the library.

Access to the Internet, either on your course or at home, will help you with your research, enabling you to access a wide range of up-to-date information. It will often give you a synopsis of books that you might want to read. Organisations such as the NSPCC and Kidscape have web sites, and this is helpful in providing information quickly. Check what CD ROMs are available at your library, as these can be invaluable in your understanding of certain topics.

OTHER RESOURCES

NCMA organises regular conferences at national, county, regional and borough level that will keep you up to date with all childminding issues. These conferences are particularly valuable as they not only keep you up to date, but may offer programmes of workshops and seminars on current issues, and allow you to meet a number of childminders involved in working with young children. Once a year, usually in September, the magazine *Nursery World* organises an exhibition of resources, books and equipment, for under-eights in London, and once a year in another part of the country.

Organising your work

FILING WORK

One way of making sure that your course is a success is to have easy access to your material. All those handouts given to you and those activities that you have planned and carried out – all this needs to be carefully sorted and filed. All written work that you complete needs to be dated, titled and carry your name.

There are several methods of filing your coursework. Within each subject you may choose one or both of the following methods:
- date order (chronological). Each piece of work is added to the file in date order, with the date in the top right-hand corner of the page
- topic headings. Most subjects are broken down into topics. For example, in one file, you might put pre-school provision and Early Years Curriculum. In another file, you might put nutrition and physical growth and development. In a third, you might put the Children Act 1989, and handouts on the family. This is a convenient method of filing but be careful not to view each topic in isolation.

Some childminders might find it useful to keep a list of contents at the front of the file for quick access. The use of dividers in different colours, with the name of each topic clearly depicted is another useful way of finding what you need quickly.

ASSIGNMENT PLANNING

You will be assessed on the DCP course by assignments that you will be expected to complete by a given date. These tasks require careful long-term planning, research and recording. Your tutors will make clear their expectations, and help you with the format.

Having been set an assignment, clarify:

- what you are required to do
- what information you need to complete the assignment
- where you will find this information
- the date of submission of the work.

If the assignment requires you to undertake a piece of work or research in your home involving the children, you should discuss it with the parents before starting the project. Try to have a clear idea of how long it will take, allowing time to proofread the first draft and make any necessary amendments before submitting the finished assignment. It is important to follow instructions for the presentation of your work.

PORTFOLIOS

The word 'portfolio' is used to describe the folder that contains evidence demonstrating your ability to work competently and skilfully with young children. Candidates for NVQ will have their competence assessed in various ways. The portfolio, where evidence of your work is stored, is one of the essential tools for making assessments. Your tutor/assessor will indicate as you commence the course/assessment how you should compile your portfolios. It is important to listen to your tutor/assessor, question anything you do not understand, and follow instructions carefully when compiling portfolios.

REFERENCING

You will obviously need to use and refer to other people's work when writing any type of assignment. You must, however, be very careful to avoid the temptation to plagiarise. This means copying chunks of text and using it as your own work, without any acknowledgement.

Committing yourself to, and completing a course of study is hard work, but well worthwhile. When you are qualified, you will feel immense satisfaction in your new professional status.

APPENDIX A
Developmental norms

0 to 1 year

	Physical development – gross motor	Physical development – fine motor	Social and emotional development	Intellectual and communication development
At birth	Reflexes: ■ Rooting, sucking and swallowing reflex ■ Grasp reflex ■ Walking reflex ■ Moro reflex If pulled to sit, head falls backwards If held in sitting position, head falls forward, and back is curved In supine (laying on back), limbs are bent In prone (laying on front), lies in fetal position with knees tucked up. Unable to raise head or stretch limbs	Reflexes: ■ Pupils reacting to light ■ Opens eyes when held upright ■ Blinks or opens eyes wide to sudden sound ■ Startle reaction to sudden sound ■ Closing eyes to sudden bright light	Bonding/attachment	Cries vigorously, with some variation in pitch and duration
1 month	In prone, lifts chin In supine, head moves to one side Arm and leg extended on face side Begins to flex upper and lower limbs	Hands fisted Eyes move to dangling objects	Watches mother's face with increasingly alert facial expression Fleeting smile – may be wind Stops crying when picked up	Cries become more differentiated to indicate needs Stops and attends to voice, rattle and bell
3 months	Held sitting, head straight back and neck firm. Lower back still weak When lying, pelvis is flat	Grasps an object when placed in hand Turns head right round to look at objects Eye contact firmly established	Reacts with pleasure to familiar situations/routines	Regards hands with interest Beginning to vocalise

continued

0 to 1 year continued

	Physical development – gross motor	Physical development – fine motor	Social and emotional development	Intellectual and communication development
6 months	In supine, can lift head and shoulders In prone, can raise up on hands Sits with support Kicks strongly May roll over When held, enjoys standing and jumping	Has learned to grasp objects and passes toys from hand to hand Visual sense well established	Takes everything to mouth Responds to different emotional tones of chief caregiver	Finds feet interesting Vocalises tunefully Laughs in play Screams with annoyance Understands purpose of rattle
9 months	Sits unsupported Begins to crawl Pulls to stand, falls back with bump	Visually attentive Grasps with thumb and index finger Releases toy by dropping Looks for fallen objects Beginning to finger-feed Holds bottle or cup	Plays peek-a-boo – can start earlier Imitates hand-clapping Clings to familiar adults, reluctant to go to strangers – from about 7 months	Watches activities of others with interest Vocalises to attract attention Beginning to babble Finds partially hidden toy Shows an interest in picture books Knows own name
1 year	Walks holding one hand, may walk alone Bends down and picks up objects Pulls to stand and sits deliberately	Picks up small objects Fine pincer grip Points at objects Holds spoon	Cooperates in dressing Demonstrates affection Participates in nursery rhymes Waves bye-bye	Uses jargon Responds to simple instructions and understands several words Puts wooden cubes in and out of cup or box

1 to 3:11 years

	Physical development – gross motor	Physical development – fine motor	Social and emotional development	Intellectual and communication development
1 year	Walks holding one hand, may walk alone Bends down and picks up objects Pulls to stand and sits deliberately	Picks up small objects Fine pincer grip Points at objects Holds spoon	Cooperates in dressing Demonstrates affection Participates in nursery rhymes Waves bye-bye	Uses jargon Responds to simple instructions and understands several words Puts wooden cubes in and out of cup or box
15 months	Walking usually well established Can crawl up stairs frontwards and down stairs backwards Kneels unaided Balance poor, falls heavily	Holds crayon with palmar grasp Precise pincer grasp, both hands Builds tower of 2 cubes Can place objects precisely Uses spoon which sometimes rotates Turns pages of picture book	Indicates wet or soiled pants Helps with dressing Emotionally dependent on familiar adult	Jabbers loudly and freely, with 2–6 recognisable words, and can communicate needs Intensely curious Reproduces lines drawn by adult
18 months	Climbs up and down stairs with hand held Runs carefully Pushes, pulls and carries large toys Backs into small chair Can squat to pick up toys	Builds tower of 3 cubes Scribbles to and fro spontaneously Begins to show preference for one hand Drinks without spilling	Tries to sing Imitates domestic activities Bowel control sometimes attained Alternates between clinging and resistance Plays contentedly alone near familiar adult	Enjoys simple picture books, recognising some characters Jabbering established 6–20 recognisable words May use echolalia (repeating adult's last word, or last word of rhyme) Is able to show several parts of the body, when asked Explores environment energetically
2 years	Runs with confidence, avoiding obstacles Walks up and down stairs both feet to each step, holding wall Squats with ease. Rises without using hands Can climb up on furniture and get down again Steers tricycle pushing along with feet Throws small ball overarm, and kicks large ball	Turns picture book pages one at a time Builds tower of 6 cubes Holds pencil with first 2 fingers and thumb near to point	Competently spoon feeds and drinks from cup Is aware of physical needs Can put on shoes and hat Keenly interested in outside environment – unaware of dangers Demands chief caregiver's attention and often clings Parallel play Throws tantrums if frustrated	Identifies photographs of familiar adults Identifies small-world toys Recognises tiny details in pictures Uses own name to refer to self Speaks in 2- and 3-word sentences, and can sustain short conversations Asks for names and labels Talks to self continuously

continued

1 to 3:11 years continued

	Physical development – gross motor	Physical development – fine motor	Social and emotional development	Intellectual and communication development
3 years	Competent locomotive skills Can jump off lower steps Still uses 2 feet to a step coming down stairs Pedals and steers tricycle	Cuts paper with scissors Builds a tower of 9 cubes and a bridge with 3 cubes Good pencil control Can thread 3 large beads on a string	Uses spoon and fork Increased independence in self-care Dry day and night Affectionate and cooperative Plays cooperatively, particularly domestic play Tries to please	Can copy a circle and some letters Can draw a person with a head and 2 other parts of the body May name colours and match 3 primary colours Speech and comprehension well established Some immature pronunciations and unconventional grammatical forms Asks questions constantly Can give full name, gender and age Relates present activities and past experiences Increasing interest in words and numbers
3:11 years	All motor muscles well controlled Can turn sharp corners when running Hops on favoured foot Balances for 3–5 seconds Increasing skill at ball games Sits with knees crossed	Builds a tower of 10 cubes Uses 6 cubes to build 3 steps, when shown	Boasts and is bossy Sense of humour developing Cheeky, answers back Wants to be independent Plans games cooperatively Argues with other children but learning to share	Draws person with head, legs and trunk Draws recognisable house Uses correct grammar most of the time Most pronunciations mature Asks meanings of words Enjoys verses and jokes, and may use swear words Counts up to 20 Imaginative play well developed

4 to 7:11 years

	Physical development – gross motor	Physical development – fine motor	Social and emotional development	Intellectual and communication development
4 years	All motor muscles well controlled Can turn sharp corners when running Hops on favoured foot Balances for 3–5 seconds Increasing skill at ball games Sits with knees crossed	Builds a tower of 10 cubes uses 6 cubes to build 3 steps, when shown	Boasts and is bossy Sense of humour developing Cheeky, answers back Wants to be independent Plans games cooperatively Argues with other children but learning to share	Draws person with head, legs and trunk Draws recognisable house Uses correct grammar most of the time Most pronunciations mature Asks meanings of words Enjoys verses and jokes, and may use swear words Counts up to 20 Imaginative play well developed
5 years	Can touch toes keeping legs straight Hops on either foot Skips Runs on toes Ball skills developing well Can walk along a thin line	Threads needle and sews Builds steps with 3–4 cubes Colours pictures carefully Can copy adult writing	Copes well with daily personal needs Chooses own friends Well-balanced and sociable Sense of fair play and understanding of rules developing Shows caring attitudes towards others	Matches most colours Copies square, triangle and several letters, writing some unprompted Writes name Draws a detailed person Speaks correctly and fluently Knows home address Able and willing to complete projects Understands numbers using concrete objects Imaginary play now involves make-believe games

continued

4 to 7:11 years continued

	Physical development – gross motor	Physical development – fine motor	Social and emotional development	Intellectual and communication development
6 years	Jumps over rope 25 cm high Learning to skip with rope	Ties own shoe laces	Eager for fresh experiences More demanding and stubborn, less sociable Joining a 'gang' may be important May be quarrelsome with friends Needs to succeed as failing too often leads to poor self-esteem	Reading skills developing well Drawings more precise and detailed Figure may be drawn in profile Can describe how one object differs from another Mathematical skills developing, may use symbols instead of concrete objects May write independently
7 years	Rides a 2-wheel bicycle Improved balance	Skills constantly improving More dexterity and precision in all areas	Special friend at school Peer approval becoming important Likes to spend some time alone Enjoys TV and books May be moody May attempt tasks too complex to complete	Moving towards abstract thought Able to read Can give opposite meanings Able to write a paragraph independently

APPENDIX B

Sequence of language development

Children's language develops through a series of identifiable stages. These stages are sequential, as outlined below. The level of children's development depends partly on their chronological age, but their experience of language from an early age is, however, just as important a factor. If children are exposed to a rich language environment this will be reflected in their language development. Children who have not had this opportunity will not have had the same chances for development. It is important to take this into account when assessing a child's stage of language development.

Children who are bilingual may develop their languages at a slightly slower rate than children who are monolingual. This is to be expected as they have much more to learn. Given an environment that promotes language development, bilingual children will become proficient in both languages.

Approximate age	Developmental level
Birth	Involuntary cry
2–3 weeks	Signs of intentional communication: eye contact
4 weeks onwards	Cries are becoming voluntary, indicating for example, unhappiness, tiredness, loneliness Children may respond by moving their eyes or head towards the speaker, kicking or stopping crying
6 weeks onwards	Children may smile when spoken to Cooing and gurgling begin in response to parent's or carer's presence and voice, also to show contentment
1–2 months	Children may move their eyes or head towards the direction of the sound
3 months	Children will raise their head when sounds attract their attention
4 months	Playful sounds appear: cooing, gurgling, laughing, chuckling, squealing; these are in response to the human voice and to show contentment Children respond to familiar sounds by turning their head, kicking or stopping crying Shouts to attract attention

Approximate age	Developmental level
6 months	The beginning of babbling: regular, repeated sounds, e.g. *gegegegeg*, *mamamam*, *dadada*; children play around with these sounds. This is important for practising sound-producing mechanisms necessary for later speech Cooing, laughing and gurgling become stronger Children begin to understand emotion in the parent or carer's voice Children begin to enjoy music and rhymes, particularly if accompanied by actions
9 months	Babbling continues and the repertoire increases Children begin to recognise their own name May understand simple, single words, e.g. *No*, *Bye-bye* Children continue to enjoy music and rhymes and will now attempt to join in with the actions, e.g. playing Pat-a-Cake
9–12 months	Babbling begins to reflect the intonation of speech Children may imitate simple words. This is usually an extension of babbling, e.g. *dada* Pointing begins. This is often accompanied by a sound or the beginnings of a word. This demonstrates an increasing awareness that words are associated with people and objects
12 months	Children's vocabulary starts to develop. First word(s) appear, usually names of people and objects that the child is familiar with. They are built around the child's babbling sound repertoire Children understand far more than they can say. This is called a passive vocabulary They begin to be able to respond to simple instructions, e.g. 'Give me the ball', 'Come here', 'Clap your hands'
15 months	Active vocabulary development remains quite limited as children concentrate on achieving mobility Passive vocabulary increases rapidly Pointing accompanied by a single word is the basis of communication
18 months	Children's active vocabulary increases; this tends to be names of familiar things and people Children use their language to name belongings and point out named objects Generalisation of words is difficult, e.g. cat can only be their cat, not the one next door One word and intonation is used to indicate meaning, e.g. cup may mean, 'I want a drink', 'I have lost my cup', 'Where is my cup?'. The intonation (and possibly the situation) would indicate the meaning to people who are familiar with the child Children will repeat words and sentences

Approximate age	Developmental level
21 months	Both passive and active vocabularies rapidly increase; the passive vocabulary, however, remains larger than the active
	Children begin to name objects and people that are not there: this shows an awareness of what language is for
	Sentences begin. Initially as two word phrases, e.g. 'Mummy gone', 'Coat on'
	Gesture is still a fundamental part of communication
	Children begin asking questions, usually 'What?', 'Who?' and 'Where?'
2 years	Both active and passive vocabularies continue to increase
	Children can generalise words but this sometimes means that they over-generalise, e.g. all men are *daddy*, all furry animals with four legs are *dog*
	Personal pronouns (words used instead of actual names) are used, e.g. I, she, he, you, they. They are not always used correctly
	Sentences become longer although they tend to be in telegraphic speech, i.e. only the main sense-conveying words are used, e.g. 'Mummy gone work', 'Me go bike'
	Questions are asked frequently, 'What?' and 'Why?'
2 years 6 months	Vocabulary increases rapidly; there is less imbalance between passive and active vocabularies
	Word use is more specific so there are fewer over- and under- generalisations
	Sentences get longer and more precise, although they are still usually abbreviated versions of adult sentences
	Word order in sentences is sometimes incorrect
	Children can use language to protect their own rights and interests and to maintain their own comfort and pleasure, e.g. 'It's mine', 'Get off', 'I'm playing with that'
	Children can listen to stories and are interested in them
3 years	Vocabulary develops rapidly; new words are picked up quickly
	Sentences continue to become longer and more like adult speech
	Children talk to themselves during play: this is to plan and order their play, which is evidence of children using language to think
	Language can now be used to report on what is happening, to direct their own and others' actions, to express ideas and to initiate and maintain friendships
	Pronouns are usually used correctly
	Questions such as 'Why?', 'Who?' and 'What for?' are used frequently
	Rhymes and melody are attractive

Approximate age	Developmental level
3 years 6 months	Children have a wide vocabulary and word usage is usually correct; this continues to increase They are now able to use complete sentences although word order is sometimes incorrect Language can now be used to report on past experiences Incorrect word endings are sometimes used, e.g. *swimmed, runned, seed*
4 years	Children's vocabulary is now extensive; new words are added regularly Longer and more complex sentences are used; sentences may be joined with *because*, which demonstrates an awareness of causes and relationships Children are able to narrate long stories including the sequence of events Play involves running commentaries The boundaries between fact and fiction are blurred and this is reflected in children's speech Speech is fully intelligible with few, minor incorrect uses Questioning is at its peak. 'When?' is used alongside other questions. By this stage children can usually use language to share, take turns, collaborate, argue, predict what may happen, compare possible alternatives, anticipate, give explanations, justify behaviour, create situations in imaginative play, reflect upon their own feelings and begin to describe how other people feel
5 years	Children have a wide vocabulary and can use it appropriately Vocabulary can include colours, shapes, numbers and common opposites, e.g. big/small, hard/soft Sentences are usually correctly structured although incorrect grammar may still be used Pronunciation may still be childish Language continues to be used and developed as described in the section on 4-year-olds; this may now include phrases heard on the television and associated with children's toys. Questions and discussions are for enquiry and information; questions become more precise as children's cognitive skills develop Children will offer opinions in discussion

Source: Beaver M. et al., *Babies and Young Children, Book 1: Early Years Development*, 2nd edition, Stanley Thornes, 1999. Reproduced with permission

APPENDIX C

DCP1 Course Guidelines

National Childminding Association

PRINCIPLES OF EXCELLENCE IN
CHILDMINDING PRACTICE

1 The welfare of the child

The welfare of the child is paramount. Childminders must give precedence to the rights and well-being of the children they work with. Children should be listened to, and their opinions and concerns treated seriously.

2 Keeping children safe

Young children are very vulnerable.

Childminders should organise the environment and activities with careful attention to safety and hygiene, and work practices (including level of supervision) should help to prevent accidents and to protect health. They should be aware of the dangers of passive smoking.

Each childminder should make a detailed personalised plan to be put into operation in an emergency, including keeping records of accidents. Every childminder has a responsibility to contribute to the protection of children from abuse, and should be aware of signs and symptoms of possible abuse and appropriate procedures to follow, including the recording of incidents.

3 Commitment

Young children need stability.

Childminders should recognise the nature of the commitment of agreeing to care for other people's children and should enter minding arrangements with the intention and determination to sustain the arrangement. Plans should be made for back-up cover in emergencies.

4 Children's behaviour

Childminders should establish a framework of clear boundaries and limits for children's behaviour, emphasising positive expectations for that behaviour. This should be shared with parents and applied firmly and consistently. Praise and encouragement should be given when children live up to expectations, and responses to unwanted behaviour should be suited to the child's stage of development and understanding.

A child must never be slapped, smacked, shaken or humiliated.

5 Working in partnership with parents/families

Caring for young children involves sharing responsibilities with their parents and families, recognising the prime role they play in their children's upbringing. Childminders must never try to take over the parents' role, or see themselves as substitutes for parents. Parents and families should be listened to as expert on their own child.

Information about children's development and progress should be shared regularly with parents to ensure consistency of care between the family's home and the childminding setting.

Respect must be shown for families' traditions and childcare practices, and childminders' practice should be in harmony with the values, practices and wishes of parents, as far as is possible in the context of caring for children from several different families.

Respect should be shown for parents' choices about working outside the home.

6 Children's learning and development

Childminders should be aware of their role as educators.

Children learn more and faster in their earliest years than at any other time in life. Their development and learning in these earliest years lay the foundations for abilities, characteristics and skills later in life.

Learning begins at birth. Caring for children and contributing to all aspects of their development are intertwined.

Childminders should plan relevant and appropriate play and other activities and experiences (the 'curriculum') to support and stimulate all aspects of children's development: social, physical, intellectual, communication, emotional. Besides periods of planned play, aspects of domestic routines should be used as learning opportunities. The value of play and activities initiated by children themselves should be recognised, as well as those planned by the childminder.

Activities and experiences should be chosen to suit each child's stage of development. The stage of development reached by a child should be assessed on the basis of observation and discussion with families. The 'curriculum' should set high but realistic expectations for children's progress and build on their achievements and interests.

Simple written records should be kept of children's progress, and these records should be shared with parents.

7 Equality of opportunity

Each child should be offered equality of access to opportunities to learn and develop, and so work towards her/his potential. Each child is a unique individual; childminders must respect this individuality; children should not be treated 'all the same'. In order to meet a child's needs, it is necessary to treat each child 'with equal concern': some children need more and/or different support in order to have equality of opportunity. It is essential to avoid stereotyping children on the basis of gender, racial origins, cultural or social background (including religion, language, class and family pattern), disability or special educational needs: such stereotypes may act as barriers to equality of access to opportunity.

Childminders should demonstrate their valuing of children's personal characteristics (derived from gender, racial origins, etc.) in order to help them develop self-esteem.

8 Anti-discrimination

Childminders must not discriminate against any child, family or group in society on the grounds of gender, racial origins, cultural or social background (including religion, language, class and family pattern), disability, health, age or sexuality. They must acknowledge and address any personal beliefs or opinions which prevent them respecting the value systems of other people, and comply with legislation relating to discrimination.

Childminders have a great influence on the development of children's understanding of and attitudes towards other people. They have a powerful role to play in nurturing greater harmony amongst various groups in our society for future generations.

Childminders have a particular responsibility in helping children to develop positive attitudes towards children and adults who are different from themselves, and should use practices and materials which emphasise the equal value of all individuals whatever their racial origin, cultural grouping, family background, gender, disability, health, age or sexuality.

Children learn prejudice from their earliest years, and must be provided with accurate information to help them avoid prejudice. Expressions of prejudice by children or adults should be challenged, and support offered to those children or adults who are the objects of prejudice and discrimination.

9 Celebrating diversity

Britain is a multi-racial, multi-cultural society. The contributions made to this society by a variety of cultural groups should be viewed in a positive light, and information about varying traditions, customs and festivals should be presented to children as a source of pleasure and enjoyment. Children should be helped to develop a sense of their identity within their racial, cultural and social groups, as well as having the opportunity to learn about cultures different from their own. No one culture should be represented as superior to any another.

10 Confidentiality

Information about children and families must never be shared with others, without the permission of the family, except in the interests of protecting children – for instance, in the case of suspected abuse. In the latter case, correct procedures must be followed, and information passed only to appropriate personnel or agencies as set out in such procedures.

11 Working with other professionals

Advice and support should be sought from other professionals in the best interests of children and families, and information shared with them, subject to the principle of confidentiality. Seeking advice and support to help resolve queries or problems should be seen as a form of strength and professionalism. Respect should be shown for the roles of other professionals.

12 Reflecting on practice

Childminders should use any opportunity they are offered or which arises to reflect on their practice and principles, and make use of the conclusions from such reflection in developing and extending their practice. Opportunities for in-service training/continuous professional development should be used to the maximum.

Childminders must be aware of current legislation and guidance concerning their work.

13 Business practice

Records of attendance, information about children and their development and progress, records of accidents and incidents, and financial records should be kept in a well-organised way, and written contracts with parents reviewed regularly. All necessary insurance cover must be kept up to date.

Written policy statements on equal opportunity and anti-discriminatory practice, managing children's behaviour and other issues should be based on these Principles for Excellence in Childminding Practice.

GLOSSARY OF TERMS

Anti-discriminatory practice
Examining all areas of practice to ensure no discrimination occurs, that all resources project positive images and that the language used is appropriate and correct, and that all prejudice and discrimination is challenged.

Appraisal
A term used to describe the procedure of assessing people on their work and practice on a regular basis. This helps them to look at their progress and self-development and identify training needs.

Bibliography
The listing of books read and used in an essay or a piece of research.

Bullying
Attacks on a child, which can be physical, emotional, verbal, racist and/or sexual, and is the main cause of school refusal. It can leave emotional scars that remain for life.

Challenging behaviour
Describes the child displaying behaviour that is inappropriate and attention-seeking.

Child protection
Protecting children from abuse and neglect is the duty of the whole community. There are many statutory and voluntary agencies involved, such as the law, the police, social services, the health service, the NSPCC, ChildLine and education services.

Child-rearing practices
Children are brought up in many different ways with, for example, some families believing in firm discipline for even the mildest infringement of the rules, while other parents have far fewer rules and allow the children a great deal of freedom. A good understanding of such practices is necessary for any person working with children.

Children Act 1989
An act drawn up to resolve the conflicting areas of family privacy, professional power and the rights of children. The three main principles are: the welfare of the child is paramount; there should be as little delay as possible by the courts in deciding issues; and the court has to be satisfied that it is better to make an order

than not to do so. It brings together the care and upbringing of children in both private and public law. This has had an impact on childcare provision with firm guidance on registration and inspection.

Comfort object
An object, often a blanket or a soft toy, which a child carries around as a comforter, and usually takes to bed with him or her. It may be used until it disintegrates.

Development
The acquisition of new skills, ideas, and attitudes that lead to progressive change.

Disability
Any restriction, or lack (resulting from impairment) of ability to perform an activity in the manner or within the range considered normal for a human being (World Health Organisation, 1980).

Discrimination
Treating certain people or groups of people in an unfair manner based solely on prejudice.

Equal opportunities
Along with other professionals, childminders need to recognise that no member of society should be discriminated against because of his or her gender, race, disability, culture, religion, age, class or sexual orientation.

Evaluation
The term used by childcare practitioners to assess and appraise observations and activities, so as to plan for the future.

Exploration of the outside world
As young children venture outside their family home, they learn about different environments and different value systems. Most children adapt very quickly to outside stimulation and learn a great deal.

Learning environment
When positive, this describes an environment that is stimulating and exciting, offering opportunities for learning new skills and for exploration.

Literacy
The ability to read and write. Literacy is attained in many ways, using reading schemes, (look and say, phonics, real books) and other techniques.

Parental rights and responsibilities
Parents should have responsibility for their children, rather than rights over them. Parental responsibility is defined as the rights, duties, powers,

responsibilities and authority that, by law, a parent of a child has in relation to the child and to his or her property.

Partnership with parents
The Children Act 1989 has laid down firmly that parents have rights and responsibilities, and all professionals are expected to work with them in partnership for the benefit of the child.

Positive images
Developing a positive environment that reflects all the children in a positive way, for example showing women carrying out what traditionally have been thought of as men's roles. It is against stereotyping by race, gender and disability. It is reflected in books, posters, food, festivals and artifacts and in the involvement of all the parents.

Reconstituted family
Resulting from divorce, separation, and re-marriage. The coming together of groups of children into families with new parents/carers.

Regressive behaviour
When a child is ill, or emotionally upset, his or her behaviour may be more suitable for someone younger. For example, a child who can normally concentrate well, finds it impossible to do more than play with toys and equipment that would normally be considered too young. He or she might start wetting the bed again, having been completely dry for more than a year.

Scapegoating
Blaming a person unfairly for the shortcomings or problems of others.

Self-esteem
Confidence in oneself as a worthwhile person. Essential to learning and achievement. Abused children often suffer from low self-esteem.

Self-reliance
Independence. From a very young age, children strive to do things for themselves, such as dressing and washing. This can be helped by adult encouragement.

Stereotypes
Generalisations about a particular group in society, for example believing that girls read earlier than boys.

FURTHER READING

Andreski R. and Nicholls S., 'Managing Children's Behaviour', *Nursery World*, 1997

Axline V., *Dibs, In Search of Self*, Penguin, 1966

Ball M., *Consulting with Parents*, National Early Years Network, 1997

Bax M. et al., *Child Development and Child Health*, Blackwell Scientific, 1990

Beaver M. et al., *Babies and Young Children, Book 1: Early Years Development* (2nd edition), Stanley Thornes, 1999

Beaver M. et al., *Babies and Young Children, Book 2: Work and Care* (2nd edition), Stanley Thornes, 1999

Bishop S., *Develop Your Assertiveness*, Kogan Page, 1996

Bowlby J., *Child Care and the Growth of Love* (2nd edition), Penguin, 1965

British Red Cross, *First Aid for Children – Fast*, Dorling Kindersley in association with the British Red Cross, 1994

Brown B., *All our Children*, BBC Educational Publishing, 1993

Unlearning discrimination in the early years, Trentham Books, 1998

Butler D., *Babies Need Books*, Penguin Books, 1988

CAPT, *Accident Prevention in Daycare and Play Settings*, CAPT, 1994

Corbett P. and Emmerson S., *Dancing and Singing Games*, Kingfisher Books, 1992

Dare A. and O'Donovan M., *A Practical Guide to Child Nutrition*, Stanley Thornes, 1996

A Practical Guide to Working with Babies (2nd edition), Stanley Thornes, 1998

De'Ath E., *Changing Families*, National Early Years Network, 1991

Deakin M., *Children on the Hill*, Quartet Books, 1973

Department of Health, *Child Health in the Community*, HMSO, 1996 Immunisation Fact Sheets, HMSO, 1997 (A free copy can be obtained from the health literature line: 0800 555 777)

Donaldson M., *Children's Minds*, Fontana, 1978

Einon D., *Child Behaviour*, Viking, 1997

Elliott M., *Keeping Safe: a practical guide to talking to children*, Coronet, 1994

EYTARN, *Partnership with Parents: an anti-discriminatory approach* EYTARN, 1997

Goldschmied E., and Jackson S., *People Under Three*, Routledge, 1994

Goodnow J., *Children's Drawings*, Developing Child Series, Fontana, 1980

Griffin S., *Keeping and Writing Records*, National Early Years Network, 1994

Hall D. et al, *The Child Surveillance Handbook* (2nd edition), Radcliffe Medical Press, 1994

Harris J., *The Nurture Assumption*, Bloomsbury, 1998

Hobart C. and Frankel J., *A Practical Guide to Child Observation* (2nd edition) Stanley Thornes, 1999

Good Practice in Child Protection, Stanley Thornes, 1998

A Practical Guide to Activities for Young Children (2nd edition), Stanley Thornes, 1999

A Pratical Guide to Working with Young Children (3rd edition), Stanley Thornes, 1999

Hyder T. et al., *On Equal Terms*, National Early Years Network/Save the Children, 1997

Jackson V., *Racism and Child Protection*, Cassell, 1996

Kidsone I., *Tax Facts* (5th edition), Kogan Page, 1996

Kurtz Z. and Bahl V., (Eds) *The Health and Health Care of Children and Young People from Minority Ethnic Groups in Britain*, NCB and DoH, 1997

Leach P., *Babyhood*, Penguin Books, 1983

Levene S., *Play It Safe – the complete guide to child accident prevention*, BBC Books, 1992

Lindon J., *Understanding Child Development*, Macmillan Caring Series, Macmillan, 1998

Lindon J. and L., *Caring for Young Children*, Macmillan Caring Series, Macmillan, 1994

Millam R., *Anti-discriminatory Practice*, Cassell, 1996

Moore J., *The ABC of Child Protection*, Arena, 1992

Mortimer H., *Playladders*, Ainderby Hall, Northallerton, N. Yorkshire DL7 9QJ

NCMA *Children's Learning: a framework for delivering desirable learning outcomes*, NCMA, 1996
   The Members Handbook, NCMA, 1998 (available to members only)

NCMA and NES Arnold, *The Use of All About Me with Parents*, NCMA and NES Arnold, 1992

Neaum S. and Tallack J., *Good Practice in Implementing the Pre-school Curriculum*, Stanley Thornes, 1997

Northedge A., *The Good Study Guide* , Open University, 1990

O'Hagan M., *Geraghty's Caring for Children* (3rd edition), Ballière Tindall, 1997

Petrie P., *Communication with Children and Adults*, Edward Arnold, 1989

Sheridan M., *From Birth to Five Years* (revised and updated by Frost M. and Sharma A.), Routledge, 1997

Smith C., *Care for Under Eights: a guide to daycare services and standards under the Children Act*, National Early Years Network in partnership with the NCMA, 1991

Stoppard M., *Complete Baby and Child Care*, Dorling Kindersley, 1995

Tizard B. and Hughes M., *Young Children Learning*, Fontana, 1984

Valman H., *ABC of 1–7 years* (2nd edition), BMJ Publishing Group, 1993

Valman H.B., *The First Year of Life* (4th edition), BMJ Publishing Group, 1995

Whiting M. and Lobstein T., *The Nursery Food Book*, Edward Arnold, 1992

Williams F., *Babycare for Beginners*, HarperCollins, 1996

Winnicott D., *The Child, the Family and the Outside World*, Penguin, 1964

Wolfe L., *Safe and Sound*, Hodder and Stoughton, 1993

Wolfendale S., *All About Me*, NES Arnold, 1990

Wragg T., *Key Stage 1 of the National Curriculum*, Longman, 1993

Zealey C., 'The Importance of Names', in *Equal Opportunities, the Co-ordinate Collection*, National Early Years Network, November 1995

ADDRESSES AND HELPLINES

Anaphylaxis Campaign
PO Box 149, Fleet, Hampshire GU13 9XU
Telephone: 01252 542 029

Association for Spina Bifida and Hydrocephalus (ASBAH)
42 Park Road, Peterborough PE1 2UQ
Website: www.asbah.demon.co.UK

British Deaf Association
1–3 Worship Street, London EC2 2AB
Website: www.bda.org.UK

Child Accident Prevention Trust (CAPT)
Clerks Court, 18/20 Farringdon Lane, London EC1R 3AU
Telephone: 0171 608 3828

ChildLine
Telephone: 0800 1111

Community Playthings Catalogue – 'Criteria for Play Equipment', Community
Playthings, Robertsbridge, East Sussex TN32 5DR
Telephone: 0800 387 457

Contact a Family
170 Tottenham Court Road, London W1P 0HA

Council for Awards in Children's Care and Education (CACHE)
8 Chequer Street, St. Albans, Herts AL1 3LX
Telephone: 01727 867 333

Council for Disabled Children
8 Wakely Street, London EC1V 7QE

Disabled Living Foundation
380–384 Harrow Road, London W9 2HU

Down's Syndrome Educational Trust
Website: www.downsnet.org

HAPA, Play for Disabled Children
Bishop's Avenue, London SW6 6EA
Telephone: 01604 792 300

Kidscape
Telephone: 0171 730 3300
Website: www.solnet.co.UK/Kidscape/

MIND (National Association for Mental Health)
Granta House, Broadway, London, E15
Telephone: 0181 519 2122
Website: www.mind.org.UK

Muscular Dystrophy Group
Nattrass House, 35 Macaulay Road, London, SW4 0QP
Website: www.sonnet.co.UK/muscular-dystrophy.html

National Association of Toy and Leisure Libraries
68 Churchway, London NW1 1LT
Telephone: 0171 387 4592

National Childbirth Trust (NCT)
Alexandra House, Oldham Terrace, Acton, London W3 6NH
Telephone: 0181 992 8637

National Childminding Association (NCMA)
8 Masons Hill, Bromley, Kent BR2 9EY
Telephone: 0181 464 6164

NSPCC
Telephone: 0171 825 2500
Helpline: 0800 800 500
Website: www.NSPCC.org.UK

Parentline
Telephone: 01702 554 782

Royal National Institute for the Blind (RNIB)
224 Great Portland Street, London W1N 6AA
Website: www.rnib.org.UK

Royal Society for the Prevention of Accidents (RoSPA)
Cannon House, The Priory, Queensway, Birmingham BF 6BS
Telephone: 0121 200 2461

Save the Children Equality Learning Centre
356 Holloway Road, London N7 6PA
Telephone: 0171 700 8127

SCOPE (Cerebral Palsey Society)
London and SE Regional Office, Shackleton Square, Priestley Way, Crawley, Sussex
Telephone: 01293 522 655
Helpline: 0800 626 216)
Website: www.nspcc.org.UK

SENSE (The National Deaf Blind and Rubella Association)
11–13 Clifton Terrace, Finsbury Park, London N4 3SR

Social Security and National Insurance Information
Freeline: 0800 666 555

St John Ambulance
National Headquarters, 1 Grosvenor Crescent, London SW1X 7EF

The Letterbox Library
Unit 2D, Leroy House, 436 Essex Road, London N1 3QP
Telephone: 0171 226 1633

The National Association for Special Educational Needs
Nasen House, 4–5 Amber Business Village, Amber Close, Amington, Tamworth B77 4RP

The Terence Higgins Trust
52–54 Grays Inn Road, London WC1X 8JU
Telephone: 0171 831 0330

The Vegetarian Society
Parkdale, Dunham Road, Altrincham, Cheshire WA14 4QG

The Working Group Against Racism in Children's Resources
460 Wandsworth Road, London SW8 3LX
Telephone: 0171 627 4594

INDEX

absences   132
abuse   3, 61, 92,
abuse and neglect   136–155
accident report forms   144, 109, 110,
   151, 201
accident types   95–96
accidents   96, 97, 99, 105, 150, 173, 199
accounts   195, 200
activities with children   45
after school care   87, 197
AIDS   117
All About Me   188, 193
allegations of abuse   147, 149, 151
allergies   17, 18, 36, 38, 76, 103, 105,
   106, 124, 131
anaphylactic shock   105, 106
annual inspection   8, 13, 165, 202
anti-discriminatory practice   3, 164, 228
antiseptics   107
appendicitis   124
appetite   34, 36, 55, 75, 78, 123, 150,
   175
application form   7
appraisal   5, 157, 158, 228
assertiveness   24, 113, 154, 165, 176,
   177, 178, 179, 207
assessment   45, 58, 114, 154, 201, 204,
   213
assessment procedures   203, 205
assignments   206, 207, 211, 213
assistant (childminder)   7
associative play   45
assumptions   182
assumptions   189
asthma   102, 108, 111, 131
attachment   28, 43, 159, 160
attendance register   200, 201
autism   68

babies (developmental norms)   214, 215
babies   7, 26, 27, 28, 31, 33, 38, 42–45,
   49, 50, 59, 64, 73–86, 90, 98, 99, 119,
   126, 127, 134, 135, 139, 140, 149,
   150, 154, 168, 169, 170, 174, 197, 200

balanced meals   48
baseline assessment   56
bathtime   76, 77, 81
behaviour   17, 23, 28, 34, 35, 51, 60–72,
   74, 75, 83, 88, 90, 93, 113–115, 126,
   143, 147, 150–155, 162, 175, 182,
   183, 184, 185, 188, 194
behaviour modification   68
behavioural indicators/bullying   92
bibliography   210, 211, 228
bleach solution   117, 118
blood disorders   133
board games   52
body language   43, 59, 115, 159, 168,
   169, 172, 174
bonding   28, 43, 149
book lists   211
books   18, 31, 32, 43, 49, 53, 54, 55, 82,
   85, 163, 164, 165, 170, 171, 172, 211
boredom   66
bottle feeding   78, 79
breast-feeding   75, 78, 117
bricks, blocks and construction sets   52
bullying   91, 92, 93, 139
burns and scalds   95, 96
business basics   195, 200
business management   9, 12
business matters   16, 195–202
business needs   13
business records   199

car   17
car insurance   101, 195, 199,
care order   21
cash book   200
challenging behaviour   61, 228
changes in behaviour   142
checklists   188, 190, 191, 192, 193
chicken pox   125
child abuse statistics   138, 139
child protection   13, 136–155, 208, 228
child protection conference   147, 148,
   182, 209,
child protection plan   147, 148, 155

child protection register   138, 147, 148
Child Record Form   103, 109
child's individual preferences   18
child-centred play   45
Childline   138
childminding groups   156, 157
childminding networks   12, 57
child-rearing practices   3, 22, 23, 24, 26, 55, 61, 183, 228
Children Act, 1989   4, 21, 89, 140, 154, 164, 184, 212, 228
children with disabilities   111–118
children's rights   165
choking   96, 122, 131, 150
chronic illness   96
chronic medical conditions   108, 129–135
closed questions   171
coeliac disease   134
cold sores   107, 125
comfort behaviour   24, 63, 71
comfort habit   142
comfort object   16, 20, 23, 27, 31, 63, 75, 85, 229
comfort seeking   143
common cold   121, 122, 124, 126, 143
communcs   22
communication   5, 14, 29, 23, 24, 25, 26, 43, 59, 66, 75, 84, 88, 112, 113, 115, 153, 154, 159, 205, 207, 209
communication skills   168–179
concussion   106
confidentiality   12, 17, 91, 118, 120, 136, 159, 183, 194, 201
conflict   69, 71, 120, 136, 172, 177, 178, 179, 207
conjunctivitis   107
consistency of care   2, 3, 22, 74, 123, 138
consistent approach   32, 60, 63, 66, 67, 72, 73, 75, 81, 88, 112, 152, 155
constipation   127
contract   19, 23, 120, 157, 179, 159, 195, 196, 197, 198, 201
convulsion   119, 132
cooking   48, 49
co-operative play   45, 52, 83
coughs   122, 124, 131, 143
court order   201
cradle cap   76, 124, 125, 143
creative play   45, 84

creativity   59, 210
criminal record   4
cross infection   76, 119, 121, 122, 135,
croup   124
crying   34, 74, 80, 92, 126, 150, 220
cultures   5, 22, 23, 30, 34, 36, 41, 43, 48, 49, 54, 55, 60, 61, 66, 75, 90, 138, 142, 160, 161, 162, 164, 169, 183, 190, 194
curiosity and exploration   64, 150
curriculum   57, 91, 169
cuts   96
cystic fibrosis   127, 134

daycare advisor   24, 179
definitions of abuse and neglect   137–138
dehydration   126, 127, 133
dental hygiene   32
Developing Childminding Practice   13, 157, 203, 204, 207, 211, 213
development   40–59, 229
developmental norms (1–3:11)   216–217
developmental norms (4–7:11)   218–219
developmental norms (babies)   214–215
developmental stages   40, 149, 150, 182
diabetes   111, 127, 130
diet   36, 38, 42, 123, 130, 131, 134, 135, 163, 164, 165, 176, 207
disability   54, 55, 61, 111–118, 139, 160, 161, 163, 164, 165, 189, 197, 229
discipline   67, 72, 90
disclosure   144, 152
disinfectant   107, 108, 117, 121
domestic play   45, 51, 83
domestic violence   138
dough   48
drowning   96
DSS   200

ear infections   126
early years curriculum   56, 212
eczema   3, 30, 111, 125, 131, 132
educational neglect   137
emergencies   17, 101, 102, 124, 129, 130, 131, 133, 201
emergency contact   103
emergency cover   9, 12
emergency protection order   21

emotional abuse 138, 142
emotional development 28, 41, 43, 44, 81, 85, 188, 214–219
emotional neglect 138
empathy 210
epilepsy 111, 113. 132, 133
equal opportunities 8, 13, 17, 90, 158, 160, 162, 202, 229
equality of opportunity 3, 4
evaluation and assessment 189
event sample 185, 186
exercise 28, 29, 30, 31, 55, 56, 130, 131, 132, 176, 207
Existing Injuries Form 144
expenses 198
experimental play 85, 86
exploratory play 85, 86
extended family 22, 61

factors which contribute to abuse and neglect 149
failure to thrive 134, 138
falls 95
family behaviour 154
fees 197
feral children 40, 41, 43
fever 122
filing work 212
fine manipulative skills 83, 84
fine motor skills 42
fire drill 97, 98
First Aid 102, 105, 106, 117, 121, 198, 201
First Aid kit 100
'fit' person 4
fits 127, 132, 133, 140
fleas 128, 129
food additives 38
foreign bodies 96
formula feeds 75, 77, 79
fresh air 31
fruitarian 38

gender 4, 22, 54, 60, 61, 65, 90, 160, 161, 162, 164, 183, 189
German measles 125
gluten fee diet 134
good practice 21, 28, 44, 224–227
grand mal 132
'grazing' 35
grievance procedure 207

gross motor skills 42
growth 30, 42, 78, 121, 123, 130, 150, 212
Gulbenkian Foundation Report 139

haemophilia 133
hair care 30, 164
hand foot and mouth disease 125
hand-eye co-ordination 42, 81, 83
handouts 212
HASS 95
hay fever 131
hazards 96, 97, 101, 110, 133, 136, 182
head lice 128
health checks 80
health visitor 12, 17, 80, 103, 137, 148, 174
healthy diet 32
healthy eating habits 35
hearing impairment 111, 189
hearsay 182, 189
heat rash 76, 125
HIV 111, 117, 118
holiday activities 93
holistic approach 25
home insurance 195, 199
home language 43, 54, 103, 165, 169, 181, 187
home visits 7, 8, 27
homosexual family 22
House Information 102, 104
hygiene 7, 23, 28, 30, 33, 48, 49, 77, 87, 106, 117, 122, 128, 136, 143, 165
hyperactivity 111, 114
hyperglycaemia 131
hypoglycaemia 130, 131

imaginary play 45, 49, 50, 51, 55, 84, 143
imitative play 45
impairment 111, 112, 114
impetigo 107, 125
incubation period 64, 121, 182
independence 29, 30, 33, 44, 46, 53, 57, 64, 65, 87, 88, 95, 115, 123, 150, 151, 188, 230
indicators of abuse 140
indicators of sexual abuse 142
infection 31, 55, 64, 74, 75, 77, 82, 107, 110, 117, 118, 120, 121, 122, 124, 125, 129, 131, 132, 133, 134, 140, 165, 182

infestation   120, 128, 129
information technology   212
Inland Revenue   200
inspection   19, 21, 29
insulin   130
insurance   12, 17, 101, 198
intellectual (cognitive) development
     42, 43, 45, 46, 81, 84, 137, 214–219
interactive learning   208
investigation of possible child abuse   148

jealousy   28, 44, 113

keeping up-to-date   166
Key Stages   91
key worker   147, 148
Kidscape   152, 212

lacto-ovo vegetarians   38
lacto-vegetarian   38
language development   40, 43, 81,
     137, 170, 171, 188, 214–223
learning   40–59, 83, 84, 85, 86, 114,
     115, 134, 152, 153, 165, 182, 184,
     188, 189, 190
learning aids   211
learning environment   229
legal advice   195
legal expenses insurance   195, 199
legal liability   199
libraries   211
listening skills   172
literacy   229
lone-parent family   22, 24
lower respiratory tract infection   124
Lymes disease   129

manipulation skills   42, 53, 55, 171
masturbation   63, 71
maternity leave   20
mealtimes   18, 28, 30, 34, 35, 69, 112,
     134, 182
measles   125
media   12, 61, 136, 138, 161
medical conditions   111
medical referral   189
medication   17, 98, 106, 108, 109, 112,
     119, 120, 123, 129, 130, 131, 132,
     134
meningitis   121
messy play   30, 31, 45, 46, 85, 132, 183

middle ear infection   124
milk refunds   195, 200
minor ailments   122
modelling materials   48
Mongolian blue spot   142
mud   47
Munchausen's syndrome by proxy
     138

nappy rash   76, 124, 143
naps   17, 28, 31, 53, 63, 69, 70, 150
national childcare strategy   20
National Curriculum   91
National Insurance   200
natural materials   45, 46
NCMA   1, 4, 6, 8, 10, 12, 13, 16, 22,
     24, 56, 57, 59, 103, 105, 108, 109,
     137, 142, 144, 147, 148, 151, 155,
     156, 157, 159, 162, 166, 173, 179,
     188, 195, 196, 197, 198, 199, 200,
     203, 204, 212, 227, 297
needs of children   26–39
neglect   3, 61
nettle rash   125
nits   128
non-accidental injury   141
NSPCC   137, 138, 152, 212
nuclear family   22, 55
nutrition   34, 36, 38, 49, 77, 87, 165,
     212
NVQ   13, 166, 203, 213

objective approach   180, 182, 184, 185,
     189
observation   13, 45, 66, 112, 114, 123,
     147, 151, 152, 154, 157, 158, 159,
     173, 201, 206, 210
observation techniques   184, 188
observing and assessing children
     180–194
open-ended questions   171
organised abuse   138
organised games   45
outside play   55

painting and drawing   51, 52
parallel play   45
parental responsibility   21, 147, 230
Parentline   154
parents   27, 31, 32, 36, 40, 61, 64, 65,
     69, 87, 91, 102, 116, 120, 121, 124,

126, 128, 136, 137, 143, 147, 151, 155, 165, 168, 178, 180, 184
partner (childminder)   7, 9, 10
partnership with parents   3, 57, 75, 123, 130, 152, 154, 230
peer group   61, 71, 87, 89, 90, 91, 169, 205, 207
perception   180, 182
permission to administer medicine/ treatment   108
petit mal   132
pets   6, 10, 16, 17, 61, 108, 122, 129, 131, 132
phenylketonuria   134, 135
physical abuse and injury   137
physical development   42, 83, 188, 214–219
physical injury   138
physical neglect   137
physical play   45
physical punishment   139
plagiarise   213
plasticine   48
play   17, 28, 45, 46, 49, 50, 56, 57, 59, 61, 66, 74, 76, 81, 84, 89, 114, 137, 152, 161, 162, 165, 188, 190
playladders   188, 190, 191
poetry   53
poisoning   96, 137
police check   7
portfolio   19, 206, 213
positive images   54, 55, 160, 163, 164, 230
presentations   209
principles of excellence in childminding practice   224–227
professional approach   3, 13, 6, 23, 26, 28, 71, 96, 97, 120, 136, 137, 140, 149, 156–167, 173, 180, 195, 206
professional practice   154
professional role   9
professional support   12
professionalism   156
promotion of health   34, 55, 119, 123
protection   26, 111, 123
public liability insurance   8, 195, 199, 201
puzzles   52, 53

quarantine period   122

questionnaire for new childminder   10, 11

racial origin   162
racism   162, 163
raised temperature   123, 127
rashes   30, 80, 121, 123, 124, 125, 143, 182
recognition of abuse and neglect   140–144
re-constituted family   22, 61, 230
record keeping   8, 13, 24, 34, 47, 58, 112, 120, 144, 147, 148, 151, 155, 157, 159, 166, 173, 180, 183, 184, 188, 195, 200, 201, 210,
Record of concerns   144–146
record of training   167
recovery position   102, 105, 106
referencing   213
referral and investigation of abuse and neglect   147–148
referral to GP   124, 126, 129, 176
registers   151
registration   3, 4, 7, 8, 13, 17, 19, 21, 71, 102, 120, 199, 201
registration officer   6, 7, 12, 106, 137, 142, 147, 151, 155, 197
regression   24, 28, 44, 88, 114, 123, 153, 230
relationships with parents   14–25
religion   163, 164, 165
repetitive play   45
re-registration   8
rest and sleep   23, 30, 31, 74, 123
rest times   69, 70
return to learning   203–213
ringworm   107, 129
road safety   90, 100
role play   49, 51, 83, 209
RoSPA   95
routine domestic activities   46
routine physical care   26, 30, 111
routines   17, 23, 26, 28, 30, 31, 33, 56, 74, 75, 77, 80, 81, 87, 88, 89
rubella   125
rules of safety   100

safe environment   95–110
safety   6, 7, 8, 10, 13, 17, 36, 49, 55, 58, 64, 74, 76, 81, 82, 83, 84, 120, 123, 136, 150, 154, 158, 159, 165, 179

sand 47
scabies 125, 129
scapegoating 149, 230
scarlet fever 125
school-aged children 18, 28, 87–94, 114, 124, 159
school day 88
school liaison 90
Schools Curriculum and Assessment Authority 58
seborrhoeic eczema 125
senses 42, 43, 44, 55, 80, 86, 168
sensory 48
sensory activities 81, 82
sensory development 44, 86
sensory impairment 86
separation 18, 24, 54, 55, 61, 60, 149, 175
separation anxiety 74, 150
settling in 19, 25, 26, 27, 28, 35, 43, 48, 74, 169
sexual abuse 138, 139, 142
shaking babies 140, 141
shock 105
sickle cell 111, 133
SIDS 77
significant harm 147
signs and symptoms of illness 121, 127, 128
signs of abuse 141
signs of abuse and neglect 140
signs of good and poor health 122, 123
signs of good health 122, 123
signs of ill health 80, 123
signs of neglect 143
signs of sexual abuse 142, 143
signs of shock 105
signs of stress 175–176
skin 55
skin care 30, 76, 117, 123, 132, 164
sleep 17, 18, 30, 55, 64, 71, 74, 75, 76, 77, 123, 132, 150
smacking 19, 62, 68, 71, 72, 137, 150, 151, 154
snack 17, 34, 35, 36, 38, 88, 150
snapshot observation 180, 181
social development 40, 41, 46, 83, 188, 192, 214–219
social security benefits 195, 199
social worker 155

solitary play 45, 83
special diets 34, 111
speech 169
SPICE 40
spontaneous play 45, 46
staff:child ratio 6
stages of development 51, 57, 60, 184, 189, 214–219
stereotyping 51, 54, 55, 61, 90, 161, 162, 164, 189, 230
sterilising equipment 75, 77, 78, 107
stimulation 7, 26, 42, 66, 73, 80, 81, 87, 111, 123, 137, 150, 154, 165, 180
stomach aches 124, 130
stools 80, 124, 127, 128, 134
stories 53, 54, 55, 59
stranger abuse 138
stranger anxiety 74
strangers 152
stress (causes) 175
stress (coping strategies) 176–177
stress 9, 14, 23, 24, 95, 96, 124, 131, 147, 150, 155, 195, 208
stress management 175–179, 207
structured play 45
Sudden Infant Death Syndrome 77
support groups 158
support systems 10
swearing 70, 171
sweat test 134
symptoms of illness 124, 134, 135

table of contents 211
tax and national insurance 195, 199
teacher 12, 57, 90, 91, 93
teeth 30, 32
television 18, 28, 45, 88, 133, 164, 182
temper tantrums 62, 63, 67, 68, 85, 143, 186
thalassaemia 111, 133
therapies 112, 123, 129, 130, 131, 134, 174
threadworms 127, 128
ticks 129
time management 29, 176, 206, 207
time sample 185, 187, 188
toddlers (developmental norms) 215, 216
toddlers 7, 60, 64, 73–86, 90, 99, 140, 154, 168,

toilet training   17, 18, 32, 33, 60, 64, 150

tonic/clonic seizures   132

tonsillitis   124

training   3, 7, 8, 12, 13, 17, 19, 58, 66, 96, 112, 154, 156, 157, 158, 163, 166, 197, 203, 204, 208, 211

travellers   22

treasure basket   82

types of play   45

under-eights advisors   12, 151, 174, 176

upper respiratory tract infections   122, 124

urinary tract infection   124, 127

urine   80, 127, 130, 143

vacancies   157, 200

value judgements   182, 183, 189

vegan   38

vegetarian   38

violence   137, 139, 140, 154, 179

vomiting   121, 122, 124, 126, 130, 134, 182

water play   46

weaning   77, 80, 134

well-balanced diet   34

whistle-blowing   136

worksheets   210

written contract   17

written permission   17, 91, 101, 108, 119, 120, 129, 201

written record observation   185

Zen macro-biotic diet   38